HE, TOO,
SPOKE FOR
DEMOCRACY

William H. Hastie, Civilian Aide to the Secretary of War, 1940–1943. Photograph courtesy of Moorland-Spingarn Research Center, Howard University.

HE, TOO, SPOKE FOR DEMOCRACY

Judge Hastie, World War II, and the Black Soldier

PHILLIP MCGUIRE

CONTRIBUTIONS IN AFRO-AMERICAN AND
AFRICAN STUDIES, NUMBER 110

GREENWOOD PRESS
NEW YORK
WESTPORT, CONNECTICUT
LONDON

Library of Congress Cataloging-in-Publication Data

McGuire, Phillip, 1944–
  He, too, spoke for democracy : Judge Hastie, World War II, and the black soldier / Phillip McGuire.
       p.   cm.—(Contributions in Afro-American and African studies, ISSN 0069–9624 ; no. 110)
  Bibliography: p.
  Includes index.
  ISBN 0–313–26115–6 (lib. bdg. : alk. paper)
  1. Hastie, William. 2. Afro-American judges—Biography. 3. Afro-American soldiers—Civil rights. 4. Race discrimination—United States. 5. United States—Armed Forces—Afro-Americans. 6. World War, 1939–1945—Participation, Afro-American. I. Title. II. Series.
KF373.H38M35   1988
355'.008996073—dc19
[B]   87–24943

British Library Cataloguing in Publication Data is available.

Copyright © 1988 by Phillip McGuire

All rights reserved. No portion of this book may be reproduced, by any process or technique, without the express written consent of the publisher.

Library of Congress Catalog Card Number: 87-24943
ISBN: 0–313–26115–6
ISSN: 0069–9624

First published in 1988

Greenwood Press, Inc.
88 Post Road West, Westport, Connecticut 06881

Printed in the United States of America

The paper used in this book complies with the Permanent Paper Standard issued by the National Information Standards Organization (Z39.48–1984).

10 9 8 7 6 5 4 3 2

To
Moses Green
in
Painful Memory

Contents

	Acknowledgments	ix
	Introduction	xi
1.	On the Eve of Progress: Hastie and Black Protest Leadership	1
2.	The Anguish of Hastie's War Department Experiences	25
3.	Hastie and the Nadir of Uncle Sam's Black Soldiers	53
4.	Hastie and the Apparent End of a Painful Quest	83
5.	The Conclusion: Shifts in Military Policy	97
	APPENDIX. The Gillem Report (March 4, 1946): Report of Board of Officers on Utilization of Negro Manpower in the Post-War Army	117
	Bibliography	131
	Index	149

Acknowledgments

This book could not have been written without the help of many people who recognized that the late Judge William H. Hastie had a significant and historical impact on policies affecting the treatment and use of black soldiers during and after the Second World War. They shared with me the desire to place Hastie in his rightful place among the principals in the nascent civil rights movement in the post–World War II era. To these individuals I wish to express my most sincere gratitude.

Since I began the research in 1973, the work has undergone many changes. Helpful suggestions were made by the members of my former dissertation committee, which included Arnold H. Taylor as chairman, Harold T. Pinkett, Martha Putney, Harold O. Lewis, and Roland C. McConnell. To these former teachers, I wish to express my sincere thanks for their unselfish support and encouragement since my days as a graduate student at Howard University. I am also especially grateful to Professor Emeritus Benjamin Quarles of Morgan State University, Professor A. Russell Buchanan of the University of California at Santa Barbara, and my colleague, John H. Haley. These historians read parts of the work and provided detailed and useful criticism that were used to improve the manuscript.

The comments of close friends, colleagues, and Professor Sam Barber of North Carolina A&T State University helped me considerably to maintain my enthusiasm while I completed the manuscript. In addition, I am deeply indebted to the late Bell I. Wiley of Emory University for the suggestions made at the inception of this study.

A list of all the institutions and individuals to whom I am indebted for assistance would be unreasonably long. I feel obliged, however, to acknowledge gratefully the kind assistance rendered by staff members of the following libraries: the National Archives, the Library of Congress, the Moorland-Spingarn Research Center of Howard University, the Franklin D. Roosevelt Library, the Harry S Truman Library, Yale University Library, the Schomburg Center for Research in Black Literature of the New York Public Library, Howard University Law School Library, and the staff, especially the diligent and constant assistance of Reference Librarian Lana D. Taylor, of the University of North Carolina at Wilmington.

Gratitude is also due Cynthia Harris, history editor, my production editor, John Donohue, copyeditor Trisha Taylor, and the entire Greenwood Press staff for aiding me in the final preparation of this work for publication.

The major portion of the research for this book was made possible through the generosity of the History Department of Howard University with three Ford Foundation Teaching Assistantships, and grants from the American Philosophical Society and the National Endowment for the Humanities. To these institutions I am deeply grateful.

Finally, Mrs. Barbara H. Christmas of the History Department of the University of North Carolina at Wilmington deserves my special thanks for a fine typing job. She typed the entire manuscript, and her skill and occasional editing contributed greatly to this book.

Introduction

The Civil War changed the status of blacks in the American armed forces. No longer would they be officially excluded from the Regular Army. As President Abraham Lincoln freed slaves and fostered the changing position of black Americans in the larger society, Congress and the military established the 24th and 25th Infantry and the 9th and 10th Cavalry as permanent black units of the Regular Army. But the overall perceptions and status of black soldiers would change little during the next 50 years of military service. As blacks rallied to the nation's call for manpower, they were met head-on with an entrenched tradition of segregation and discriminatory practices that had characterized the standing of blacks in the military from the American Revolutionary War to and including the Second World War.

Historically, the status of black soldiers was nurtured by personal and institutional racism. Even as military auxiliaries, blacks faced segregation and insurmountable discrimination on and off the military posts. Just as white Americans had traditionally devised and established legal and extralegal social and political barriers to maintain a servile class of black civilians, the military accepted and incorporated these practices into the armed services. From the beginning of black participation in foreign and domestic wars, the military believed that maximum efficiency of the armed services and high soldier morale required an uncompromising allegiance to the race relations that existed between black and white Americans in the larger society.

Thus the segregation and the unequal treatment black soldiers faced as the United States entered World War II were maintained because of their deep traditional roots in race relations and in the institutions of an American society unwilling to make the democratic rhetoric and the "American dream" a reality for its black citizens. Such was the case, for example, when the War Department's General Staff collectively advised Secretary of War Henry L. Stimson that "every effort should be made by the War Department to maintain in the Army the social and racial conditions which exist in civil life in order that normal customs of white and colored personnel now in the Army may not be suddenly disrupted." The staff went on to say that "the Army can, under no circumstances, adopt a policy which is contrary to the dictates of a majority of people [because] to do so would alienate the people from the Army and lower their morale at a time when their support of the Army and high morale are vital to our national needs."[1]

In spite of the Staff's position, most soldiers and black civilians had an unswerving faith that the hallowed principles of the Declaration of Independence and of the U.S. Constitution would eventually lead the armed forces and indeed the larger American community to live out the true meaning of their creeds. Professor Benjamin Quarles (author of *The Negro in the American Revolution* and *The Negro in the Civil War*) said it best in 1983 when he wrote: "Like blacks during former wars, those of World War II believed that their condition as armsbearers and homefront workers, along with the spirit of the times, would ameliorate their lot and that changes favorable to their group would result from the war; ... it was hope, not despair, that bred black soldier dissatisfaction."[2]

Like previous wars, blacks viewed World War II as an opportunity for a better day, despite long-held beliefs such as those of Chief of Staff George C. Marshall who asserted (though his stance would change by the end of the war) that integration was "fraught with danger to efficiency, discipline, and morale."[3] Unlike the past, however, black Americans had finally gained enough solidarity and political muscle by 1940 to force the government and the War Department into making unheralded military concessions. Colonel Benjamin O. Davis, Sr., was promoted to brigadier general, the first black American elevated to the rank of general. Major Campbell C. Johnson was appointed special assistant to the Director of the Selective Service, and Judge William H. Hastie was appointed Civilian Aide to Secretary of War Henry L. Stimson.

Hastie's appointment—unbeknownst to Stimson, War Department personnel, and the military's top brass—was viewed by the black leadership and others as the single most important appointment of the three for achieving their objective—the integration of the armed forces. Hastie would become the catalyst who would help revolutionize the status and treatment of blacks in the armed services.

Hastie, one of America's most outstanding black reformers and civil rights activists, was born into a middle-class family in Knoxville, Tennessee, on November 7, 1904. His father, William Henry Hastie, was a graduate of Howard University College of Pharmacy but worked as a clerk in the United States Pension Office until his death. His mother, Roberta Childs Hastie, was a college-trained schoolteacher, educated at Fisk University and Talladega College. When the father was transferred to Washington, D.C., young Hastie completed his public school education, graduating from the famed Paul Laurence Dunbar High School. Dunbar was known at the time for its college prepatory curriculum, and as an institution for producing outstanding and recognized black leaders in America. Hastie distinguished himself at Dunbar and graduated as valedictorian in 1921. He attended Amherst College on an academic scholarship, won numerous academic prizes, was elected to Phi Beta Kappa in 1924, and graduated from Amherst as the magna cum laude valedictorian of his 1925 class.[4]

After working for two years at a black high school in Bordentown, New Jersey, Hastie entered Harvard University Law School, where he had obtained the L.L.B. and J.D. degrees by 1932. At Harvard, Hastie once more performed demonstratively well. Such as the case that prompted Felix Frankfurter, Hastie's constitutional law professor and former Associate Justice of the U.S. Supreme Court, to say that he was "not only the best colored man we have ever had but he is as good as all but three or four outstanding white men that have been here during the last twenty years."[5]

Frankfurter's remarks were meant as compliments, but Hastie viewed them with offensive disgust. Perhaps as an indication of his future attitudes on race relations, Hastie commented as early as 1931 that "this notion that Negroes have to be better than other people is about as disgusting as the notion that Negroes are inferior. As a matter of fact, I very much fear that they are rationalizations of the same thing."[6]

From 1932 to 1937, Hastie worked as a partner in the Houston and Houston Law Firm of Washington, D.C., while serving as Assistant Solicitor in the Department of Interior. In 1937 President Roosevelt appointed him federal judge of the U.S. District Court in the Virgin Islands, the first black elevated to the federal bench. Hastie resigned this post in 1939 to become dean of Howard University Law School. He was granted a leave of absence from Howard to accept his new position as civilian aide to the Secretary of War on November 1, 1940.[7]

When Hastie assumed his new post in the War Department, he had already distinguished himself as a member of Roosevelt's "black cabinet" and as a public statesman. His greatest recognition, however, would result from his civil rights activities both within and outside of the department. As a lawyer for the National Association for the Advancement of Colored People (NAACP) and civil rights activist, he skillfully used his intellectual and legal abilities and sources of public and private strength within both the black and white communities to publicize the racial discrimination against and segregation of black Americans. Before state courts, appellate federal courts, and in the U.S. Supreme Court, Hastie argued against state statutes and traditional practices that barred, segregated, and discriminated against black Americans in public and professional education, public accommodation facilities, public transportation, public housing, voting, employment, teachers' pay, and organized labor. Judge Constance Baker Motley (Chief Judge of the U.S. District Court for Southern New York) perhaps described Hastie best when she recalled "that of the nineteen cases that Thurgood Marshall, representing the NAACP or the NAACP Legal Defense and Educational Fund, Inc., argued before the Supreme Court between 1939 and 1949, Hastie figured as co-counsel or consultant in twelve. Asked to specify the ones in which Hastie was important, Marshall said, 'all of them.' "[8] And as Hastie's only biographer, Gilbert Ware, claimed that "there were, in the forties, two citadels of civil rights in the United States: one was the NAACP, the other was Howard University Law School; and both were what they were largely because of William Hastie, whose admirers prayed that the gods would favor the champion who came forward, 'a fighter for us.' "[9]

Because Hastie was an integrationist and committed to the concept and practical application of equal opportunity, he challenged the racial tradition of the military and initiated actions for correcting the racial inequalities of the armed services. He worked toward this end in spite of the cries from the War Department, race-baiting politicians, and army officers who insisted that the armed forces would not be used as a "sociological laboratory" for effecting social change. Hastie thought otherwise, however. In fact, he did exactly what Secretary Stimson's appointment letter charged him to do: to assist the War Department in developing administrative policies that would insure the fair and most effective usage of black manpower in the armed services.

As civilian aide to the secretary, Hastie began immediately implementing Stimson's charge, but the secretary, the department's staff, and the Army's top brass viewed Hastie's recommendations, which called for integration or which would have had the effect of creating an integrated military, as unrealistic and visionary. Such proposals were rejected outright or manipulated to maintain segregation. Yet, faced with overwhelming odds, Hastie exerted himself to have ended or modified many of the discriminatory policies that permeated the armed services. He attacked these policies posthaste. Hastie's basic strategy consisted, within the confines of segregation, of locating the problem, investigating it, and achieving quick remedial action where discrimination could be proved.

The basic direction of this study has been strongly influenced by six major categories of primary sources: the military archives, manuscript collections of private papers, the diary of Henry L. Stimson, personal correspondence and interviews with Judge William H. Hastie, the black press, and the black soldiers' letters, which attest to segregation, racial discrimination, anger and their beleaguered patriotism.

Of the military archives, the records of the Civilian Aide to the Secretary of War (National Archives Record Group [NARG] 107), which contain correspondence to and from Judge Hastie and his assistant, Truman K. Gibson, Jr., was the most useful. Various collections of private papers were significant in getting the official and personal points of view of the military's racial situation from Hastie's perspective and from those with whom he was directly and indirectly involved within and outside of the War Department. Black newspapers were also used extensively to note press reaction and the overall response of the black leadership to Hastie's activities as a civilian aide and to the issues that dealt mainly with segregation and the official and customary military policies that sanctioned racial discrimination. Stimson's diary was a godsend, for it provided his personal, military, and political feelings on Hastie, race, politics, and black soldiers. The correspondence and personal interviews with Hastie were likewise deeply meaningful and blessed this study with the only firsthand account of Hastie's War Department experiences, frustrations, successes, and failures. In addition, the soldiers' letters were invaluable. According to them, black soldiers were humiliated, despised, denied regular army privileges, insulted by post commanders, subjected to military and civilian police brutality, constrained by traditional mores, court-martialed excessively, and denied access to adequate recreational facilities.[10] In an effort to capture and preserve the authenticity, character, spirit, content, and flavor of the correspondence, the letters were typed exactly as they were written and typed by the soldiers themselves. This accounts for inaccuracies in grammar, spelling, punctuation, capitalization, style and structure.

Throughout this study, some of the soldiers' comments and those of Hastie and Stimson and other major military and civilian figures deemed essential in presenting a story of the complex matter of democratic idealism and the alleged practical realities of segregation and racial discrimination are penetrating and deserved to be quoted at length. Perhaps more so than usual, the quotes were used deliberately to voice thoughts otherwise often left out when historians paraphrase and interpolate the social and racial history of the Second World War. They were likewise used to preserve the authenticity, character, spirit, and language flavor of the persons speaking in a given context. In the correspondence of war department officials, for example, oftentimes the word Negro was written with a small n. Although I cannot prove it, the use of the small n probably indicated contempt for blacks in and out of uniform.

It is not my intention to subject readers to, for example, atrocities committed against black soldiers or to their military valor and wartime achievements. This study is rather one of a man who worked within the War Department's mind-set—segregation and racial discrimination—and used his sources of power to modify and/or eliminate institutional racism while simultaneously recommending policy changes that would have effectively integrated blacks into the armed services on an equal basis. Hastie's story in the War Department is also one of a "persistent warrior" who fought uncompromisingly for the rights of black soldiers to serve their country in an unblemished armed forces. It is an account of a man who spoke for democracy with glaring clarity and who helped to hasten more changes in the placement, training, and promotion of black soldiers than any other single individual in the history of American armed forces prior to World War II.

Social histories of the Second World War have been voluminous over the last two decades. Unfortunately, the literature on Hastie's participation has been grossly silent. Those writing these accounts have either ignored or chose to minimize Hastie's role in the complexities of American race relations during the war. Of several recognized studies to date, *not one*, including a well-publicized 1986 book, has utilized the availability of primary documents that tell the racial story of World War II from the perspective of the man solely appointed in 1940 to insure equality and the fair and most effective usage of black manpower in the armed forces. These scholars simply have failed (perhaps because of his persecution of the unsavory nature of the story and the embarrassment of a nation fighting for democracy and freedom abroad while consciously denying them to a substantial segment of its own population) to place Hastie in proper historical perspective. To claim that he, as the majority of these histories do, was visionary and ineffective does injustice to a man who sought to change the status and institutional rejection of black soldiers. The fact of the matter is that the War Department and the Army's top brass made Hastie's work ineffective as they deliberately waged a campaign to dishearten him.

I do not attempt to claim that Hastie was solely responsible for the changing status of black soldiers, nor do I hide my esteem for a remarkable man. But I have labored cautiously not to make my study into a book of hagiography. Instead, this work will supply a missing part to the uncompleted human and racial story of the Second World War. It focuses on the interaction of Hastie and the people and events to suggest how that interaction shaped the course of the American Armed Forces.

Further, I believe this story is a major contribution to the social literature of World War II.

NOTES

1. Quoted in Ulysses Lee, *United States Army in World War II: Special Studies: The Employment of Negro Troops* (Washington, D.C.: United States Government Printing Office, 1966), 140.

2. Quoted from Phillip McGuire, *Taps for a Jim Crow Army: Letters from Black Soldiers in World War II* (Santa Barbara, Calif.: ABC-Clio, 1983), xvi, xviii.

3. Quoted in Lee, *The Employment of Negro Troops*, 140–141.

4. Judge William H. Hastie, interview with author, March 8, 1974; Anna Rothe, ed., *Current Biography* (New York: H. W. Wilson Company, 1944), 77; Richard Bardolph, *The Negro Vanguard* (New York: MacMillan Company, 1959), 357; Phillip McGuire, "Black Civilian Aides and the Problems of Racism and Segregation in the United States Armed Forces: 1940–1950" (Ph.D. diss., Howard University, 1975), 67–68.

5. Quoted in Gilbert Ware, *William Hastie: Grace Under Pressure* (New York: Oxford University Press, 1984), 28.

6. Ibid.

7. Hastie, interview with author, March 8, 1974; Rothe, *Current Biography*, 77; United States Committee on the Interior and Insular Affairs, 79th Congress, *Report on the Proceedings Held Before the Committee on Territories and Insular Affairs— Nomination of William H. Hastie For Appointment As Governor of the Virgin Islands*, March 20, 1946–April 5, 1946, National Archives Record Group (hereafter cited as NARG) 46, 1–5; Bardolph, *The Negro Vanguard*, 357.

8. Ware, *William Hastie: Grace Under Pressure*, 190.

9. Ibid., 191.

10. See McGuire, *Taps for a Jim Crow Army.*

1

On the Eve of Progress: Hastie and Black Protest Leadership

The integration and use of black Americans in the armed forces became grave questions for both the military and the black community during World War II. While segments of black America demanded integration and full opportunity for its black soldiers, War Department officials and politicians insisted that the military would not be used as a "sociological laboratory" for effecting social change.[1] Although this attitude reflected the overall policies of the War Department, the Army, however reluctantly and belatedly, did undergo some noteworthy shifts during the war.

But just as black Americans in the larger society found the "American dream" an illusion, black soldiers in particular experienced racial discrimination in the armed forces. Most of them were never accepted as military equals to white soldiers. Blacks were relegated to segregated and distinct combat units, to separate training schools, and to segregated camp facilities. More often than not they made up the service and supply units and, even within these, the black troops faced what they considered to be unwarranted degrees of discrimination. The soldiers claimed they did their duty and fought proudly to make the world "safe for democracy." Yet, for them, the vestiges of racism were inescapable. In their letters, for example, to Judge Hastie, and to other private and public individuals stateside, the soldiers told of these debilitating experiences from the day they entered the Army to the day of their discharge.[2]

In 1941, when the United States entered the war, black soldiers joined an army in which the parameters of their world already had been established. It was in 1937 that the War Department's personnel division concluded an extensive study on black participation in the armed forces. The plan indicated that the military wanted to avoid the "grave" mistakes made in the use of black troops in World War I.[3] A ban prohibiting the induction of black volunteers was lifted, and the training of 50 percent more white officers was authorized to handle the projected increase in black personnel. Other features of the new policy included plans to raise the number of black personnel in the Army to equal the proportion of blacks in the total population, to mobilize more black troops before an actual national emergency existed, to reserve portions of warrant officers, chaplains, and reserve officers in black units for blacks, to confine black officers in the National Guard to positions authorized for blacks, to restrict black officer candidates to the number required to fill authorized positions in black units, and to limit blacks assigned to reception, placement, and training centers to the general corps area from whence they came.[4]

Except for one major addition in 1940, the 1937 plan provided the guidelines for the Army's treatment of black personnel throughout World War II. Although not classified, the contents of the 1937 plan were known only to high-level officials in the War Department. Details were not disclosed because Commandant of the Army War College Major General H. E. Ely convinced Secretary of War Harry H. Woodring and the military chiefs of staff that the plan should remain secret. As a rationale, the Commandant explained that he doubted "the wisdom of the War Department announcing this policy at large. Its early announcement will give time for its careful study by those seeking political capital, for points on which the War Department may be attacked, or embarrassed."[5]

Events in the black community suggested that Commandant Ely understood the potentially explosive nature of the Army's plan. Charles H. Houston, veteran of World War I and special counsel to the National Association for the Advancement of Colored People (NAACP), was one of the first black leaders in the late 1930s to address the issue of fair treatment for blacks in the military. On October 8, 1937, he appealed to President Roosevelt to issue an executive order that would ban all racial discrimination in the armed forces. Houston respectfully asked the President "to give Negro citizens the same right to serve their country as any other citizen, and on the same basis."[6]

On the same day Houston reminded Secretary Woodring that the United States could not hope to win a major war without the support of black manpower. He spoke for blacks, and wanted Woodring to be aware that the black community was loyal but "the Negro population will not silently suffer the discrimination and abuse which were heaped upon Negro soldiers and officers in World War I." "We urge you," stated Houston, "to remove all racial barriers to service in all branches of the Army."[7]

Houston's declaration signaled the beginning of an intense campaign by the black press. Its leading exponent was the *Pittsburgh Courier*. Under Robert L. Vann, editor and publisher, the *Courier* pressed for at least 10 percent black personnel in the Army on a nonsegregated basis.[8] The *Courier* also requested that the President appoint two blacks annually to West Point, and proposed that the War Department create an all-black army division commanded by black officers. Vann cited black loyalty, black achievements in battle, and the long-term elimination of prejudices as the major reasons for the *Courier*'s crusade. Vann's campaign for total integration was short-lived, however, and by late 1938 he had accepted the idea that segregation was a means by which blacks at least could increase their total number in the military. Vann's new position was based on the results of a nationwide *Courier* survey, which, he concluded, indicated a consensus of the black community that to attempt full military integration at this time would fail. His analysis was supported by leaders in the black community such as Charles H. Houston, Dr. Rayford Logan, historian and chairman of the Committee for the Participation of Negroes in the National Defense Program, and Roy Wilkins, assistant secretary of the NAACP, as well as most of the black press.

Vann asked New York Congressman Hamilton Fish, who had been a company commander of black troops in the 369th Infantry in World War I, to introduce to the House what Vann called the *Courier*'s Army bills. Representative Fish complied, and in 1940 the bill to end discrimination passed Congress and was made a part of the 1940 Selective Service Act; however, the provisions for an all-black army division and the annual presidential appointment of two blacks to West Point failed.[9]

In the meantime, Vann's acceptance of quotas and the policy of segregation created a rift between him and the NAACP. The executive secretary of the NAACP cautioned that "segregation in public institutions always works to the disadvantage of the segregated group and must be resisted with all the united strength we can command." Walter White felt "to do otherwise is to take the road towards being permanently labeled as a pariah group which in turn will mean spiritual defeatism and death."[10]

Roy Wilkins agreed with White's position. As editor of the *Crisis*, the official news organ of the NAACP, Wilkins published a statement that left no doubt as to his stance: "The *Crisis* wants Negroes all through the

Army, and the Navy, and other defense services. There is no reason why we should not have Negro aviators or generals or admirals." Thus, in contrast to Vann's acceptance of segregation, the idea of fully integrating every branch of the armed forces became the single most important campaign for the *Crisis*, and the NAACP used it continually to rally support from the black community.[11]

In September 1939, for example, White addressed a lengthy letter to President Roosevelt. In it he reviewed the crisis in Europe and expressed fears that the United States would be drawn into the war. He then asked Roosevelt to take steps to correct the evils of prejudice that permeated every aspect of the military; in particular, he emphasized the creation of an interracial commission to investigate alleged discriminatory practices in the military.[12]

The president, through his aide General Edwin Watson, rejected White's idea of an interracial commission, denying that discrimination existed in the armed services. Watson referred to the four black regiments in the Regular Army as proof of black participation in the defense of their country and ended his letter with the assurance to White that Roosevelt was committed to including blacks in the country's future mobilization plans.[13]

White responded to the president after first rallying support in the black community from such notables as Thurgood Marshall, counsel for the NAACP; William H. Hastie, dean of Howard University Law School; Roy Wilkins; and Charles H. Houston. Houston, however, supported Vann and the *Courier*'s position, and did not respond to White. Wilkins and Marshall suggested that White stress the point that the NAACP was diametrically opposed to the separate black units in the Regular Army, and Hastie prepared a list of discriminatory practices and complaints from black soldiers that he thought White should emphasize. Both suggestions were included in White's next message to the president.[14]

Momentum for an integrated military gathered force during 1940. A resolution of the National Negro Congress, entered in the Congressional Record in April, actively urged young blacks to refuse to fight for democracy abroad when they continued to suffer from the effects of discrimination and segregation in the United States.[15] Although the War Department still kept confidential its plan for mobilizing black manpower, a form letter to answer inquiries on the matter had been written. To charges of segregation and discrimination against black soldiers, the department responded that "the War Department is not an agency which can solve national questions relating to the social and economic position of the various racial groups composing the nation." The department then reminded dissidents that it "administers the laws affecting the military establishment; it cannot act outside the law, nor contrary to the will of the majority of the citizens of the nation."[16]

As the year wore on, black leaders became increasingly cynical and more militant in their demands for equal opportunity and the integration of the armed forces. Some wondered if the War Department would allow the same World War I prejudices against black soldiers to impede their full participation in the defense of the country in the Second World War. The black press posed questions such as: In the event of war, what proportion of blacks would serve in the armed forces? Would blacks be used in combat or be restricted to labor and supply units? Were blacks going to be admitted to officer candidate schools? Would blacks serve in segregated or mixed units? Until these questions were answered, black leaders expressed a lack of enthusiasm for military preparedness. Even the *Pittsburgh Courier* revised its position after the death of its publisher, Robert L. Vann, on November 1, 1940. The new editor, Percival L. Prattis, joined White, Wilkins, and other integrationists, editorializing the day following Vann's death: "We must stop asking for more segregation even if there is a prospect of having complete Negro units in every branch of the service; we must start fighting segregation sincerely."[17]

Stafford King, Minnesota state auditor and a civilian aide to the secretary of war, warned Secretary of War Woodring that unless blacks were accorded the same privileges as white enlistees, they might become victims of Axis propaganda.[18] King's warning generated some concern in the War Department. Speaking for the black cause, Adjutant General Emory S. Adams told Woodring that form letters would not satisfy black leaders, and further insisted that "the colored race is entitled to greater and better representation in our Army for obvious reasons, many of which are set forth in Mr. King's letter, and this whole subject should have careful and immediate study to determine the future policy of the War Department in the premises. It is recommended that this study be initiated without delay." The department's general staff made the study that Adams suggested but the final recommendation consisted only of more of the same, that is, that more black units be added to the Regular Army.[19]

When the Selective Service and Training Act became law on September 16, 1940, black leaders considered it a milestone for black soldiers because of two antidiscrimination clauses. The first provided that all men between the ages of 18 and 36 were eligible to volunteer for service in the land and naval forces of the United States. The second clause prohibited discrimination (based on race and color) in the selection and training of men. However, a third provision gave the War Department final authority in deciding who would or would not be accepted in the military, prompting leaders in the black community to voice their concern about the intention of the legislation. Sensitive to racist implications, they argued that the provision could be implemented so as to leave blacks desiring to enlist no redress if they were rejected, possibly rendering the antidiscrimination clauses in the Selective Service Act virtually ineffective.[20]

Evidence suggests that such concern was appropriate. As blacks were given the opportunity to serve in the Army, they volunteered for induction in record numbers. Many were turned away, however, as the black community had feared. The law provided no method or means to redress the grievance of any black American on rejection.

The reasons for rejection ranged from overt army actions to more subtle excuses. The First Army Headquarters (one of nine geographical service commands that included Maine, Connecticut, Massachusetts, New Hampshire, Rhode Island, and Vermont) sent secret orders to its draft boards requesting that no blacks be inducted in the first draft. Although the order to Connecticut was rescinded when Governor Raymond Baldwin threatened to expose it to the public and to President Roosevelt, the antiblack request did not fade away. Late in 1940 the War Department itself ordered Connecticut's draft boards to fill their quotas with white men only, and it fell to Governor Robert Hurley, Baldwin's successor, to instruct the draft boards to ignore the War Department's order.[21] A survey by Roy Wilkins showed that 25 cities in 17 states had no blacks on the draft boards; moreover, white recruiting officers often failed to serve induction notices to black I-A registrants, despite the War Department's promise to create more black ground units to absorb the new inductees. When pressed, the War Department claimed that separate facilities were inadequate to house the new inductees.

Another factor in these rejections may have been the absence of black advisors in the office of the director of the Selective Service and in the War Department. One who addressed this issue was Mary McLeod Bethune, founder and president of the National Council of Negro Women and director of the Division of Negro Affairs of the National Youth Administration in Roosevelt's administration. Bethune asked Eleanor Roosevelt, whom Secretary of War Henry L. Stimson regarded as an agitator, to urge the president to appoint black advisors to the office of the director of the Selective Service and to the War Department. She stressed that the request was a result of long consultation with other black leaders, all of whom agreed that these appointments were necessary to ensure that the policies of the War Department were effectively carried out. Bethune also assured Eleanor Roosevelt that she and the other leaders were prepared to offer the names of the best qualified men for these positions.[22]

Illiteracy was another major factor that prevented the inclusion of blacks. Over 75 percent of the black inductees who failed the Army Classification Test came from the South and border states, an area that accounted for only 25 percent of the white inductees. According to a study conducted by Professors Eli Ginzberg and Douglas Bray of Columbia University, 90 percent of the blacks who failed the test had been deprived of adequate educational and cultural opportunities. Their conclusions were anticipated by Major Campbell C. Johnson, who later became special assistant to the director of the Selective Service. As early as 1944, Johnson blamed the South for the high rate of illiteracy among black inductees.[23]

Furthermore, the War Department apparently seized the opportunity to use illiteracy as a tactic to discriminate against blacks, while accepting illiterate whites without question. According to his diary, Secretary of War Henry L. Stimson had sanctioned this policy. He admitted that "the Army had adopted rigid requirements for literacy mainly to keep down the number of colored troops and this is reacting badly in preventing us from getting in some very good but illiterate [white] recruits from the southern mountain states." To solve the manpower shortage, at least from the southern region of the country, Stimson recommended that the Army embark upon a voluntary recruitment program aimed at bringing more whites into the service. Thus the War Department was willing to actively recruit illiterate whites but unwilling to do the same for illiterate blacks.[24]

On October 9, 1940, the War Department finally announced the confidential guidelines established in 1937 for the treatment of black personnel in the Army. The policy itself might have received a favorable response from Hastie and the other black leaders had it not been accompanied by a general statement that "the policy of the War Department is not to intermingle colored and white enlisted personnel in the same regimental organization. This policy has proven satisfactory over a long period of years and to make changes would produce situations destructive to morale and detrimental to the preparation for National defense." The statement continued:

For similar reasons the department does not contemplate assigning colored Reserve Officers other than of the Medical Corps and Chaplains to existing Negro combat units of the Regular Army. These regular units are going concerns, accustomed through many years to the present system. Their morale is splendid, their rate of reenlistment is exceptionally high and their field training is well advanced.

The final sentence was probably the most devastating to the hopes of Hastie and the other black leaders. The department refused to accept the idea of experimenting with mixed units and used as its rationale the war as a time too critical for such experimentation.[25]

Because the War Department had rejected the idea of integration, blacks renewed their challenges to President Roosevelt and to the War Department for failure to end segregation. Hastie and the other black leaders based their protest on three basic principles: (1) segregation was morally wrong since it embodied an undemocratic doctrine of racial inferiority; (2) segregation denied full military opportunities to black soldiers, relegated them to an inferior status, and destroyed their *esprit de corps*; and (3) segregation was an unnecessary luxury. These leaders also believed that had the War Department been aware of the considerably greater expense involved in maintaining a segregated army, official zeal for a black and white military would have wavered.[26]

Eugene K. Jones, successor to George E. Haynes as executive secretary of the National Urban League, sent a letter to President Roosevelt in protest of the October 9 announcement. He declared: "We deny that the segregationist policy of the War Department, though it has been pursued over a long period of years, has been satisfactory to thoughtful Negro citizens. We deny also that to make changes in this policy would produce situations destructive to morale." Jones also called the president's attention to a unanimous resolution adopted at the League's thirtieth annual conference. In summary, the resolution stated: "The National Urban League is unalterably opposed to the policy and practice of racial discrimination and segregation in the Army, Navy, Air Force, and Marine Corps of the United States."[27]

More adamant in its tone than the Urban League, the Citizens' Nonpartisan Committee for Equal Rights in National Defense demanded that the War Department's policy be revised. In telegrams to President Roosevelt and to the War Department, the committee stated: "We want no discrimination or segregation in the Army, Navy, Air Corps, or Industrial Defense. This is our just dessert in a democratic government, and the need for national unity demands immediate revision of the stated policy."[28]

In an effort to quiet or delude the black community, Roosevelt's press secretary, Stephen Early, released a statement to the press implying that military segregation had been sanctioned by A. Philip Randolph, president of the Brotherhood of Sleeping Car Porters, Walter White, and T. Arnold Hill, director of the National Urban League's Department of Industrial Relations, at their White House meeting on September 27. Randolph, White, and Hill, however, denounced Early's statement as a gross fabrication of the truth and demanded that Roosevelt make a public statement exculpating them of any participation in such an agreement.

In a letter to White, Early made it clear that the White House could not be held responsible for inferences drawn from press releases.[29] White was not satisfied, insisting that Early's words, "as a result of that conference," conveyed to the public that he, Randolph, and Hill supported segregation in the armed forces when in fact they were diametrically opposed to it. The moral implications of the statement worried these leaders, who feared that if Roosevelt did not exonerate them publicly the black community would think the struggle for integration had come to a halt. Therefore, they reiterated to President Roosevelt that whatever Early's intention, Americans, black and white, would accept the erroneous inferences as truth. Roosevelt finally capitulated and wrote a letter to each of the men, which was reprinted in the official news organ of their respective organizations. The President assured them that he regretted that Early's remarks had been misunderstood, and expressed sorrow that their positions, the position of the White House, and the position of the War Department had not been made clear to the public. Roosevelt ended his letter remarking that "these measures [components of the October 9 policy statement] represent a very substantial advance over what has been the practice in past years. You may rest assured that Negroes are given fair treatment on a non-discriminatory basis."[30] Roosevelt's letter notwithstanding, Walter White and Roy Wilkins subsequently went on a nationwide speaking tour. They spoke in every major city in an effort to solidify black support, which had fluctuated because of Early's statement.[31]

Meanwhile, shortly before the 1940 presidential election, two damaging incidents occurred that proved politically advantageous for the black community. First, the *New York Age* editorialized rumors that Colonel Benjamin O. Davis, Sr., was resigning his commission because President Roosevelt had ignored him in appointing 34 white colonels to brigadier general. The second incident was a political embarrassment. Following a speech Roosevelt had delivered in Madison Square Garden, Stephen Early kicked James Sloan, a black policeman, in the groin for unknowingly blocking Early's entrance to a presidential train bound for Washington, D.C. This incident made news headlines in major newspapers across the country. Although Early had publicly apologized to Sloan and to the New York Police Commissioner, black leaders were outraged.[32]

President Roosevelt also apologized publicly for Early's conduct. But black leaders were not satisfied. Hastie, White, Robert C. Weaver (special advisor to Secretary of Interior Harold Ickes), Hill, Jones, Marshall, Randolph, Houston, Will W. Alexander (presidential advisor on black affairs), and Wilkins formulated strategy to quell the crisis, but they used the incident and the threat of the black vote to gain some military concessions from the government. Secretary of War Stimson apparently felt pressure from the leaders as he noted in his diary that "there is a tremendous drive going on by the Negroes, taking advantage of the last weeks of the campaign in order to force the Army and Navy into doing things for their race which would not otherwise be done and which are certainly not in the interest of sound national defense." Finally, Stimson wrote, "but they are making such progress in their drive that the friends of Mr. Roosevelt are very much troubled and are asking us to do anything we can."[33]

In the meantime, Roosevelt and his aides were discussing and mapping strategy at the White House. Because they felt the black vote was important to the outcome of the 1940 presidential election, Harry Hopkins, chief aide, called in Will Alexander to help resolve the president's dilemma. Black leaders had already met with and instructed Alexander to state four basic demands in return for the black vote. Thus he informed Hopkins that the black community wanted segregation abolished in the armed forces, Colonel Benjamin O. Davis, Sr. promoted to brigadier general, Major Campbell C. Johnson appointed assistant to the selective service director, and Judge William H. Hastie appointed assistant secretary in the War Department.[34]

Except for the abolition of segregation, the government yielded to black demands, and shortly after the political crisis three significant appointments were made: National Director General Lewis B. Hershey announced the appointment of Major Johnson as executive assistant to the office of the Selective Service; President Roosevelt promoted Colonel Davis to brigadier general; and the War Department announced the appointment of Hastie as Civilian Aide to the Secretary of War. Johnson and Davis accepted their positions without hesitation. Their appointments were praiseworthy mainly because they were firsts for black Americans. However, Secretary Stimson considered Davis's promotion political appeasement having no substantive value. Stimson remarked sarcastically, "I had a good deal of fun with Knox over the necessity that he was facing the possibility of appointing a colored Admiral and a battle fleet full of colored sailors according to a Resolution passed by the Colored Federal Employees Association and I told him that when I called next time at the Navy Department with my colored Brigadier General I expected to be met with the colored Admiral."[35]

Unlike the appointments of Davis and Johnson, Hastie's appointment became a controversial issue, and he delayed acceptance of the post. Hastie's attitude toward the newly created position was based largely on his conviction that the office of the civilian aide was just another bureaucratic office established to appease the black community and capture its vote in the 1940 presidential election. Then, too, his knowledge of Emmett J. Scott's role as the black special assistant to Secretary of War Newton Baker during World War I worried him. He viewed Scott as an adjuster of racial ills and black complaints rather than a leading voice for justice and social change within the military establishment. Hastie was particularly concerned that the black community might view him as an appeaser on racial matters. He made his feelings known to Supreme Court Associate Justice Felix Frankfurter, who was Hastie's former law professor at Harvard University and who had recommended Hastie as the best man for the job to Roosevelt and Assistant Secretary of War Robert P. Patterson. Hastie also discussed his appointment with Thurgood Marshall, who was Special Legal Counsel to the NAACP.[36]

Justice Frankfurter told Huntington Thomas, special aide to Patterson, that Hastie felt that his acceptance of the appointment would indicate his support of segregation in the armed forces. To arrest Hastie's concerns, Frankfurter suggested that the War Department release a public statement to the effect that Hastie was persuaded to represent blacks in the department although he strongly opposed a segregated military. Finally, the Justice recommended that Patterson express to Hastie privately his regret over the War Department's policy.[37]

Thurgood Marshall regarded Hastie's anxiety with similar apprehensions. He, too, was concerned that blacks would view Hastie's appointment as political appeasement. Thus in response to a Hastie memo, Marshall wrote him a detailed letter outlining his position. It stated:

I have no doubt concerning the integrity of Mr. Patterson, or of the people associated with him, who are so well recommended by many people as being fair and just. At the present time there is a young war on between the Negroes and the War Department and White House. An appointment at this time will be viewed by the public in one of two ways; either as (a) a victory for Negroes in their fight for full integration into the armed forces without discrimination or segregation or (b) as an act appeasement, as an effort to fool the Negroes and to use a Negro leader for this purpose. At this stage of the fight the odds are that such an appointment will be considered as an act toward appeasement on the part of the War Department without them actually giving up anything.

Of course we are opposed to appeasement. The point is, however, what will the reaction of the Negro public be? What will be the reaction of the membership of the N.A.A.C.P.? I am convinced that the Negroes believe that the fight against the program of the War Department is one of the most important fights we have ever waged and they are anxious to maintain a good fight rather than to consent to any method of appeasement.

If the above statements are true, you start off with the odds against you and the only way to counteract this is by actually showing concrete gain for Negroes. With this in mind, here are my suggestions: *Title.* Any title other than that of Assistant Secretary of War is appeasement. On one hand, Negroes are convinced that *all* of the titles suggested by your memorandum, with the notable exception of Bob Weaver's mean nothing. On the other hand the War Department is so peculiarly set up that actually rank and title means more than anything else under the sun. I cannot imagine a Brigadier General giving any respect to an administrative assistant to the Secretary of War. This goes for the other departments as well. *Responsibilities.* I think your responsibilities should be limited to the Secretary of War only.

The statement accompanying the appointment should set forth that the appointment is for the express purpose of working out a program for the elimination of discrimination and segregation. This, I think, is most important and unless such a statement is made I believe you will be on the spot.[38]

Using advice from Marshall, having Justice Frankfurter intercede on his behalf, and insisting on a title that would not suggest appeasement, Hastie accepted the post with the title of Civilian Aide to the Secretary of War. In his letter of appointment, Secretary Stimson spelled out Hastie's duties in detail. They included aid to the department in developing plans that would ensure the most effective use of black manpower, recommending ways to improve the departments' plans to organize black units in all branches of the services, assisting in the employment of civilian blacks at military installations, investigating discriminatory complaints of black soldiers as well as those of black civilians, and cooperating with blacks on the Selective Service Committee and other agencies concerned with blacks in the Armed Forces.[39]

Hastie was not exactly sure what Stimson's letter meant. He noted, however, that it did not include a specific statement that the War Department was committed to the elimination of segregation and the other discriminatory policies that were major sources of frustration in the black community. He and other black leaders were anxious to have such a commitment in writing. But Stimson refused to provide one, either in writing or verbally. In fact, the War Department's official position regarding black and white relations remained the same: "The Army would not be used as a sociological laboratory for effecting social change within the military establishment." In light of the department's stance, Hastie publicly (as Marshall had suggested) responded to his appointment in such a way as to ensure that his opposition to segregation and discrimination was well known. He declared: "I have always been constantly opposed to any policy of discrimination and segregation in the Armed Forces of this country. I am assuming this post in the hope that I will be able to work effectively toward the integration of the Negro into the Army and to facilitate his placement, training, and promotion."[40]

Hastie's public response to his appointment found considerable support within the black community. Most of the black press and the black leadership were especially pleased with his appointment. The press regarded it as being politically expedient, but "indicated that the black vote would no longer be taken for granted, and could be used as leverage in seeking advancements for the race." The black leadership voiced similar feelings. For instance, T. Arnold Hill congratulated President Roosevelt on Hastie's appointment as well as those of Davis and Johnson. Hill assured Roosevelt that he would find support in the black community for the upcoming presidential election.[41]

Mary McLeod Bethune was equally elated over Hastie's appointment. In a letter to Eleanor Roosevelt, she suggested that if the President ordered the War Department to activate a few black army officers in New York, it would be an incentive for black New Yorkers to vote democratically in the election. Bethune concluded that "if the announcement could come out Saturday, Sunday, or Monday, it will mean a great deal for our cause. The tide of loyalty among my people is rising high. I think we can feel assured 75 percent." In the same spirit, Roy Wilkins exclaimed:

The President came through and gave us a channel through which we can fight. Of course it was political. Of course it was hammered out under pressure. All concessions in government are the result of pressure. Through Hastie we can fight toward the objective we want. We have cracked the toughest department in the whole government. If anything should happen now to put Hastie out, we would have to begin the long, weary fight all over again—and we would not have the advantage of an election campaign in our favor.[42]

The white press made no comments because they considered Hastie's appointment insignificant. Without editorial discussions, most of the newspapers simply reported that Hastie had been appointed civilian aide to the Secretary of War. In contrast, Republican politicians such as Congressman Thomas Reed, Jr. of Maine accused President Roosevelt of befriending blacks because "he knew their votes held the balance of power in some states."[43]

Shortly after Hastie's appointment, Secretary Stimson remarked that "he seems like a rather decent negro who is now Dean of Law in the Law School of Howard University in this city." By October 1942, Stimson would accuse Hastie of having an unrealistic attitude toward solving the race problem in the armed forces, but at the time of Hastie's appointment, Stimson was probably aware that black leaders, the black press, and the black community expected Hastie to be "more than a rubber stamp official" who would work toward integration and the elimination of the inequalities blacks experienced in the armed services. Stimson probably was also aware that Hastie's determination to do an effective job stemmed from his sources of power and his previous career as a public servant and lawyer for the NAACP. Drawing on his capacity to articulate the facts and the immorality of racism and segregation, Hastie was always supported by a majority of the black press and black leaders. All the black national pressure organizations, many white liberals and, to some degree, white national organizations also supported Hastie. As nongovernmental opponents of racism and segregation, these elements were instrumental in exposing the discriminatory policies and practices of the armed forces.[44]

Since Hastie and the other black leaders expected little sympathy from the War Department, they felt it was equally important for them to stress constantly to black soldiers that while they fought for the elimination of discrimination within and outside the government, it was necessary to maintain good discipline and the highest possible rate of military efficiency. Hastie summed up the leaders' aspirations as he prepared to lead the campaign for integration within the War Department. He said: "The man in uniform must grit his teeth, square his shoulders and do his best as a soldier, confident that there are millions of Americans outside the armed forces, and more persons than he knows in high places within the military establishment, who will never cease fighting to remove all social barriers and every humiliating practice which now confronts him. But only by being, at all times, a first-rate soldier can the man in uniform help in this battle which shall be fought and won."[45]

Thus Hastie and the black leaders all agreed that the time was right for them to put pressure on the federal government to take the initiative in promoting equal opportunity and the integration of the armed forces. To this end, Hastie suggested to Walter White and A. Philip Randolph that in their upcoming meeting with President Roosevelt they should emphasize three major points: (1) that blacks vigorously opposed segregated army units; (2) that many whites supported this opposition; and (3) that the Army was not, as Congress had mandated, training blacks for the Army Air Corps. He also wanted them to inquire whether all black units would be officered by blacks; whether blacks would be included in medical training programs; and whether the War Department would make sincere efforts to prevent discrimination against civilian blacks in awarding defense contracts. In all these matters, Hastie urged White and Randolph to convey to the President as strongly as they could the idea that the black community was diametrically opposed to segregation and to the attitude of the federal government toward its black soldiers. Hastie then noted, "If such inquiries are made, I will undoubtedly be asked what the situation is with reference to particular matters. I think between us we will be able to give a more comprehensive picture of the seriousness and diversity of the problems than the persons in authority now have."[46]

Although Hastie and the other black leaders demonstrated solidarity on the issue of army integration, the NAACP and the National Urban League, sensing some confusion and antipathy in the black community, called a black leadership conference in New York City shortly after the Japanese attack on Pearl Harbor. Sixty prominent blacks met to consider the black community's part in the war effort. Judge Hastie, then in his position as civilian aide to the Secretary of War, introduced a resolution (passed with only five dissenting votes) that stated that "colored people are not wholeheartedly and unreservedly all out in support of the present war effort." Walter White summed up the sentiments of the group and attributed the apathy among blacks to discrimination and segregation in the armed services and war industries.[47]

A faction, however, had developed in the black community. A small group of black accommodations opposed integration while the war was in progress. For example, Eddie W. Reevers, editor of the *Messenger*, voiced the sentiments of conservative blacks who felt that such men as Hastie, White, and Randolph, as well as the leading black press such as the *Pittsburgh Courier*, had incited racial hatred among the black masses. As early as August 1941, Reevers had written to Secretary of War Stimson claiming that millions of loyal blacks supported the policies of the War Department. In the same spirit, Charles M. Thomas, editor of the *Washington Tribune*, sent a letter to Stephen Early, stating that there was general dissatisfaction with Hastie's performance as civilian aide. Dr. William Pickens, former director of branches for the NAACP, echoed the same feelings. In May 1942, he was quoted in the *Richmond Times-Dispatch*, a southern white newspaper, as having said that the black community was loyal as a group but suffered from the traitorous influences of some foolish leaders in its midst. Pickens further stated: "It [the Army] is planning to win a war in spite of segregation or those who oppose segregation. Blacks could demand their full citizenship rights after Hitler and the Axis Powers had been defeated. Everything must be sacrificed in winning this war. Such sacrifices are not sacrifices at all."[48]

While Pickens, Thomas, Reevers, and the conservative black press supported segregation during the war, their position did not arouse much enthusiasm among the black masses. Instead, integrationists such as Hastie, White, and Randolph, major civil rights organizations, and an overwhelming majority of the black press wielded the most influence. Thus, in spite of the black conservatives, the integrationists continued to spearhead the black community's thrust toward desegregating the armed forces.[49]

When the war broke out in 1941, black Americans as well as black soldiers seized the opportunity to press the government and the armed forces more vigorously to end a legacy of entrenched segregation and racial discrimination both in the military and on the home front. Blacks were no longer willing to fight and die for the "Four Freedoms" in Europe while they were denied to blacks in America. They found "it simply too difficult to reconcile their treatment with the announced war aims" of the Roosevelt Administration.[50]

Thus the war for black Americans in and out of uniform crystalized into a "Double V" campaign—a campaign to stop the spread of totalitarianism in Europe and to destroy the vestiges of racism in America. Like black soldiers, black Americans on the home front took advantage of the war to register their protest against "a domestic enemy as well as an overseas one."⁵¹

This attitude of stateside blacks was summed up best in 1942. In an editorial, Roy Wilkins reaffirmed black loyalty but stated that black sacrifices in the war should be for a

new world which not only shall not contain a Hitler, but no Hitlerism. And to thirteen million of American Negroes that means a fight for a world in which lynching, brutality, terror, humiliation and degradation through segregation and discrimination, shall have no place—either here or there.⁵²

In March 1942, however, the black press startled its white colleagues by assuming a more determined stance, one that was made visible by the adoption of the "Double V" symbol for victory *at home* as well as abroad. Despite admonitions from the Director of the Office of War Information, Archibald MacLeish, and criticism from members of their own community, black editors insisted that they would not cease the "Double V" campaign until blacks in the military and in the larger community were accorded their full constitutional rights as citizens and soldiers. Besides, said the editors, 91.2 percent of the black community approved of their efforts to force the government to integrate the military.⁵³

The case of Winfred W. Lynn furnished an example of blacks' dedication to eliminating segregation and racial discrimination in the military. Lynn was notified in June 1942 by Local Board 261 of Jamaica, New York, that he had been classified I-A. He replied "Gentlemen: I am in receipt of my draft reclassification notice. Please be informed that I am ready to serve in any unit of the armed forces of my country which is not segregated by race. Unless I am assured that I can serve in a mixed regiment and that I will not be compelled to serve in a unit undemocratically selected as a Negro group, I will refuse to report for induction."⁵⁴

Not receiving the assurances he wanted, Lynn refused to report for duty, claiming that his induction into segregated units violated Section 4(A) of the 1940 Draft Act, which states: "In the selection and training of men under this act, and in the interpretation and execution of the provisions of this act, there shall be no discrimination against any person on account of race or color." The Act also states that " . . . in classifying a registrant there shall be no discrimination for or against him because of his race, creed, or color." Subsequently, Lynn was arrested and indicted for draft evasion. Thus with his case began a two-year saga of the only legal challenge to the jim crow practices of the military in the Second World War.⁵⁵

A lower court judge informed Lynn that to have his case heard he had to submit to induction and then file suit against his superior officer. He did so, and the Federal District Court in New York ruled against him by refusing to hear the case. Thereupon the case was appealed to the U.S. Circuit Court of Appeals. There, the lower court's decision was upheld. Finally, his case reached the U.S. Supreme Court in 1944. The justices refused to hear the case on grounds that Lynn was on active duty overseas and therefore outside the jurisdiction of the court, and that the military officer against whom he had originally brought the suit had retired from the service. The Supreme Court also declared that "...if Congress had intended to prohibit separate white and Negro quotas and calls we believe it would have expressed such intention more definitely than by the general prohibition against discrimination appearing in Section 4."[56]

Although Lynn's case generated almost no press coverage, Selective Service Director General Lewis B. Hershey reacted to his charge that discriminatory segregation and racial quotas violated the Draft Act by commenting publicly that he regretted the case, "but unfortunately the army gets the final say." Hershey went on to say, "What we are doing, of course, is simply transferring discrimination from everyday life into the army. Men who make up the army staff have the same ideas [about blacks] as they had before they went into the army."[57]

In view of Lynn's case, Hastie and other black leaders had raised questions in 1940 about the Draft Act clause that made the Army the final arbiter in determining the circumstances under which it could draft men. Lynn's case confirmed their earlier fears—that the Army could strip virtually all force from the antidiscrimination clause of the Draft Act.[58]

Unfortunately for blacks, the Supreme Court had come down on the side of the Army and adopted discriminatory segregation and racial quotas as official military policy. The Lynn case nevertheless dramatized the extent to which blacks were willing to go to redress their grievances. So the battle went on between the black advocates of integration and those military and political voices who maintained that military efficiency demanded segregation. Throughout the war, changes were being made in the way black soldiers were traditionally treated, but segregation and patterns of racial discrimination continued to manifest themselves on and off the military posts. According to Hastie and others, black soldiers were humiliated, despised, denied regular army privileges, insulted by post commanders, subjected to military and civilian police brutality, accused of crimes they did not commit, constrained by traditional mores, unfairly discharged from military service, denied adequate medical services, court-martialed excessively, and denied adequate entertainment. Their treatment often suggested that they were viewed not as American soldiers but as wards of the armed forces.[59]

18   He, Too, Spoke for Democracy

As a result of these practices the *esprit de corps* of black soldiers remained low throughout the war. But their burdens became easier to bear because Hastie, along with other black leaders and the nongovernmental forces, never wavered from his efforts "to work effectively toward the integration of the Negro into the Army and to facilitate his placement, training, and promotion" on a nondiscriminatory basis.[60]

NOTES

1. "Colonel Eugene Householder's Remarks at the Conference of Negro Newspaper Representatives," Washington, D.C., December 8 and 9, 1941, Civilian Aide to the Secretary of War Subject File, 1940–1947, NARG 107; Judge William H. Hastie, private interview with author, March 6, 1974.

2. For a fuller view see Phillip McGuire, *Taps for a Jim Crow Army: Letters from Black Soldiers in World War II* (Santa Barbara, Calif.: ABC-Clio Press, 1983).

3. Because the War Department had not adequately planned for the drafting, training, and assignments of black soldiers as combatant and noncombatant troops in World War I, much of their performance record was marred during and after the war with official reports and racist innuendo as ineffective soldiers. For more detail, see Arthur E. Barbeau and Florette Henri, *The Unknown Soldiers: Black American Troops in World War I* (Philadelphia: Temple University Press, 1974).

4. Ulysses Lee, *United States Army in World War II: Special Studies: The Employment of Negro Troops* (Washington, D.C.: United States Government Printing Office, 1966), 37–41.

5. Quoted in Lee, *The Employment of Negro Troops*, 39; Lee Finkle, "Forum for Protest: The Black Press and World War II," (Ph.D. dis., New York University, 1971), 73.

6. Letter, Charles H. Houston to President Franklin D. Roosevelt, October 8, 1937, Box C–376, National Association for the Advancement of Colored People Papers, Manuscript Collection, Library of Congress, Washington, D.C. (hereafter cited as NAACP Papers).

7. Letter, Houston to Harry H. Woodring, October 8, 1937, Box C–376, NAACP Papers; Finkle, "Forum for Protest: The Black Press and World War II," 170–171.

8. The 10 percent figure was based on the black percentage of the total population.

9. Andrew Buni, "Robert L. Vann of the *Pittsburgh Courier*." Paper intended for the annual meeting of the Association for the Study of Afro-American Life and History, October 25, 1974, 4–7; *Pittsburgh Courier*, February 16, 1938; Finkle, "Forum for Protest: The Black Press and World War II," 171–177, 182.

10. Letter, Walter White to the Editor of the *Pittsburgh Courier*, June 11, 1938, Box C–377, NAACP Papers.

11. Buni, "Robert Vann of the *Pittsburgh Courier*," 10; Roy Wilkins, "National Defense and Negroes," *The Crisis* 46 (February):49.

12. Letter, White to Roosevelt, September 15, 1939, Box C–377, NAACP Papers. Copies of the letter were sent to Roy Wilkins, Thurgood Marshall, Charles

H. Houston and William H. Hastie; Buni, "Robert L. Vann of the *Pittsburgh Courier*," 8–10.

13. Letter, General Edwin Watson to White, October 17, 1939, Box C–377, NAACP Papers.

14. Letter, William H. Hastie to White, October 26, 1939; Memorandum, Thurgood Marshall and Roy Wilkins to White, October 28, 1939; White to Roosevelt, October 29, 1939, all in boxes C–376 and C–377, NAACP Papers.

15. The text of the National Negro Congress resolution was reprinted in the Congressional Record, 76th Congress, 3rd Session, April 30, 1940, 5253; Horace M. Bond, "Should the Negro Care Who Wins the War?" *The Annals of the American Academy of Political and Social Science* 223 (September 1942): 81–84; Adam C. Powell, Jr., "Is This a White Man's War?" *Common Ground* (April 1942): 111–113.

16. Quoted in Lee, *The Employment of Negro Troops*, 49; Colonel Eugene R. Householder, Assistant Adjutant General, voiced the same sentiments to twenty black newspaper editors on December 8, 1941; he was quoted in the *Chicago Defender*, December 13, 1941.

17. Editorial, *Pittsburgh Courier*, December 28, 1940; *Pittsburgh Courier*, November 2, 1940; Finkle, "Forum for Protest: The Black Press and World War II," 299.

18. By Axis propaganda, King meant that unless black soldiers received fair treatment in the army, the Germans would seize the opportunity to use psychological warfare on the troops in an effort to destroy their morale, and the will to fight for the allied cause.

19. Quoted in Lee, *The Employment of Negro Troops*, 67–69. Similar warnings from R. J. Reynolds of the *Topeka Daily Capitol* were reprinted in the *Congressional Record*, 76th Congress, 3rd Session, May 28, 1940, appendix, 40–48; Elmer A. Carter, "The Negro and Nazism," *Opportunity* 17 (July 1940); 194–195.

20. Jean Byers, "A Study of the Negro in Military Service" (Washington, D.C.: Department of Defense, 1947): 6–9; John P. Davis, "The Negro in the Armed Forces of America," in John P. Davis, ed. *The American Negro Reference Book* (Englewood Cliffs, N.J.: Prentice-Hall, 1966): 627; "Army Can Dodge Anti-Discrimination Clause on Selective Service System," *Pittsburgh Courier*, November 30, 1940.

21. "Secret Army Orders Barred," *Pittsburgh Courier*, November 23, 1940; "Army Jim Crow Orders Defied by Connecticut," *Pittsburgh Courier*, January 4, 1941.

22. Letter, Mary McLeod Bethune to Eleanor Roosevelt, October 5, 1940, Box 151, Judge Robert P. Patterson Papers, Manuscript Division, Library of Congress, Washington, D.C.; Henry L. Stimson Diary, January 24, 1942, Yale University Library, New Haven, Conn.; Walter White, *A Man Called White: The Autobiography of Walter White* (New York: The Viking Press, 1948), 186–187; Colonel Campbell C. Johnson, *Selective Service System Special Groups: Special Monograph No. 10* (Washington, D.C.: United States Printing Office, 1953), 3, 94; Roy Wilkins, "No Negro Draft Board Members in Many States, Says NAACP Survey," *The Crisis* 48 (January 1941): 22; "U.S. Plans New Units of Race Troops," *Norfolk Journal and Guide*, July 6, 1940; Charles S. Johnson, *To Stem This Tide: A Survey of Racial Tension Areas in the United States* (Boston: The Pilgrim Press, 1943), 81; "Only Whites Are Called: Boards All White," *Pittsburgh Courier*, January 4, 1941.

23. Byers, "A Study of the Negro in Military Service," 17; Eli Ginzberg and Douglas W. Bray, *The Uneducated* (New York: Columbia University Press, 1959), 240–245; Colonel Noel F. Parrish, "The Segregation of Negroes in the Army Air Forces" (M.A. thesis, Air University, 1947), 10–11; War Department Pamphlet, *Command of Negro Troops* (Washington, D.C.: United States Government Printing Office, 1944), 9.

24. Stimson Diary, May 12, 1942.

25. "War Department Press Release," The Adjutant General's Office, October 9, 1940, NARG 407.

26. Byers, "A Story of the Negro in Military Service," 80–82; Horace R. Cayton, "Fighting for White Folks?" *The Nation* 45 (September 26, 1942: 267–269; Evelyn P. Meyers, *The Case Against Our Jim Crow Army Demands Investigation By the U.S. Congress* (Washington, D.C.: United States Government Printing Office, 1947), 5; "President O.K.'s Strange Request as Fellowmen Fight for Equality," *Chicago Defender*, October 9, 1940.

27. *New York Age*, October 26, 1940. The letter from Jones and the resolution adopted by the National Urban League were reprinted in this black newspaper.

28. Telegrams, Citizens' Nonpartisan Committee for Equal Rights in National Defense to Roosevelt, October 20, 1940, Franklin D. Roosevelt Papers, Franklin D. Roosevelt Library, Hyde Park, N.Y.; to War Department, October 20, 1940, Box 151, Patterson Papers.

29. Letter, Stephen Early to White, October 18, 1940, Roosevelt Papers; James C. Evans, private interview with author, October 6, 1974. James C. Evans was the last black American to hold the position titled Civilian Aide to the Secretary of War. He assumed the post in 1947.

30. Letters, White to Early and Roosevelt, October 21, 1940; Roosevelt to Randolph, Hill, and White, October 25, 1940, Roosevelt Papers.

31. *New York Amsterdam Star-News*, October 26, 1940.

32. *New York Age*, October 12, 1940. On November 1, 1940, the "Stephen Early Incident" made headlines in the following: *New York Times, New York Amsterdam Star-News, Oregon Statesman, Norfolk Journal and Guide, Washington Afro-American, Pittsburgh Courier, Washington Post, Chicago Defender, Richmond Times-Dispatch, Los Angeles Times, Greensboro Daily News, Vicksburg Herald, Baltimore Sun, New Orleans Times, Savannah Morning News, Montgomery Advertiser, Boston Daily Globe, California Eagle, Chicago Daily News, Philadelphia Tribune, Houston Post, Detroit News, Atlanta Daily World, Atlanta Constitution, Philadelphia Record, People's Voice, Cleveland Gazette,* and *Indianapolis News.*

33. White, *A Man Called White*, 188–189; Samuel A. Stouffer and others, *The American Soldier: Adjustment During Army Life*, Volume 1 (Princeton, N.J.: Princeton University Press, 1949), 489–490; Richard Bardolph, *The Negro Vanguard* (New York: Vintage Books, 1959), 353; Stimson Diary, October 23, 1940; Finkle, "Forum for Protest: The Black Press and World War II," 197.

34. Bardolph, *The Negro Vanguard*, 354; Richard M. Dalfiume, *Desegregation of the United States Armed Forces: Fighting on Two Fronts, 1939–1953* (Columbia, Mo.: University of Missouri Press, 1969), 40–41; White, *A Man Called White*, 187.

35. Press Release, Democratic National Committee Publicity Department Colored Division, October 30, 1940; Stimson Diary, October 22, 25, 1940; Lee, *The*

Employment of Negro Troops, 79; "First Race General in History of United States Appointed," *Norfolk Journal and Guide*, November 2, 1940.

36. Hastie, private interview with author, March 4, 1974; Memorandums, Associate Justice Felix Frankfurter to Robert P. Patterson, n.d., and Huntington Thomas to Patterson, October 21, 1940, Box 151, Patterson Papers. Thurgood Marshall is presently an Associate Justice of the U.S. Supreme Court.

37. Ibid.

38. Letter, Thurgood Marshall to Hastie, October 21, 1940, Box 264, NAACP Papers.

39. Letter, Stimson to Hastie, October 25, 1940, Box 151, Patterson Papers. My research did not reveal whether Patterson spoke to Hastie privately, or if the War Department publicly announced that Hastie had been persuaded to represent the interests of blacks in the department although he strongly opposed a segregated military.

40. Hastie, private interview with author, March 6, 1974; "Colonel Eugene Householder's Remarks at the conference of Negro Newspapers Representatives," December 8 and 9, 1941, NARG 107; *New York Amsterdam Star-News*, November 2, 1940; *Norfolk Journal and Guide*, November 2, 1940.

41. Finkle, "Forum for Protest: The Black Press and World War II," 197–198; Letter, Hill to Roosevelt, October 31, 1940, Roosevelt Papers; *New York Age*, November 2, 1940; Editorial, *Baltimore Afro-American*, November 2, 1940; Editorial, *Pittsburgh Courier*, November 2, 1940.

42. Letter, Mary McLeod Bethune to Eleanor Roosevelt, November 1, 1940, Box 151, Patterson Papers; Editorial, *New York Amsterdam Star-News*, November 2, 1940.

43. Finkle, "Forum for Protest: The Black Press and World War II," 199–200. Finkle revealed that the white press considered Hastie's and the other appointments insignificant and thus did not bother to comment. Editorial, *Greensboro Daily News*, October 26, 1940. The following white newspapers reported Hastie's appointment with few if any comments: *New York Times, Oregon Statesman, Los Angeles Times, Vicksburg Herald, Baltimore Sun, Richmond-Times Dispatch, New Orleans Times Picayune, Savannah Morning News, Montgomery Advertiser*, and *Shreveport Times*.

44. Stimson Diary, October 23 and 28, 1940, and October 19, 1942; Editorial, *New York Age*, November 9, 1940; Editorial, *Cleveland Gazette*, November 2, 1940; Editorial, *Chicago Defender*, November 2, 1940; Editorial, *Norfolk Journal and Guide*, November 2, 1940; *Pittsburgh Courier*, November 2, 1940; Finkle, "Forum for Protest: The Black Press and World War II," 197; White, *A Man Called White*, 188–189; Bardolph, *The Negro Vanguard*, 353; Henry L. Stimson and McGeorge Bundy, *On Active Service in Peace and War* (New York: Harper, 1948), 463; Office Memorandum, "Conference of the Chicago Council of Negro Organizations with Under Secretary Robert P. Patterson," March 29, 1941, NARG 107.

45. Memorandum, Huntington Thomas to Patterson, October 21, 1940, Box 151, Patterson Papers; Hastie, private interview with author, March 6, 1974; William H. Hastie, *On Clipped Wings: The Story of Jim Crow in the Army Air Corps* (New York: NAACP, 1943), 1.

46. Letter, Hastie to White and Randolph, December 21, 1940, Box 264,

NAACP Papers; Rackham Holt, *Mary McLeod Bethune* (New York: Doubleday and Company, 1964), 196–197.

47. Roi Ottley, *'New World A-Coming': Inside Black America* (Boston: Houghton Mifflin Company, 1943), 314–315.

48. *Richmond Times-Dispatch*, May 17, 1942; Letter, Eddie W. Reevers to Henry L. Stimson, August 8, 1941; Letter, Charles M. Thomas to Stephen Early, March 3, 1942, Roosevelt Papers; Warren H. Brown, "A Negro Looks At The Negro Press," *Saturday Review of Literature* 25 (December 19, 1942): 5; Finkle, "Forum for Protest: The Black Press and World War II," 172; Sheldon B. Avery, "Up From Washington: William Pickens and the Negro Struggle For Equality 1900–1954" (Ph.D. diss., University of Oregon, 1970), 243–246.

49. For detailed discussion of the black community's consensus on army integration see Ottley, *'New World A-Coming': Inside Black America*; Hastie, *On Clipped Wings: The Story of Jim Crow in the Army Air Corps*; Richard J. Stillman, *Integration of the Negro in the U.S. Armed Forces* (New York: Praeger, 1968); Dalfiume, *Desegregation of the United States Armed Forces, 1939–1953*; McGuire, "Black Civilian Aides and the Problems of Racism and Segregation In the United States Armed Forces: 1940–1950"; Neil A. Wynn, *The Afro-American and the Second World War* (New York: Holmes & Meier Publishers, 1976); A. Russell Buchanan, *Black Americans in World War II* (Santa Barbara, Calif.: ABC-Clio Press, 1977); Alan M. Osur, *Blacks In The Army Air Forces During World War II* (Washington, D.C.: United States Government Printing Office, 1977).

50. Robert W. Mullen, *Blacks in America's Wars: Shift in Attitudes from the Revolutionary War to Vietnam* (New York: Monad Press, 1973), 55; Buchanan, *Black Americans in World War II*, 113–129; Dalfiume, *Desegregation Of The U.S. Armed Forces*, 105–131.

51. Bernard C. Nalty, *Strength for the Fight: A History of Black Americans in the Military* (New York: The Free Press, 1986), 141; John H. Franklin, *From Slavery to Freedom: A History of Negro Americans*, 5th ed. (New York: Alfred A. Knopf, 1980), 422–444; Buchanan, *Black Americans in World War II*, 113–129; McGuire, *Taps for a Jim Crow Army*, 80.

52. Roy Wilkins, "Now Is the Time Not To Be Silent," *The Crisis* 49 (January 1942): 7.

53. Roi Ottley, "The Negro Press," *Common Ground* 3 (Spring 1943): 11–16; Ottley, *'New World A-Coming'*, 269–270.

54. Quoted in Dwight MacDonald, "The Novel Case of Winfred Lynn, *The Nation* 46 (February 20, 1943): 263.

55. Memorandum of Law, United States ex rel. Winfred W. Lynn against Colonel John W. Downer, William H. Hastie Papers, Howard University Law School, Washington, D.C.; Gerald R. Gill, "Religious, Constitutional, and Racial Objections to the United States Involvement in World War II 1939–1945" (M.A. thesis, Howard University, 1974), 52; MacDonald, "The Novel Case of Winfred Lynn," 263–264.

56. Quoted in S. P. Breckinridge, "The Winfred Lynn Case Again: Segregation in the Armed Forces," *Social Service Review* 18 (September 1944): 370; MacDonald, "The Novel Case of Winfred Lynn," 264–270; MacDonald, "The Supreme Court's New Moot Suit," *The Nation* 159 (July 1, 1944): 13–14; Letter, Winfred L. Kerr,

Chairman of the Lynn Committee To Abolish Segregation In The Armed Forces, to Hastie, April 4, 1944, Hastie Papers.

57. MacDonald, "The Novel Case of Winfred Lynn," 268.

58. Byers, *A Study of the Negro in Military Service*, 6–9; Davis, "The Negro in the Armed Forces of America," 627; "Army Can Dodge Anti-Discrimination Clause on Selective Service System," *Pittsburgh Courier*, November 30, 1940.

59. For detailed discussion of the complaints of black soldiers see McGuire, *Taps for a Jim Crow Army*.

60. Hastie, interview with author, March 6, 1974.

2

The Anguish of Hastie's War Department Experiences

Much of Judge Hastie's first three months in office was spent studying the manner in which black soldiers were being utilized in the armed services. By February 1941, he had prepared a lengthy memorandum entitled "The Integration of the Negro Soldier in the Army" in which he spelled out in detail his observations. Hastie sent the memo to Under Secretary of War Robert P. Patterson and explained that the report represented a critical and unbiased analysis of matters affecting black soldiers, and that it was sent because its contents would not ordinarily come to his attention nor to that of Secretary Stimson. Privately, Hastie said that "the report was written in such a manner as to indicate to the War Department that he intended to attack segregation and discrimination head-on despite the traditional civilian and military practices toward blacks in and out of uniform."[1]

The personnel chart of the percentage breakdown of the number of blacks in the military submitted with the report showed that a decrease of 16, 683 in black manpower would occur by June 1941 if the proposed manpower revisions in the branches of the armed forces were put into effect. The War Department had announced in October 1940 that the total strength of black personnel in the Regular Army would be capped at 92,316. According to Hastie's figures, the percentage breakdown of arms and services, as proposed for June 30, 1941, would result in a black manpower level of 75,633. This meant, argued Hastie, that the total strength of black personnel would be less than 6 percent of the total strength of the Regular Army, despite the War Department's promise in October 1940 to utilize blacks based upon a 10 percent ratio of the total American population. To Hastie the personnel chart revealed even more important forecasts: the Army Air Corps and the Armored Forces were the branches of the military in which blacks would be least represented, while the Quartermaster and Engineering Corps would have disproportionate increases.[2]

Increasing the number of blacks in the Army Air Corps was particularly important to Hastie. At first his top priority was to get more blacks in this branch of the armed services by way of integrated air corps units; however, his efforts in this regard were unsuccessful. Nevertheless, Hastie continued his drive to get more blacks accepted. By 1941, however, getting this branch to accept blacks even on a segregated basis became a major problem for Hastie. The Air Corps quota on black enlisted men unfortunately remained in effect until the early 1950s. Although Hastie knew that Congress had authorized the quota and that the War Department had promised to utilize blacks as early as 1939, he was baffled and made known his feelings to Under Secretary Patterson. Hastie told him that "in view of the tremendous efforts being made to expand the Army Air Corps, the insistence of that Corps upon the segregated training of Negroes should be allowed to result in a plan so circumscribed, that no militarily significant addition of Negroes to the Air Corps can be anticipated for several years."[3]

In the 1941 memo, Hastie also stated that he wanted the Army to make good its promise to train apprentices and black line officers. He told Patterson that he had Secretary Stimson's assurance that apprenticeship programs would be opened, and that black officers would be accepted and accorded the benefits of training in existing army schools on a nonsegregated and nondiscriminatory basis. Hastie finally suggested to Patterson that local commanders of Corps Areas be approached regarding black applicants since they would be primarily responsible for recommending soldiers for such training. Hastie favored the same approach for securing black enlisted men for officer candidate schools. Hastie's anxiety over the possibilities of local commanders, who were all white, denying blacks the opportunities to participate in the officer candidate schools and the specialized training programs stemmed from his knowledge of the fate of blacks at the hands of white commanders during World War I.[4]

The use of blacks in the medical services also concerned Hastie. He suggested to Patterson that the heretofore closed Medical Reserve open its doors to black medical personnel. Hastie based this argument on the fact that the Personnel Division and the Surgeon General's office had projected a need for additional medical manpower in the expanding armed services. Thus he argued that the policy which prevented qualified blacks from obtaining commissions in the Medical Reserve was contrary to personnel projections and "certainly," Hastie wrote, "contradictory to the future needs of the armed services." He wrote of the efforts of his office to encourage the Medical Reserve to open its facilities to blacks without further delay. Hastie then suggested to Patterson that a committee of black medical professionals be created to advise the Medical Corps on problems peculiar to some 75,000 new black enlistees.[5]

Rather than comment in specific terms on Hastie's observations and recommendations, Patterson submitted the memorandum to Chief of Staff George C. Marshall for evaluation and comment. Marshall in turn forwarded it to Major Edwin W. Chamberlain, Chief of the Operations and Organizational-Mobilization Staff. On March 21, 1941, Chamberlain reported on Hastie's memorandum. He suggested that a general comprehensive policy be formulated, pending approval of Secretary Stimson, defining the War Department's policy on the future utilization of black soldiers. Until that was done, stated Chamberlain, "the War Department should rigidly adhere to its present policy." And that policy was segregation. Rather than outline specific policies to support or to counter Hastie's recommendations, Chamberlain commented somewhat generally, reminding General Marshall that "the efforts of the Civilian Aide and the organizations backing him have secured numerous small concessions and are likely to secure more." For example, "the proposal of the Civilian Aide to visit commanders in the field is a case in point," and, said Chamberlain, "the probable demand for a negro percentage of the entire Army equal to the population percentage, a requirement that this percentage extend to all arms and services and to three-year men as well as selectees, has been indicated." Chamberlain concluded: "It appears that these and many other demands are likely to be forced on the War Department with increasing pressure; [however], these demands can best be taken care of by their early recognition and the formulation of a policy which will both discourage their growth and prevent its function."[6]

Chamberlain's memo suggested from the beginning that the War Department's top brass, with whom Hastie would be directly involved in his attempt to promote nondiscriminatory usage and the integration of black soldiers, were determined to maintain the status quo of black/white military relations rather than implement policies leading to the abolition of discrimination and racial segregation. Hastie always felt his recommendations as civilian aide would suffer manipulations during their journey through the bureaucratic maze in the offices of the Assistant and Under Secretaries of War, but he continued to press the War

Department with the hope that, at least, some remedial action toward his objectives for black soldiers would be put into operation. To this end, and in spite of Chamberlain's memo, he, though not optimistic, again recommended to the War Department in September 1941 the integrating of small army units. The department strenuously objected to this recommendation. Hastie countered that the War Department did not comprehend the growing opposition to segregation from both black and white civilians. Moreover, he warned the department that unless segregation was ended the nation would not be effective in a war against foreign enemies.[7]

Hastie's warning stemmed from his conviction that segregation and the racial discrimination of black soldiers were contrary to the American creed. He maintained that he attempted to convince Secretary Stimson and various other War Department officials that the treatment of black soldiers was morally inconsistent with the democratic ideology and rhetoric of the nation and indeed the Roosevelt Administration. Thus, along with his constant efforts to identify and investigate the specifics of the discriminatory nature of the armed services, Hastie believed that his use of moral suasion might have helped to persuade the War Department to relax its racial policies if the Japanese had not attacked Pearl Harbor. "Because of the Japanese attack," he stated, "I was no longer optimistic that it would be possible to persuade the military to eliminate existing racial segregation while World War II was in progress."[8]

The Japanese bombing of Pearl Harbor did indeed create a national emergency, and (to Hastie's dismay but as a confirmation of his belief) it also provided the department and the top military commanders a strong rationale for maintaining segregated army units. For instance the General Staff advised the War Department to reject Hastie's proposal on the grounds that it was based largely upon racial and social principles rather than military expertise. Besides, the staff contended, "every effort should be made by the War Department to maintain in the Army the social and racial conditions which exist in civil life in order that the normal customs of white and colored personnel now in the Army may not be suddenly disrupted." The staff continued, "The Army can, under no circumstances, adopt a policy which is contrary to the dictates of a majority of the people." The staff thought that "to do so would alienate the people from the Army and lower their morale at a time when their support of the Army and high morale are vital to our national needs."[9]

As Chief of Staff, General Marshall sent the official response to Hastie's proposals to Secretary Stimson. Marshall summarized them as being "tantamount to solving a social problem which has perplexed the American people throughout the history of this nation," and, for this reason alone, Marshall insisted that the Army should not attempt to solve a major social problem by such recommendations that Hastie had submitted to the War Department. To do so, according to him, the task of the War Department and the discipline and morale of the Army would be jeopardized, especially during a time of war. With specific reference to Hastie's proposals, Marshall urged Secretary Stimson to recognize the following facts: "First, that the War Department cannot ignore the social relationships between negroes and whites which has been established by the American people through custom and habit; second, that either through lack of educational opportunities or other causes the level of intelligence and occupational skill of the negro population is considerably below that of the white; third, that the Army will attain its maximum strength only if its personnel are properly placed in accordance with the capabilities of individuals; and fourth, that experiments within the Army in the solution of social problems are fraught with danger to efficiency, discipline, and morale."[10]

Hastie was disappointed that the War Department did not act favorably on his recommendations. He made his feelings known to the black press at a scheduled press conference on December 8, one day after the Japanese attack on Pearl Harbor. General Marshall and Assistant Adjutant General Colonel Eugene Householder were also present at the conference. Both men stated clearly that the Army was not and could not be used as a "sociological laboratory" for effecting social change but claimed that steps were being studied to utilize the black soldier in the most efficient capacities.[11]

The black press was also disappointed with the position of the War Department. P. L. Prattis, editor of the *Pittsburgh Courier*, declared that segregation would not end overnight, but the War Department should be aware that the black press strenuously opposed it. Besides, he said, "if we are to have a democratic army, dividing the selectees according to so-called race is scarcely the way to do it." *Norfolk Journal and Guide* editor P. B. Young was conciliatory in his remarks. He stated he believed that "it was the general consensus of those attending the conference that a surprisingly new outlook was vouchsafed by the men in the War Department setup, that they seem openminded to a new deal in relation to the colored American in the armed forces." Claude A. Barnett, president of the Associated Negro Press, disagreed with Young and claimed that the more than twenty editors doubted that segregation in the armed forces was necessary, as General Marshall and Colonel Householder maintained. Barnett supported Hastie but called for a mixed battalion of black and white soldiers rather than small army units as Hastie had suggested. A staff writer for the *New York Amsterdam Star-News*, Roi Ottley, was openly more militant in stating categorically that the black press was the strongest and most articulate voice in the struggle against segregation, and that the press supported Hastie 100 percent.[12]

Although a majority of the black press indeed supported Hastie, John

Sengstacke attacked his credibility as civilian aide. The editor of the *Chicago Defender* viewed Hastie as "a very capable gentleman," but as civilian aide, Sengstacke felt that he had "no appreciable authority and scarcely any influence with the big wigs of the War Department." He saw Hastie as a department official who "can make no commitments [regarding black soldiers], and he cannot explain away segregation and discriminatory practices to which the high officials of his own department are clinging." Sengstacke eventually questioned the purpose of the conference and declared: "It is an obvious attempt to appease belligerent Negro editors who have taken a critical view of the whole panorama of national defense."[13]

Hastie was shocked and surprised at Sengstacke's remarks, but he claimed that he was undaunted. By far they were unfounded, for Hastie was working vigorously on behalf of black soldiers. In fact he had called a secret meeting of the National Legal Committee of the NAACP as early as May 1941 in an effort to map out legal strategy for ending segregation in the armed services. The legal maneuvers surrounding the draft case of Winfred Lynn (discussed in Chapter 1) probably resulted from this meeting. But inasmuch as he was on the inside, Hastie's major efforts, after meandering through a maze of general staff bureaucracy, were directed toward War Department officials. Because he felt that his recommendations were being ignored and/or manipulated, Hastie repeatedly threatened to resign. But Secretary Stimson and Under Secretary Patterson repeatedly promised to make adjustments and remedy some of the inhibitions and discriminatory practices against soldiers and black defense workers if he would not resign. Ironically Stimson agreed in large part with Hastie. His diary indicated that most of Hastie's charges were well-founded, but that integration represented "the hopeless side of the insoluble problem of the black race in this country."[14]

By June 1942, Hastie began to experience periods of anxiety and disillusionment because of the lack of progress he was making toward integrating black soldiers throughout the armed services on a nondiscriminatory basis. Privately he remarked that "I was never optimistic that it would be possible to persuade the military to eliminate existing racial segregation while World War II was in progress." Nonetheless, he worked toward this end. In fact Hastie boldly wrote to Assistant Secretary of War John J. McCloy on June 30 that black protest against racial segregation in the armed forces would continue despite McCloy's warnings that it was more harmful than good.[15]

Whether or not black protest was harmful did not bother Hastie or the black leadership. They made integration of the armed services their highest priority. In spite of the national emergency, while Hastie pressed within the War Department, the black vanguard used various propaganda methods that represented a solid phalanx against racial segregation and the discriminatory practices heaped upon black soldiers. Roy Wilkins editorialized in the *New York Age* that rather than save democracy and destroy Hitlerism the defense program of the country operated deliberately to keep blacks in their places by denying them training, employment, and the opportunity to serve in the armed forces honorably. Mary McLeod Bethune appealed to Eleanor Roosevelt to put pressure on President Roosevelt to come to the aid of black Americans in general and black soldiers in particular. A. Philip Randolph scorned the military's racial policies on nationwide radio. Dr. Charles H. Wesley of Howard University's Department of History challenged the War Department and the White House to implement the "Four Freedoms" at home as forcibly as they were attempting to do so abroad. Walter White and John P. Davis urged the President to meet with them (Roosevelt never did) in an effort to work out a compromise for ending racial segregation and racial discrimination both in the armed services and in the defense plants. And Congressman Arthur W. Mitchell asked the U.S. House of Representatives to consider the patriotism and heroic deeds of black Americans at home and abroad while they sustained the undemocratic racial policies of the War Department. In another speech, Mitchell asked if white America really concerned itself with blacks in the war effort.[16]

The comments of these leaders indicated that they and their respective national organizations gave full support to Hastie's integrationist stance. Of the national organizations, The National Association for the Advancement of Colored People, The March-on-Washington Committee, The National Urban League, and The National Negro Congress advocated stopping at nothing short of full integration of the armed services. The Washington, D.C. Branch of the NAACP, for example, sent a lengthy memorandum to the War Department on January 14, 1942 that spelled out in detail its views on American racism. The branch urged the department to stop paying lip service to antiquated theories of military efficiency, and proposed that institutional racism be abolished in all agencies of the federal government, and in those directly or indirectly associated with it. In the same spirit, the Chicago Branch of the National Urban League and the Chicago Council of Negro Organizations met with Under Secretary Patterson and voiced similar complaints. Patterson's response to the group was negative. Rather than give official support, he told them that he was very disturbed over the development of national organizations opposing anything but complete integration of the armed forces.[17]

The March-on-Washington Committee wielded the most influence during this period. In the spring and early summer of 1941, it sent letters to President and Mrs. Roosevelt and Secretary Stimson. A. Philip Randolph, its director, urged them to support the March-on-Washington by speaking to the marchers at a rally scheduled at the Lincoln Memorial. Randolph claimed that 50,000 or more blacks would march into Washington to demonstrate peacefully the need for jobs, equal opportunity, and the integration of American army and navy forces.[18]

In conjunction with the March-on-Washington Committee, Hastie had requested that Secretary Stimson or some high level official in the War Department speak briefly but candidly to the marchers about segregation and discrimination in the Army and defense industries. He also suggested that the department representative be prepared to explain the following: the failure of the President to ban discrimination in defense industries; why the Senate continued to delay action on Senate Resolution 75, which called for an investigation of discriminatory practices in employment and the exclusion of blacks from the Navy, Marine, and Air Corps; why the Army refused to modify racial segregation; and why widespread discriminatory practices continued in civil service appointments. Although Stimson did not respond to Hastie's memo one way or the other, he did meet with Randolph and Walter White at the White House on June 18, 1941. Stimson's diary indicated only that a discussion of the impending march took place.[19]

Meanwhile President Roosevelt experienced a great deal of anxiety over the impact that the threatened march might have on the nation and the democratic countries of the world. Subsequently he asked Eleanor Roosevelt to ask Under Secretary Patterson what could be done to prevent the march. Mrs. Roosevelt discussed the issue with Patterson, and he recommended that she and General Edwin M. Watson, Roosevelt's secretary, meet with Hastie and Randolph. Patterson prepared two memos: one for Eleanor Roosevelt and the other for General Watson. Watson was instructed to tell Hastie and Randolph to inform the black leadership that the War Department had implemented its policy announced on October 9, 1940; that black units had been organized in all branches of the armed forces (not true according to Hastie); and that Benjamin O. Davis, Sr. had been promoted to brigadier general, a rank never before attained for which blacks should be proud. General Watson was advised to say further that "the complaints that we have not mingled white troops and Negro troops in the same units are unfounded [because] such a mingling was not a part of the President's policy, and for practical reasons it would be impossible to put into operation." Patterson then instructed Watson to emphasize and end his discussion with these words: "It would seem that Negroes might be inspired to take pride in the efficiency of Negro units in the Army, as representing their contribution to the armed forces."[20]

To Eleanor Roosevelt, Patterson suggested that she say to Randolph that Judge Hastie had constantly advised her and the War Department on questions involving black servicemen and, by June 30, 1941, that the total number of blacks in the armed forces would exceed 80,000. Finally, Patterson instructed her to tell Randolph that black soldiers were attending all of the regular service schools on a nondiscriminatory basis (not true according to Hastie) except those of the Air Corps because a separate school would be established in this branch of the armed forces.[21]

It was folly to think that this appeasing language would persuade Randolph to call off the march. Nonetheless he listened to Mrs. Roosevelt and General Watson but did not abandon his plans for the march. Randolph maintained that if the President did not issue an executive order banning segregating and discrimination the march would proceed as scheduled. Rather than chance the disruptive nature of a mass march, Roosevelt issued Executive Order 8802. It prohibited discrimination, not racial segregation, in the nation's defense industries and in the armed forces.[22] Although the order was not enforced adequately, it provided a psychological stimulant to black morale, and validated another strategy—mass marches—for winning concessions from the federal government. This tactic was never used, however, for integrating the armed services.

By 1942 the integration of the armed services had become a major topic of discussion among the white segment of the population. Several of its recognized liberal leaders supported Hastie and his efforts to integrate the armed services. The "Committee of 100," for example, appealed to the American public to support Hastie. Such notables as Alice G. Brandeis, Edwin R. Embree, Helen Keller, Paul Kellogg, Cornelia B. Pinchot, Arthur S. Spingarn, Oswald Garrison Villard, and Justice James H. Wolfe, to name a few, made up its membership.[23]

But the forces of racism were too strong at this time for the Roosevelt Administration to implement what would have been a social revolution within the military, a development that probably would have impacted greatly on the social institutions of the nation as a whole.

The main separatist forces that advocated against Hastie and his supporters included: (1) the powerful southern politicians who headed the House Military Appropriations and Senate Armed Services Committees; (2) the War Department; (3) the White House; (4) Southern Congressmen; and (5) white supremist groups.

In spite of the position voiced by these anti-integrationists, there existed a white minority whose support of Hastie was very strong. For instance, the Union of Democratic Action sent a petition with 50,000 signatures to President Roosevelt asking for the elimination of all segregation and racial discrimination in the armed services. These personalities included Governors Charles Edison of New Jersey, Herbert B. Maw of Utah, Sam C. Ford of Montana, and former Governor Culbert Olson of California. Mayors signing the petition were Fiorello LaGuardia of New York City, George J. Harter of Akron, and Leo J. Promen of

Fund du Lac. Among the clergy were Bishops Guy K. Sherrill of Massachusetts, G. G. Bennett of Rhode Island, and Benjamin M. Washburn of New Jersey. Some college presidents were Frank P. Graham of the University of North Carolina, Algo D. Henderson of Brooklyn College, Paul Klapper of Queens College, and Henry Sloan Coffin of the Union Theological Seminary. John Dewey and Daniel Gregory Mason of Columbia University, Marion E. Park of Bryn Mawr, Preston W. Slossom of the University of Michigan, and F. Ernest Johnson at Columbia University Teachers College were among the college and university professors who signed the petition. Actress Joan Bennett and producer Walter Wagner were signers from the entertainment world.[24]

Hastie also had the support of The American Youth for Democracy. This group censured the War Department for its racial policies, and warned the department on October 17, 1943 that it would work vigorously "for full integration and unconditional equality for the Negro people in the armed services, factories and every phase of social and political life."[25]

Although in the minority, several western newspapers supported Hastie and the struggle against the racial policies of the War Department. But their endorsements were minimal when compared to the opposition of the press, especially the southern press, who opposed Hastie. Their opposition represented a powerful and effective voice against him and the mere thought of mixing black and white troops. The *Gadsden Times* of Gadsden, Alabama, reflected the general tone of the opposition press. Unequivocally it stated that "the social equality that is utterly inobtainable even under war conditions, is sought nevertheless, and at the expense of the war effort; the pushing of such an issue in such times is a species of madness and should be stopped before great harm is done." Southern politicians expressed the same sentiments. Congressman John E. Rankin of Mississippi was quoted in the *Washington Post* as having said that "the white people of the south are on the alert, and the better element of the Negro race refused to join in such movement." And Governor Herman Talmage of Georgia declared that northern politicians were attempting to use the Army to mix the races for social equality.[26]

In spite of the position of the majority of the white press, the attitude of powerful politicians and the White House, and the intransigent stance of the War Department, Hastie intensified his efforts to force the department to increase the number of black soldiers and to utilize them on an integrated and nondiscriminatory basis in areas of the service other than in the labor and supply units. He considered the black press the best medium to aid him in accomplishing these objectives. In October 1942, Hastie recommended to General H. B. Lewis, Acting Adjutant General, that he urge Under Secretary Patterson to press the Public Relations Bureau to amplify its advertisement program in such a way that the black press could be used in the recruitment of blacks. His recommendation was indicative of complaints from black editors that the black press had not received its share of recruiting ads from the War Department. Hastie's recommendation was also supported with letters from Senator Harry F. Byrd and Representative Wender H. Harris of Virginia, both of whom asked Under Secretary Patterson to urge the Public Relations Bureau to place some recruiting advertisements in the *Norfolk Journal and Guide*. These men probably did not object to blacks being recruited for a segregated army, despite their segregationist posture. Patterson informed Byrd and Harris, however, that since the War Department's annual appropriations did not permit advertising in all newspapers and periodicals in the country, a general formula had been adopted in 1939 to insure the wisest expenditures of the available funds. Patterson also told the Congressmen that the Army's formula included only those newspapers and periodicals that appealed to the general public and were distributed in cities where army recruiting and induction stations were located. He maintained further that "papers published primarily in the interest of any political, religious, racial, or social group are uniformly excluded, [and] no exceptions have been made to this policy and it is considered unwise to depart from the formula at this time." Patterson concluded his letter by insisting that "the War Department must be able to answer any charges of discrimination which may arise, and this can be done only through strict adherence to the approved formula."[27]

Unaware of the recruitment formula, Roy Garvin, national editor of the Washington and Baltimore Afro-American Newspapers, also wrote to General Lewis. Lewis gave Garvin the same information that Patterson had given Byrd and Harris but explained the formula in more detail. Lewis assured Garvin, moreover, that the formula had been agreed to by competent advertising experts. Unfortunately the competent experts did not include Hastie or any black newspaper personnel. But the formula agreed to excluded the use of all black newspapers and magazines for advertising.[28]

The formula for newspaper advertising included all Sunday newspapers published in cities of 150,000 people or more where recruiting and induction stations were located and in which no Sunday newspapers were published. Section three of the formula stated in essence that no advertisements would be placed in weekly, semiweekly, or triweekly newspapers in any city with a population of fewer than 150,000 people where there was daily newspaper distribution. Section four related to magazines. Black magazines were excluded, for it was doubtful that one could meet the minimum requirement of 2,000,000 copies per issue in 1942. Hastie felt that the last section of the formula excluded the remotest possibility of black media participating in the recruitment program, since it specified that no advertisements would be placed in newspapers or magazines that represented the interest of a particular ethnic group.[29] Sections three and five also disturbed Hastie. He argued that these sections were particularly discriminatory because the black masses in 1942 normally read black newspapers published weekly, semiweekly, or triweekly, and which reflected the black community.[30]

Meanwhile, C. A. Franklin, editor of the *Cleveland Call and Post*, informed the United States Recruitment-Induction Station Services that although the War Department maintained its recruitment formula to avoid discriminating against other ethnic groups, white youths were being reached through the major dailies. Black youth, on the other hand, were not being reached because their experiences had taught them that advertisements in the white press were not meant for blacks. Franklin felt that advertisements placed in the black press would raise morale and increase black loyalty and support for the total war effort.[31] In a similar letter to Hastie, Franklin asked him to press hard for the cause of the black press, for "we are the daily press, the magazines and everything else to the Negro reader; we must be used if appeal is made to Negroes effectively."[32]

Hastie was more aware of the problem than Franklin and other black editors realized. He had appealed to the acting Adjutant General and to Howard C. Petersen, a special assistant to Under Secretary Patterson, to urge Patterson to have the recruitment formula modified in such a way that the black community would believe the Army sincerely wanted black youths to participate in the war effort.[33]

In addition to his efforts within the War Department, in September 1942 Hastie had asked Walter White to use the strength and influence of the NAACP to put pressure on the War Department to change its advertisement formula. Rather than change or modify the formula, the War Department agreed to a compromise. Secretary Stimson asked Hastie, White, and General Alex P. Surles, Director of the Public Relations Bureau, to work out a plan designed to minimize racial antagonisms and to encourage more blacks to join the Army and apply for the special training programs. The men agreed that letters, radio broadcasts, lectures, pamphlets, and a motion picture should be the methods for minimizing racial animosity and increasing the number of blacks in the Army.[34]

The educational pamphlet entitled *Army Talk* and the motion picture entitled "The Negro Soldier" were given top priority in the implementation of the agreement reached between the War Department, Judge Hastie, and Walter White. These aspects of the compromise were developed by the Special Service Division of the Public Relations Bureau. Under its chief, General Frederick H. Osborn, the Special Service Division distributed *Army Talk* monthly to soldiers in America and in foreign countries. Once the black soldiers became visible entities within the military establishment, such titles as "Prejudice! Roadblock To Progress," "Insecurity Breeds Prejudice," and "Prejudice Endangers Victory" were used as pamphlet headlines to ease the racial tension between black and white soldiers.[35]

Except in the South, "The Negro Soldier" was shown to soldiers as well as to civilian Americans in most of the theaters around the country. The NAACP had to file an *Amicus Curiae* brief in the District Court of New York against the War Activities Committee of the Motion Picture Industry before the American public in the South could see the achievements of black soldiers on film. Hastie and Thurgood Marshall, Chief Counsel for the NAACP, wrote the brief that convinced the court that any interference with the distribution of the film would seriously hinder the war effort.[36]

In spite of Hastie's relentless drive to get the War Department to place recruitment advertisements in the black press, it refused to modify its position. Yet the "compromise" worked out between Hastie and the Public Relations Bureau can serve as a glaring example of how the War Department tacitly admitted that racial discrimination lay at the core of its recruitment policy. Nevertheless Hastie achieved much of his objective: to increase the number of blacks and to integrate them into the armed forces. Blacks were enrolled and graduated from the Army's special training schools on an integrated basis, even though they were returned to segregated army units in the Regular Army; more black units were created to absorb the increased number of black inductees; and the number of black applicants for specialized training increased threefold.[37]

Documentary evidence revealed neither the reason why nor the date on which the advertisement policy was changed or modified to include the black press, but after 1942 a substantial number of black newspaper clippings for army recruitment were found among the papers of Colonel Campbell C. Johnson, black Special Assistant to the Selective Service Director, and in the archival records of the Civilian Aide to the Secretary of War.[38] Thus one would be reasonably safe in assuming that the ban on advertisements in the black press was lifted sometime after 1942.

Although Hastie was convinced that the advertisement policy was deliberately formulated and implemented to keep blacks out of the armed services, available evidence did not support his contention. But in examining traditional military policies regarding blacks, a *prima facie* case can be made that Hastie was more right than wrong in his belief that the recruitment policy was an army strategem to prove itself innocent of the charge of racial discrimination.

Hastie also languished over the dilemma of the black officer. He questioned more than once why the War Department disrespected black officers, questioned their leadership abilities, and made policies that perpetuated negative myths and caused the black officers to be treated so unevenly. The department never responded directly to Hastie's inquiries, but he believed that its policies concerning black officers were based upon a legacy of racial epithets. No matter how educated they were, what special training they had, or how many years they had served, black officers were viewed as men "past the stage of youthful daring and initiative, short on education, without self-confidence or any reason for it, poorly selected and inadequately trained for his army job, ridiculed by whites, uneasy with his men and perhaps not entirely trusted by them; and convinced by all his experience that the way to survive in the Army was to avoid 'causing trouble.' " The black officer also had "to agree with the white man and try not to make decisions on his own, and to employ whatever devices would protect him from the unjust, illogical, irrational hostility of the white army." He "might have bars put on his shoulders or stripes on his sleeve, but those alone would not imbue him suddenly with the shields and commanding presence needed to lead men in battle."[39]

Although the above quotation reflected the position of the War Department and the military commanders toward black officers in World War I, Hastie felt that this attitude changed only reluctantly, remaining generally the same throughout the Second World War. For example, Secretary of War Stimson wrote in 1940 that "leadership is not imbedded in the negro race yet and to try to make commissioned officers to lead the men into battle—colored men—is only to work disaster to both." He continued, "Colored troops do very well under white officers but every time we try to lift them a little bit beyond where they can go, disaster and confusion follows." Stimson went on, "In the draft we are preparing to give the negroes a fair shot in every service, however, even to aviation where I doubt very much if they will not produce disaster there." Finally, Stimson noted, "nevertheless they are going to have a try, but I hope for Heaven's sake they won't mix the white and the colored troops together in the same units for then we shall certainly have trouble."[40]

In spite of the fact that officer candidate schools were opened and R.O.T.C. continued for blacks in 1940, "production of black officers was very slow and it was not until 1942 that appreciable numbers of blacks were graduated." Nonetheless, "black officers constituted less than 1.9% of all officers in the military by 1945." Unfortunately "none achieved general officer or flag rank during the war."[41] Hastie wanted to know why this situation existed. Under Secretary Patterson claimed that even black troops preferred white officers over black officers. According to Hastie, this was not true. In addition, the only study conducted on this question during the war concluded that a majority of black troops preferred black officers over white officers. Retired Lieutenant Colonel Jesse J. Johnson remembered that "it was the War Department and the white officers who perpetrated the degradations, myths, and bad impressions of the black officer."[42] Had the War Department promoted a policy of placing black officers in command of the all-black units, the percentage of black officers may have been higher. Instead, the department adhered to a tradition of racial discrimination against its black officers.

The problem arising from the low percentage and use of black officers was vexing to the officers themselves as well as to Hastie and the War Department. It stemmed largely from reports on the performance of black officers in World War I, from Stimson's belief that black troops operated more efficiently when commanded by white officers, from the War Department's rationale that black officers were unable to get the proper respect from noncommissioned black soldiers, and from the general belief that white officers were able to obtain goods and services for their men when black officers could not. More than any other factors, these were the reasons that accounted for the discrimination practiced against black officers.[43]

Hastie approached this situation squarely. Although he faced an uphill struggle to get more black officers placed in the Regular Army, his dilemma worsened as a result of a directive from the secretary of war. Stimson ordered all commanding officers to make great efforts to select qualified blacks for officer candidate schools. For Hastie the problem with Stimson's directive stemmed from the word "qualified." To him this single word served as a loophole for commanding officers to reject those blacks who were unalterably qualified to enter the schools. In fact, Hastie stated emphatically that "Field Commanders had not been convinced that the War Department actually intended that Negroes be freely admitted to officer candidate schools."[44]

Those blacks who managed to achieve officer rank faced other discriminatory problems. Rather than move toward the effective placement of black officers in the Regular Army, the War Department became increasingly alarmed over their growing number. The department worried over the possibility of blacks being in command of white troops and especially of white officers. The answer to this dilemma was finally written into official policy for the first time in April 1942.[45]

The War Department decided that black officers could on rare occasions command white enlisted men, but they would be prohibited from commanding white officers during the war crisis. One post commander even went so far as to state that no black officer could ever hope to outrank his lowest-ranked white officer. Another commander declared that white first lieutenants would be superior to a black officer with the rank of captain. In other commands blacks who managed to rise above the rank of first lieutenant were almost always stationed among units with black staffs. If a situation occurred in which a black officer outranked white officers, the army systematically instituted a shifting program. The black officer usually ended up commanding a noncombatant black service unit.[46]

The policy that no black officer would be given a command position in charge of white officers paid homage to racism and indicated the general thinking of the War Department and the officials of the officer candidate schools, even though it contradicted in spirit Secretary Stimson's assurance to Hastie that the schools would be opened on a nonsegregated and nondiscriminatory basis. Though the schools were opened, Hastie reasoned that when a black graduated from a particular school and was then restricted to the command black and white noncommissioned officers or to noncombatant service units, this reflected the paradoxical character of the military. He believed, too, that the one difficulty with the assignment and promotion of black officers arose from the fact that white officers were routinely assigned to command duty while black officers had to wait for the War Department to indicate specifically that a particular position be filled by a black.[47]

Because Hastie had hoped to strengthen his argument for the elimination of segregated army units and facilities with the results of integrated training at the officer candidate schools, he was quick to point out the racial overtones of the War Department's announcement in 1943 that the white graduates of the schools had risen to the ranks of captains and lieutenant colonels in less than two years, while no black graduate had been promoted beyond the rank of first lieutenant.[48]

A glaring example of the discriminatory promotion system was found in the records of two officers of the 93rd Division, one black, Second Lieutenant Martin Winfield, and one white, First Lieutenant Raymond Grube. Lieutenant Winfield was assigned to the 3rd Battalion of the 25th Infantry Regiment as communications officer. He received this assignment after graduating second in his class from infantry school and first in his class from communications school. During the Bougainville Campaign, he worked on very difficult terrain with inadequate supplies and personnel. His commander turned in a report that indicated the high proficiency of Winfield's work on the island. When Winfield became crytography officer on Green Island, he again displayed exceptional skill and high efficiency. As late as February 1945, Winfield was still a second lieutenant. On the other hand, Lieutenant Grube was motor officer of the 1st Battalion of the 25th Infantry. As the motor officer, he illegally ordered and installed a motor in his civilian car. For this offense, Grube was court-martialed, found guilty of embezzling government property, and fined $300. One year later he was promoted to captain and given a command position.[49]

In numerous instances, black officers were overlooked for promotions, humiliated, denied military protocol, disrespected, and forced to be "Uncle Toms." For example, a young white private from Virginia stated: "Gosh, I just had to salute a damn nigger lieutenant. Boy, that burns me up." Black officers themselves spoke of their problems, especially in the South: "To go to a nearby city is to invite trouble. Not only from civilian police but more often from the military police, who are upheld in any discourtesy, breach of discipline, arrogance, and bodily assault they render the Negro officers."[50]

In spite of the dilemmas of black officers, Hastie sighed with relief because of his nominal success in getting blacks placed in the officer candidate schools and, when graduated, in minimal command positions of blacks and on occasion white enlisted men.

The issue surrounding black officers had hardly subsided before Hastie began working expeditiously to increase the number of black medical personnel in the Army. He pressed the War Department on this matter with equal vigor and hopeful determination to correct or modify yet another problem faced by blacks both in and out of uniform and, in this case, the difficulty black nurses faced in the Army Nurses Corps.

As Hastie pressured the War Department, his first concern was the exclusion of black physicians and dentists from local induction boards. Rather than answer Hastie directly, however, Secretary Stimson directed the Chief of Staff, in concurrence with the Surgeon General of the Army, to prepare a form letter for use when Hastie and/or his assistant, Truman K. Gibson, Jr., presented such discriminatory charges to the War Department. Brigadier General William E. Shedd, Assistant Chief of Staff, prepared the letter. He sent it to Hastie. It stated that "the War Department has not and cannot specify that induction boards be composed exclusively of either white or negro physicians [because] Corps Area Commanders have been instructed to make up induction boards from among the personnel available to them, including where necessary the hire of reputable civilian physicians." General Shedd concluded by appealing to Hastie to "understand the difficulties inherent in this problem and that you know the War Department does plan to fully utilize the services of negro doctors and dentists as rapidly as circumstances permit."[51]

Experiences with the racial prejudices of Corps Commanders, especially in the South, however, had created in Hastie the belief that these men could not be relied upon to correct discriminatory practices. Thus he consulted Under Secretary Patterson on the matter. Before a scheduled meeting with Patterson, Hastie sent him a memo outlining the areas he wanted to cover in their conversation. He contended that since the Personnel Division of the General Staff and the Office of the Surgeon General estimated that approximately from 200 to 300 black doctors and from 50 to 60 black dentists would be needed as the Army expanded, it seemed that the policy preventing qualified blacks from obtaining commissions in the Medical Reserve was unjustified. Hastie believed the Army Medical Corps was doggedly sticking to a policy of complete exhaustion of the small group of black reserve physicians before any additional officers were commissioned. He appealed to Patterson to take whatever action necessary to force the Medical Corps to grant Reserve Commissions to at least the number of black doctors and dentists projected for the expanded Army. The black press was also supportive of Hastie's position.[52]

Patterson was sensitive to this problem as he had been to others involving the fair and equal treatment of blacks in the armed forces. As a matter-of-fact, he sent a memo to the Surgeon General immediately following his talk with Hastie. He asked Dr. Norman T. Kirk to recommend that the number of 60 black doctors and 15 black dentists be increased to the black percentage of the projected expansion of the Army. Patterson said further that "it seems to me that there is sound reason for the commissioning of additional negro doctors and dentists from the men now subject to service under the Selective Service Act." He also suggested that Kirk act quickly "otherwise these men will get located into units, and it may be very difficult later on to extricate them and put them to a line of duty on which their abilities and experiences qualify them."[53]

Black nurses experienced the same fate as black physicians and dentists. As late as 1945, the Army Nurses Corps had less than 3% black representation. This meant that approximately 7% of the 9,000 available black nurses were needed to satisfy the 10% black ratio of the total population. George Marshall, chairman of the National Federation for Constitutional Liberties, concluded that the limited number of black nurses represented the exclusion policy of the Navy and a policy of discouragement on the part of the Army. He was referring to the policy of the Army to restrict black nurses to hospitals staffed exclusively by black medical personnel, and to the smaller black medical units operating within large white medical establishments. Like Hastie, Marshall urged the Surgeon General to utilize black nurses on a fully integrated basis rather than on a policy based upon race and/or the need of black troops. A biracial delegation to the War Department expressed the same sentiments in a petition, signed by 15,000 persons. These grievances were directed at Dr. Kirk and Secretary Stimson because they had announced in 1943 that the Army Nurses Corps would utilize all nurses based on the existing needs of the armed services. Yet, the need for 8,000 additional nurses announced by President Roosevelt early in 1945 did not pave the way for more black nurses, despite the War Department's lifting of its quota on black nurses. This was so because within the 50,000 ceiling established for all nurses, black nurses were disproportionately rejected based on the number of blacks inducted into the armed services, which never reached the 10% black ratio of the total population. Gibson attempted to get Assistant Secretary of War John J. McCloy to rescind the 50,000 ceiling, but he failed.[54]

Hastie and Gibson were successful in getting the Army to commission more black medical personnel and to remove the priority quota for black nurses, but they failed to persuade the Surgeon General and the War Department to initiate a nonsegregated medical corps. The establishment of two black medical facilities however at Fort Huachuca and Tuskegee Air Base marked the end of the institutional rejection of blacks in the medical services of the United States Armed Services.[55]

Besides being one of the first facilities for black medical personnel, Tuskegee Air Base was important in other ways. It symbolized partial success for Hastie in his drive to get the War Department and the command of the Army Air Corps to accept blacks for aerial combat training.

Because the Army Air Corps was relatively new, Hastie had hoped that blacks would be retained and utilized in nonsegregated facilities and nonsegregated flying units. Tuskegee Air Force Flying and Training Center was established instead. Even this separate facility met with some opposition in the House of Representatives. Congressman Ludlow of Indiana had sponsored an amendment to the 1939 Military Appropriations Bill that would have allocated funds to train white but no black pilots. The House voted on this measure and made available $1,000,000 to train black pilots.[56]

Although Hastie objected in principle to Tuskegee Air Base, he regarded it as a move toward the eventual introduction of black pilots into regular air combat when the United States would later enter the war. But his hopes and desires faded quickly when segregated training facilities were established at the base. Hastie, more than anyone else, seemed to understand the Army's plan. He believed the War Department, rather than sheltering black soldiers from the humiliation and practice that tended to make them feel inferior, had deliberately planned such a program. He discussed the Tuskegee situation with Secretary Stimson, but these talks proved fruitless since Stimson, citing official reports, insisted that the progress being made at Tuskegee was satisfactory. Hastie's attitude was unchanged, however.[57]

Shortly after his meetings with Hastie, Stimson recorded in his diary, "I was profoundly disappointed with the attitude he took." He felt that Hastie "was not realistic and I am afraid his usefulness is limited." Stimson continued that "the two interviews took a great deal of drain out of me because I did my best to win him and to reassure him as to our attitude and I felt I had not made a success of it." Stimson had not been successful because Hastie had been to Tuskegee himself and reported that "the situation there was very bad and that Negroes were being unfairly discriminated against." Stimson nevertheless rejected Hastie's claim because Tuskegee's white officers had reported otherwise.[58]

The black press and the black leadership supported Hastie's view concerning Tuskegee, but according to Sidney Walker, staff correspondent for *Pittsburgh Courier*, they had suppressed their protest "because, although the Tuskegee school is a jim-crow school in principle no matter how it is sugar-coated, they wanted their boys above all to make good airmen for Uncle Sam."[59]

Although Walker's statement was not entirely true, especially in 1943, Hastie had expressed the same sentiments to Robert A. Lovett, Assistant Secretary of War for Air, in April 1941. Perhaps as a pressure tactic, he had warned Lovett that "if in addition to the segregated training school, the Army insists upon the separation of white and colored personnel attached to the same unit, such a nationwide storm of protest and resentment will arise as to destroy all the goodwill and support of the Negro public with reference to the Army program." He continued with an appeal to Lovett to modify the Tuskegee situation, but also insisted that "no single enterprise is being watched as closely by Negroes as the Air Corps Training Program."[60]

Lovett ignored Hastie's warning, and announced publicly that the Air Corps would follow the policy established by the War Department. The black press, the black leadership, and several white leaders regarded the announcement as an incorrigible stand for which they could no longer keep silent. With Hastie's support, they launched an attack upon the War Department's Air Corps policy. The press ran a series of exposés, and both black and white leaders wrote newspaper diatribes and sent protest letters to Secretary Stimson and the chiefs of staff. They objected to the Army's continued use of white rather than black aviation instructors; to jim crow room and board facilities; to the refusal of the Air Corps to train blacks as flyers for heavy bombers; to the use of whites only in command positions; to the rejection of blacks for the Air Corps Reserve.[61]

Hastie discussed these issues with the Air Corps Command, placing major emphasis upon its instructors and training, and upon how black airmen were being utilized. His efforts along these lines created an impasse between him and the War Department, which lasted until his resignation in January 1943.

Although Hastie accepted the training school at Tuskegee, he refused to sanction what he termed the racist tactics involved in the Army's selection of its officers and training instructors. Not one officer and few instructors were black. As late as 1942, the situation at Tuskegee remained unchanged. In June of that year, Hastie finally requested that Colonel Richard T. Coiner, Air Corps executive, provide him with information on the use of blacks as training instructors, and the progress being made in replacing white officers with black officers. Coiner replied that white personnel would be replaced with black personnel as soon as they were trained. Hastie felt that Coiner's answer was perfunctory and simply a stalling device to prolong unjustified discrimination against blacks. Subsequently he asked Under Secretary Patterson to investigate the matter. Patterson apparently agreed with Hastie and asked Assistant Secretary Lovett to speed up the replacement progress. The replacements came however only after months of black protest and Hastie's resignation.[62]

The creation of separate black aviation squadrons at Tuskegee was another source of frustration for Hastie. These squadrons, according to him, were organized when the Air Command agreed to accept 2,500 black soldiers as pilot trainees. They were eventually assigned to all Army air fields to be utilized as the local commanders wished. More often than not they performed menial tasks. The War Department accused Hastie of blowing this issue out of proportion, but Patterson indirectly confirmed Hastie's accusation. In a 1942 letter to Wilbur La Roe, Chairman of the Washington Federation of Churches' Committee on Civic Affairs, Patterson revealed that blacks were indeed being used mainly as labor and maintenance crews. The letter was reprinted in the *Congressional Record*. In it, Patterson admitted that the aviation squadrons provided a place for men in the Army Air Force who did not qualify for more technical duties. He admitted further that "the duties they [blacks] perform are to a large extent labor and housekeeping jobs that have to be done at every Air Force Base." But Patterson modified his statement, explaining that "while there are no white units actually named 'aviation squadrons (separate)' there are many white headquarters squadrons which perform the same type of duties at Air Force installations."[63]

Hastie disagreed vehemently with Patterson. He believed the aviation squadrons were created to provide a place for blacks rather than mix them with the regular air force units. Thus he objected to Patterson's efforts to whitewash the fact that 95% of the blacks who had entered the Air Force had been assigned to these aviation squadrons, regardless of their ability, by announcing publicly that they did not qualify for more technical duties. Hastie had discovered that there was no attempt by the Air Command to prevent the assignment of men with superior abilities to these labor units. There was no reason to question Hastie's findings, since Secretary Stimson had admitted in his diary that "the Army had adopted rigid requirements for literacy mainly to keep down the number of colored troops."[64] The scores made on the Army Classification Tests determined the placement of men in the Army Air Force.

In addition to wasting black manpower, Hastie criticized the War Department and the Air Command for misleading the American people to believe that the aviation squadrons were receiving training as pilots, mechanics, and technical specialists when in reality the only pilot training the soldiers received came from civilian, not military, personnel at a few black colleges and universities. When the Air Corps finally decided to train black pilots, the 99th Pursuit Squadron was organized in 1941. But preconceived biases prevented it from becoming a part of the fighting defense of America until April 1943. And even then, the 99th was relegated to an escort and service unit that flew occasional reconnaissance missions. It was late in 1943 that the 99th got its chance to participate in aerial combat. This North African exercise resulted, however, in a stream of conflicting reports concerning its ability as a flying fighting unit. Some reports cited the 99th for bravery and satisfactory service. Others reported that it lacked initiative, its officers were inferior, and that it did not have the capacity for air combat. Hastie's assistant (and later Civilian Aide himself, 1943–46), Truman K. Gibson, Jr., remarked to the War Department's Advisory Committee on Negro Troop Policy that "heretofore the Air Force supported the belief that blacks could not fly; now it believed that they do not have the ability to fight successfully in the air."[65]

Hastie also felt that segregated aviation cadet training was an unnecessary proscription upon black trainees. He appealed to the War Department in May 1941 to avoid unnecessary social, military, and economic expenditures by assigning black cadets to existing contract schools and to regular army bases for their advance training. He even suggested placing blacks in one of the contracted schools located in Arizona or California where their presence would not create any substantial problems. The Air Command ignored Hastie's recommendation, and actually created more problems for him. It normally requested the Selective Service to grant deferments to soldiers in aviation training, but in November 1941, Colonel St. Clair Street, Air Corps Executive Officer, informed Hastie that the Air Command had discontinued this practice. Street's letter severely damaged the credibility of the Air Command. He not only disregarded Hastie's proof that the Selective Service was indeed granting deferments to white cadets, but his actions confirmed Hastie's belief that the Air Corps had accepted blacks only because Congress had forced it to do so.[66]

In 1942, when the Air Corps began its Air Force Enlistment Program, Hastie wanted to know if the program would include students at predominantly black colleges and universities; if so, he urged Assistant Secretary Lovett to issue a public statement to that effect. Hastie was concerned how blacks would benefit from the program since the colleges and universities selected to participate were all white and did not accept blacks on an integrated and equal basis. Some of the schools refused to accept blacks altogether. Then, too, Hastie had learned from Malcolm S. McLean, president of Hampton Institute and Chairman of the President's Committee on Fair Employment Practices, that the War Department did not intend to solicit blacks for the program because 300 were on a waiting list for the 99th Pursuit Squadron at Tuskegee. This information strengthened Hastie's belief that the Air Corps did not intend to utilize blacks as heavy bomber pilots. Under Secretary Patterson publicly validated Hastie's claim on March 13, 1943, and Lovett never responded to Hastie's original request.[67]

Meanwhile, the Air Command stopped consulting Hastie on matters affecting blacks. The War Department's Advisory Committee for Negro Troop Policy refused to invite him to scheduled meetings, the Air Corps stopped recruiting blacks, and, according to James C. Evans, Civilian Aide from 1947 to 1970, Lovett said that blacks would never fly as heavy bomber pilots as long as he was Secretary of Air.[68]

Lovett's position and the War Department's attitude on this issue left Hastie dismayed, but he pledged to continue to work tirelessly to end racial discrimination and segregation in the armed services.[69]

NOTES

1. Memorandum, William H. Hastie to Robert P. Patterson, February 7, 1941, Army General Staff, NARG 407; Judge William H. Hastie, interview with author, March 6, 1974.

2. Memorandum, Hastie to Patterson, February 7, 1941, 2–4; Charles C. Moskos, "The American Dilemma in Uniform: Race in the Armed Forces," *The Annals of the American Academy of Political and Social Science* 406 (March 1973): 96.

3. Hastie, interview with author, March 6, 1974; Letter, Hastie to author, October 8, 1974; Memorandum, Hastie to Patterson, February 7, 1941, 4; *Congressional Record*, 76th Congress, 1st Session (1939), Appendix, 7667.

4. Hastie, interview with author, March 6, 1974; Memorandum, Hastie to Patterson, February 7, 1941, 5–6; Henry L. Stimson Diary, March 5, 1941.

5. Memorandum, Hastie to Patterson, February 7, 1941, 5–6; Hastie, interview with author, March 6, 1974.

6. Memorandum, Major Edwin W. Chamberlain to Lieutenant Colonel Karlstad, Office of the Chief of Staff, March 21, 1941, Army General Staff, NARG 407; Hastie, interview with author, March 6, 1974.

7. Memorandum, "Survey and Recommendation Concerning the Integration of the Negro Soldier into the Army, Submitted to the Secretary of War by the Civilian Aide to the Secretary of War," September 22, 1941, Box 151, Judge Robert P. Patterson Papers, 19–24.

8. Letter, Hastie to author, October 8, 1974; Hastie, interview with author, March 8, 1974; Memorandum, "Survey," September 22, 1941, 15–24.

9. Quoted in Ulysses Lee, *United States Army in World War II: Special Studies: The Employment of Negro Troops* (Washington, D.C.: United States Government Printing Office, 1966), 140.

10. Ibid., 140–141.

11. "Colonel Eugene Householder's Remarks at the Conference of Negro

Newspaper Representatives," Washington, D.C., December 8 and 9, 1941, Civilian Aide to the Secretary of War Subject File, 1940–1947, NARG 107; Letter, Hastie to author, October 8, 1974.

12. P. L. Prattis, "The Horizon: Conference of Negro Editors Was Challenge to War Department Officials," *Pittsburgh Courier*, December 18, 1941; Editorial, *Norfolk Journal and Guide*, December 13, 1941; Editorial, *Baltimore Afro-American*, December 13, 1941; "Negro Editors of Nation Get Information From General Marshall," *Atlanta Daily World*, December 10, 1941; Roi Ottley, "The Negro Press," *Common Ground* 3 (Spring 1943): 11–15; Lester M. Jones, "The Editorial Policy of the Negro Newspapers 1917–1918 as Compared with That of 1941–1942," *The Journal of Negro History* 29 (January 1944): 31; Lee, *The Employment of Negro Troops*, 141–143.

13. Editorial, *Chicago Defender*, December 18, 1941.

14. Hastie, interview with author, March 8, 1974; Memorandum, Hastie, Chairman of the National Legal Committee of the NAACP, to Members of the National Legal Committee, May 19, 1941, Box 230, NAACP Papers; Stimson Diary, January 3, 1942.

15. Hastie, interview with author, March 8, 1974; Letter, Hastie to author, October 8, 1974; Memorandum, Hastie to McCloy, June 30, 1942, Civilian Aide to the Secretary of War Subject File, 1940–1947, NARG 107.

16. Editorial, *New York Age*, March 24, 1941, Box 230, NAACP Papers; Jervis Anderson and Peter Stone, *A. Philip Randolph: A Biographical Portrait* (New York: Harcourt, Brace, Jovanovich, 1973), 243; Memorandum, "Randolph Comments on Army's Race Policy," Major James S. Tatman, Acting Chief, Analysis Branch, to General F. H. Osborn, Chief, Special Service Division, Public Relations Bureau, June 14, 1943, Office of War Information, NARG 208; "Army, Navy Exclusion Is Rapped," *Pittsburgh Courier*, February 8, 1941; Letter, White to Roosevelt, March 13, 1941; Letter, Edwin M. Watson to White, April 8, 1941; Letter, White to Watson, April 11, 1941; Letter, John P. Davis to Roosevelt, April 24, 1941; Memorandum, Watson to Hastie, April 26, 1941; Letter, Hastie to Watson, April 30, 1941; Letter, Watson to Davis, May 1, 1941; Letter, Davis to Watson, May 7, 1941, all in the Roosevelt Papers; "Negro Congress Urges New Western Front: End of J. C. In Armed Units," *Pittsburgh Courier*, May 15, 1941; *Congressional Record*, 77th Congress, 2nd Session (1942), Appendix, 290, 2891.

17. Memorandum, District of Columbia Branch, NAACP to War Department, January 14, 1942, Army General Staff, NARG 407; Office Memorandum, "Conference of the Chicago Council of Negro Organizations with Under Secretary Patterson," March 28, 1941, Civilian Aide to the Secretary of War Subject File, 1940–1947, NARG 107.

18. Letter, Randolph to Roosevelt, May 29, 1941, Box 151, Patterson Papers; Letter, Randolph to Eleanor Roosevelt, June 3, 1941; to Stimson, June 23, 1941, Civilian Aide to the Secretary of War Subject File, 1940–1947, NARG 107.

19. Memorandum, Hastie to Stimson, June 17, 1941, Civilian Aide to the Secretary of War Subject File, 1940–1947, NARG 107; Stimson Diary, June 18, 1941.

20. Letter, Eleanor Roosevelt to Patterson, June 10, 1941; Patterson to Watson, June 14, 1941, Box 151, Patterson Papers.

21. Memorandum, Patterson to Eleanor Roosevelt, June 13, 1941, Civilian Aide to the Secretary of War Subject File, 1940–1947, NARG 107.

22. U.S. President. Executive Order 8802. "The Committee on Fair Employment Practice." *Federal Register* 6, no. 3109, June 25, 1941; Anderson and Stone, *A. Philip Randolph*, 257–260; Frank Freidel, *F.D.R. and the South* (Baton Rouge, Louisiana: Louisiana State University Press, 1965), 97; Virginius Dabney, "Nearer and Nearer the Precipice," *The Atlantic Monthly* 171 (January 1943): 94; Charles E. Silberman, *Crisis in Black and White* (New York: Random House, 1964), 65.

23. Letter, William Allan Neilson, Chairman of the "Committee of 100," to the American Public, January 29, 1944, Hastie Papers.

24. "President Petitioned to End Race Bias; 50,000 Sign," *Pittsburgh Courier*, February 13, 1943.

25. American Youth for Democracy, Program Adopted October 17, 1943, Hastie Papers.

26. Memorandum, Truman K. Gibson, Jr., Assistant Civilian Aide, to Colonel David P. Page, Civilian Aide to the Secretary of War Subject File, 1940–1947, NARG 107; *Arqus-Leader*, July 25, 1942; *Gadsden Times*, May 19, 1942, *Washington Post*, September 9, 1942; *New Tribune*, June 21, 1942, all in the Campbell C. Johnson Papers, Moorland-Spingarn Research Center, Howard University Library. These papers contained two legal-size boxes of white newspaper clippings of northern and southern reaction to efforts to integrate the armed services and the American society during the war period.

27. Memorandum, Hastie to General H. B. Lewis, October 6, 1942, Hastie Papers; Letters, Robert P. Patterson to Harry F. Byrd and Wender H. Harris, October 29, 1942, Box 151, Patterson Papers; Letter, Hastie to author, October 8, 1974.

28. Letter, Roy Garvin to General Lewis, October 8, 1942; Letter, Lewis to Garvin, October 12, 1942, Civilian Aide to the Secretary of War Subject File, 1940–1947, NARG 107.

29. Letter, Hastie to Howard C. Petersen, October 30, 1942; Letter, Lewis to Garvin, October 12, 1942; Hastie, interview with author, March 8, 1974.

30. Hastie, interview with author, March 8, 1974; Letter, Hastie to Petersen, October 30, 1942.

31. Letter, C. A. Franklin to the United States Army Recruiting-Induction Services, October 28, 1942, Civilian Aide to the Secretary of War Subject File, 1940–1947, NARG 107.

32. Letter, Franklin to Hastie, October 28, 1942, Civilian Aide to the Secretary of War Subject File, 1940–1947, NARG 107.

33. Memorandum, Hastie to Lewis, October 6, 1942, Box 151, Patterson Papers; Letter, Hastie to Petersen, October 30, 1942.

34. Letter, Hastie to Walter White, September 15, 1942, Box 279, NAACP Papers; Memorandum, White to Stimson and General Surles, October 5, 1942, Box 264, NAACP Papers.

35. Letter, Frederick H. Osborn to William H. Hastie, October 5, 1942; Letter, Osborn to Walter White, October 15, 1942, Box 264, NAACP Papers; *Army Talk: Orientation Fact Sheet* (Washington, D.C.: War Department, 1942), 1–8.

36. Hastie, interview with author, March 6, 1974; Negro Marches on Incorporated, Plaintiff-Against-War Activities Committee of the Motion Picture In-

dustry, Defendants, no date, Civilian Aide to the Secretary of War Subject File, 1940–1947, NARG 107. (A brief of *Amicus Curiae* is defined as a legal term meaning "friend of the court." As *Amicus Curiae*, individuals or groups not parties to a lawsuit may aid or influence the court in reaching its decision.)

37. Letter, Hastie to author, October 8, 1974; Hastie, interview with author, March 6, 1974; James C. Evans, interview with author, November 30, 1974. The increased number of blacks in the Army and in the specialized training programs was substantiated further by applications and correspondence to and from Judge Hastie, found in the records of the Civilian Aide to the Secretary of War after 1942. See also Lee, *The Employment of Negro Troops*, 111–135.

38. Johnson Papers.

39. Arthur E. Barbeau and Florette Henri, *The Unknown Soldiers: Black American Troops in World War I* (Philadelphia: Temple University Press, 1974), 68–69; Letter, Hastie to author, October 8, 1974; Hastie, interview with author, March 6, 1974.

40. Stimson Diary, September 27, 1940.

41. Department of Defense, *Black Americans in Defense of Our Nation* (Washington, D.C.: Office of Deputy Assistant Secretary of Defense for Equal Opportunity, 1981), 33.

42. Memorandum, Hastie to Patterson, February 10, 1942; Patterson to Hastie, February 17, 1942, Box 151, Patterson Papers; Jean Byers, "A Study of the Negro in Military Service" (Washington, D.C.: Department of Defense, 1947), 40; Samuel A. Stouffer et al., *The American Soldier: Adjustment During Army Life*, Vol. 1 (Princeton, N.J.: Princeton University Press, 1949), 580–582. Hastie, "The Negro in the Army Today," *The Annals of the American Academy of Political and Social Science* 223 (September 1942): 59; Jesse J. Johnson, *Ebony Brass: An Autobiography of Negro Frustrations Amid Aspirations* (New York: William Frederick Press, 1967), 56.

43. Stimson Diary, January 24, 1942; Stimson, private interview with McGeorge Bundy, Box 188, Series III, Henry L. Stimson Papers, Yale University Library, New Haven, Connecticut; Henry L. Stimson and McGeorge Bundy, *On Active Service in Peace and War* (New York: Harper, 1948), 164–165; William L. White, "Negro Officers, 1917 and Now," *Survey Graphic* 31 (April 1942): 133; James C. Evans, private interview with author, October 6, 1974.

44. Memorandum, Hastie to Patterson, February 10, 1942; Patterson to Hastie, February 17, 1942, Box 151, Patterson Papers; Byers, "A Study of the Negro in Military Service," 40; Letters, Roy Wilkins to Hastie, July 31, and October 15, 1942, Box 265, NAACP Papers; Hastie, "Negro Officers in Two World Wars," *Journal of Negro Education* 12 (Summer 1943): 323.

45. Memorandum, Hastie to Patterson, February 10, 1942; Patterson to Hastie; Byers, "A Study of the Negro in Military Service," 40.

46. Byers, "A Study of the Negro in Military Service," 41.

47. Memorandum, Hastie to Major Campbell C. Johnson, January 10, 1941, Campbell C. Johnson Papers; Stimson Diary, January 13, 1942; Hastie, interview with author, March 6, 1974.

48. Letter, Hastie to author, October 8, 1974; Hastie, interview with author, March 8, 1974; Hastie, "Negro Officers in Two World Wars," 323.

49. Byers, "A Study of the Negro in Military Service," 125–128.

50. Quoted in Lucille B. Milner, "Jim Crow in the Army," *New Republic*, 110 (March 13, 1944): 340. See also McGuire, *Taps for a Jim Crow Army*, 37–57.

51. Letter, General William E. Shedd to General Emory S. Adams, Adjutant General, January 22, 1941, Army General Staff, NARG 407.

52. Memorandum, Hastie to Patterson, February 24, 1941; Letter, Eustace Gay, editor of the *Philadelphia Tribune*, to Hastie, November 25, 1942, Civilian Aide to the Secretary of War Subject File, 1940–1947, NARG 107; *Norfolk Journal and Guide*, March 21, 1942; "No Place for You in Army," *Pittsburgh Courier*, October 12, 1941.

53. Memorandum, Patterson to Dr. Norman T. Kirk, February 24, 1941, Civilian Aide to the Secretary of War Subject File, 1940–1947, NARG 107; James C. Evans, interview with author, October 6, 1974.

54. Letter, George Marshall to Kirk, January 11, 1945, Civilian Aide to the Secretary of War Subject File, 1940–1947, NARG 107; "15,000 Sign Petition On Nurse Bias," *Washington Afro-American*, April 7, 1945; Memorandum Truman K. Gibson, Jr. to Colonel Harrison A. Gerhardt, Assistant to McCloy, January 17, 1945, Civilian Aide to the Secretary of War Subject File, 1940–1947; Memorandum, Gibson to McCloy, February 12, 1945, Military Personnel Division, General Staff, NARG 165.

55. Charles H. Garvin, "The Negro in the Special Services of the United States Army: Medical Corps, Dental Corps, and Nurses Corps," *The Journal of Negro Education* 12 (Summer 1943): 340.

56. Letter, Hastie to author, October 8, 1974; *Congressional Record*, 76th Congress, 1st Session, (1939), 7666; *Pittsburgh Courier*, September 7, 1940.

57. *New York Times*, February 1, 1943; John D. Silvera, *The Negro in World War II* (Washington, D.C.: Army War Department, 1955), 30–33; Charles E. Francis, *The Tuskegee Airmen: The Story of the Negro in the United States Air Force* (Boston: Bruce Humphries, 1955), 161–162; Hastie, interview with author, March 8, 1974.

58. Stimson Diary, October 19, 1942.

59. "Hate Rule at Tuskegee Base Charged to Colonel Frederick Kimble," *Pittsburgh Courier*, January 2, 1943.

60. Memorandum, Hastie to Robert A. Lovett, April 23, 1941, Civilian Aide to the Secretary of War Subject File, 1940–1947, NARG 107; Hastie, interview with author, March 6, 1974; A. Russell Buchanan, *Black Americans in World War II* (Santa Barbara, Calif.: ABC-Clio Press, 1977), 69.

61. Memorandum, Lovett to Hastie, April 19, 1941, Civilian Aide to the Secretary of War of Subject File, 1940–1947, NARG 107; James C. Evans, interview with author, August 6, 1974; *Washington Post*, February 13, 1943; "Army Policy Unchanged," *Pittsburgh Courier*, October 16, 1943; "Rejection of Negroes for the Air Corps Reserve," *Pittsburgh Courier*, June 20, 1942; "Famed Biologist Blasts Army's Doubts on Ability Of Negroes To Fly Bombers," *Chicago Defender*, January 6, 1943; Letter, Wilbur LaRoe, chairman of the Washington Federation of Churches' Committee on Civic Affairs, to Patterson, March 13, 1943, Box 151, Patterson Papers; J. A. Ulio, Adjutant General, to Charles C. Diggs, State Senator, Michigan, July 20, 1943; Roy Wilkins to Stimson, August 13, 1942; Gerhardt, General Staff Corps Executive, to W. R. McCarthy, Secretary-Treasurer, American Youth For Democracy, December 29, 1944; E. C. Knowlton, local leader from Arnniston, Alabama, to Stimson, to General H. H. Arnold, to Marshall,

January 12, 1945; Gibson to Eleanor Roosevelt, April 28, 1943; Malcolm S. McLean, Chairman, President's Committee on Fair Employment Practice, and President of Hampton Institute, to Marshall, May 13, 1942, all in Civilian Aide to the Secretary of War Subject file, 140–1947, NARG 107; Roy Wilkins, "Too Dark For Army Air Corps," *The Crisis* 47 (September 1940): 279; Wilkins, "Army Air Corps," *The Crisis* 47 (November 1940): 358; Wilkins, "Air Pilots, But Segregated," *The Crisis* 48 (February 1941): 39; Wilkins, "Army Air Corps Smoke Screen," *The Crisis* 48 (April 1941): 103; Wilkins, "Now Is the Time Not To Be Silent," *The Crisis* 49 (January 1942): 7; Wilkins, "U.S.A. Needs a Sharp Break with the Past," *The Crisis* 49 (May 1942): 151.

62. Memorandum, Hastie to Colonel Richard T. Coiner, June 2, 1942; Memorandum, Coiner to Hastie, June 8, 1942, Civilian Aide to the Secretary of War Subject File, 1940–1947, NARG 107; Memorandum, Patterson to Lovett, June 12, 1942, Box 151, Patterson Papers.

63. Letter, Patterson to LaRoe, March 13, 1942, Box 151, Patterson Papers, *Congressional Record*, 78th Congress, 1st Session (1943), 3691.

64. William H. Hastie, *On Clipped Wings: The Story of Jim Crow in the Army Air Corps* (New York: NAACP, 1943), 5–6; Stimson Diary, May 12, 1942; *Congressional Record*, 78th Congress 1st Session (1943), 3691; Buchanan, *Black Americans in World War II*, 71–72.

65. Evans, interview with author, August 6, 1974; Memorandum, Hastie to Lovett, May 2, 1942, Civilian Aide to the Secretary of War Subject File, 1940–1947, NARG 107; Lee, *The United States Army in World War II*, 550–560.

66. Memorandum, Hastie to Lovett, May 14, 1941, Civilian Aide to the Secretary of War Subject File, 1940–1947, NARG 107. Contract schools were private institutions contracted by the Army Air Corps to train aviation cadets in elementary flying before they were assigned to military bases for advanced training. Memorandum, Colonel St. Clair Street to Hastie, November 21, 1941, Army General Staff, NARG 407; *Congressional Record*, 1st Session (1939), Appendix, 242; Hastie, interview with author, March 6, 1974.

67. Memorandum, Hastie to Lovett, April 21, 1942; Letter, Malcolm S. McLean to Hastie, May 13, 1942, Civilian Aide to the Secretary of War Subject File, 1940–1947, NARG 107; *Pittsburgh Courier*, June 20, 1942; *Congressional Record*, 78th Congress, 1st Session (1943), 3691.

68. Memorandum, Hastie to Lovett, April 29, 1942; Memorandum, Hastie to Stimson, January 5, 1943, Civilian Aide to the Secretary of War Subject File, 1940–1947, NARG 107; Stimson Diary, November 2, 1942; Evans, interview with author, August 6, 1974; "Air Force Policy Forced Me To Resign," *Pittsburgh Courier*, February 6, 1943; Hastie, interview with author, March 8, 1974; Buchanan, *Black Americans in World War II*, 70.

69. Letter, Hastie to author, October 8, 1974; Hastie, interview with author, March 6, 1974.

3

Hastie and the Nadir of Uncle Sam's Black Soldiers

Under the Selective Service Act of 1940, Uncle Sam's black soldiers registered for the armed forces in record numbers. Never before had America witnessed such black patriotism in peacetime. For the first time in military history, blacks had greater opportunities to serve their country. Because of the nondiscriminatory clause of the Selective Service Act, which prohibited discrimination in the selection and training of men based on race and color, most black troops thought that the "armed forces of democracy" would accept their soldiery on an equal basis. But as soon as the soldiers were mustered into service, most of them were faced with a rising tide of prejudice and racial discrimination. For black soldiers this illusionment was disheartening. One, identified as a "loyal soldier," wrote:

> I learned early in life that for the Negro there is no Democracy. Of course I know the principles set forth in the Amendment and the Bill of Rights. I learned that I knew nothing of the operation of a true democratic form of government. I found that a Negro in civilian life has a very tough time with segregation in public places and discrimination in industry. I knew this and I thought that white people would react differently toward a colored soldier. I had heard and read of the cruel treatment given colored soldiers and somehow, even among

existing conditions of civilian life, I couldn't understand how white people could be so down on one who wears the uniform of the fighting forces of their country. From civilian life I was drafted and now I prepare to fight for—the continuation of discriminatory practices against me and my people.[1]

Having joined up, black troops experienced many problems that were unique to them. Often they were transferred from post to post to avoid mixing them with white troops, subjected to delayed personnel action, relegated to dilapidated and segregated recreational facilities, subjected to abusive language, beaten unfairly by military and civilian police, barred from local towns, and overtly made to feel inferior. Such flagrant procedures caused their *esprit de corps* to remain low throughout the war.

For most white Americans, democracy meant equality, liberty, fraternity, individual rights, tolerance, freedom of speech, assembly and religion, unfettered military duty, and social compromise. For most black Americans, democracy meant disillusionment. Black soldiers who served during the war epitomized this devastating, inescapable, and recurring experience. For them, democracy was a grand illusion of misleading American rhetoric. Because he believed that racial discrimination was inconsistent with the nation's democratic ideals, Private Charles Wilson, for example, spoke of the war aims espoused by President Franklin D. Roosevelt but reminded him that:

The picture in our country is marred by one of the strongest paradoxes in our whole fight against world fascism. The United States Armed Forces, to fight for World Democracy, is within itself undemocratic. The undemocratic policy of jim-crow and segregation is practiced by our Armed Forces against its Negro members. Totally inadequate opportunities are given to the Negro members of our Armed Forces, nearly one tenth of the whole, to participate with "equality" . . . "regardless of race and color" in the fight for our war aims.[2]

The racial prejudice heaped upon black soldiers was the bittersweet reality they were forced to endure as they worked and fought to make the world "safe for democracy," and all mankind free to live out their fullest potential. Black soldiers were eager to fight and extremely conscious of the lofty war aims of President Roosevelt, the War Department, and other American leaders, but most of them suffered from the actuality that they were not being treated like other American soldiers. Nevertheless, blacks went to war with the hope that the Army would recognize their worth and solidly protect and provide for them as citizen-soldiers. They knew that in this time of national emergency their service was necessary, and they hoped that their loyalty and participation would secure for them military equality and the rewards of full citizenship at home once the war was over. The black troops believed that the hallowed principles of the Declaration of Independence and the U.S. Constitution would govern the conduct of the armed forces. The military was unwilling, however, to make the democratic rhetoric of the Second World War a reality for its black soldiers.[3]

While President Roosevelt, the War Department, and the military's top brass largely ignored Hastie's appeals, Eleanor Roosevelt showed compassion for the plight of black soldiers. In a 1943 letter to Assistant Secretary of War John J. McCloy, she wrote:

The colored boys lie side by side in the hospitals in the southwest Pacific with the white boys and somehow it is harder for me to believe that they should not be treated on an equal basis. Some of them from the south are quite evidently inferior in mentality and education. Nevertheless they do the job and they get killed just the same as the white boys.[4]

According to soldiers' letters, blacks loathed the idea of having to fight and die in Europe for the "Four Freedoms" while denied them as American soldiers. They complained that democracy for them was illusory and that they were fighting for "white folks." One black soldier from Fort Huachuca (Arizona) echoed these same sentiments. Corporal J. H. Becton said,

We have an "all negro" Division in action, and we have "negro soldiers" on every front wearing "Uncle Sam's Uniform" and fighting for the safety of the country the same as all other "Soldiers" of "America," [but] last night I saw the film "This Is America" and there was not a single one of "my people" in the screen, it was a film of "Whites only," why don't the armed forces release the "negroes" and fight their own war, for if this is "America" for "whites" only, we, the "negroes" have nothing to fight for.[5]

For most black soldiers, Corporal Becton overwhelmingly represented the views of their military experiences. In fact some of them even felt that "any Negro would rather give his life at home fighting for a cause he can understand than against any enemy whose principles are the same as our so-called democracy. A new Negro will return from the war—a bitter Negro if he is disappointed again. He will have been taught to kill, to suffer, to die for something he believes in, and he will live by these rules to gain his personal rights."[6]

Thus the war for black soldiers crystallized into a "Double V" campaign—a campaign to stop the spread of totalitarianism in Europe and to destroy the vestiges of racism in America. That black soldiers went to war believing that they were fighting to secure their rights in uniform as well as those in America cannot be denied. But their dreams were shattered, and their military experiences on and off the army posts were the "nadir" of their participation in an American democracy, of which the soldiers' letters forge a strong condemnation.

Answering and investigating soldiers' complaints at various military bases and nearby towns virtually became a fulltime job for Hastie and his assistant, Truman K. Gibson, Jr. They received hundreds of complaint letters. For example, at Davis-Monthan Field in Tucson, Arizona, black soldiers bitterly complained that their housing facilities were covered with black tar paper while the barracks for white soldiers were painted white. At Camp Davis in North Carolina, only black soldiers were required to take blood tests for venereal diseases, something they despised. Soldiers at Jackson Air Base in Mississippi informed Hastie on another occasion that the word "nigger" was always used when they were addressed by both noncommissioned and commissioned white officers. These particular soldiers claimed: "We as a group of Negro soldiers, wish to be soldiers in the Army of the United States, not dogs at Jackson Air Base, nor in the state of Mississippi. I'm writing for every soldier in the service at Jackson Air Base. We are treated like wild animals here, like we are unhuman. The word Negro is never used here, all they call us are nigger do this, nigger do that. Even the officers here are calling us nigger."[7]

Blacks at Pampa Army Air Field in Pampa, Texas, had similar experiences. A letter from the 328th Aviation Squadron and the 908th Quartermaster Company stated that "every Negro man on this post is absolutely fed up and disappointed with the bad treatment and discrimination, segregation and injustice imposed upon us." These men were bitter because they believed they were viewed unfairly. According to them:

We are a group of permanent K.P.'s. We are allowed no other advancement whatsoever. It is true that K.P. pushes (head K.P.) are made Cpl. and Sgt. but the K.P.'s themselves are a miserable group that will be worked like slaves without any ratings to speak of. We are confined to this job not because we are not fit for anything else but because we are dark. We are referred to on this post as "that nigger squadron at the end of the field."

At dances for officers and white enlisted men, the soldiers also claimed that they were "subject to all kinds of abusive language such as Nigger, darkie, son of a - - - - -, and everything unmentionable."[8]

A soldier writing to the editor of the *Atlanta Daily World* also decried the abusive language he had been subjected to. In fact he asked boldly: "I would like to know if your paper approves of a General calling his soldiers 'Nigger' to their face? I think that we are in this war to fight for the rights of all minority races; the morale of this organization will be low if our soldiers are not addressed in the right manner."[9]

Hastie was particularly concerned with this situation. In a 1941 conference with Chief of Staff George C. Marshall and Acting Inspector

General Howard MacC. Snyder, he objected to post commanders accused of using racial epithets being allowed to command black troops. Thus he recommended that an order be issued banning the use of the word "nigger" at all military installations. Benjamin O. Davis, Sr., the first and only black Army general and the Assistant Inspector General of the Army, almost succeeded in blocking Hastie's recommendation. General MacC. Snyder asked him to evaluate and comment on Hastie's recommendation. Davis did so, but he believed "it would be definitely unwise to issue an order directing that the term nigger be not used, as I recalled the ill effect that resulted by the use of such an order in the early days in the Philippines."[10]

Hastie was outraged at General Davis's comments, but because of them General MacC. Snyder suggested to General Marshall that the matter be dealt with as an educational problem rather than by official Army orders. Hastie objected and took up the issue with Secretary Stimson. He and Stimson very seldom agreed on policies affecting black soldiers, but the secretary apparently sided with Hastie on this question. Three months after Hastie's initial recommendation, Stimson ordered Adjutant General R. G. Hersey to prepare a memo for the commanding generals of the Eastern Theater of Operations, the Western Defense Command, the Caribbean Defense command, and all base commanders. These commanders were instructed to observe the following:

Superiors are forbidden to injure those under their authority by tyrannical or capricious conduct or by abusive language. While maintaining discipline and thorough and prompt performance of military duty, all officers, in dealing with enlisted men, will bear in mind the absolute necessity of so treating them as to preserve their self-respect. A grave duty rests on all officers and particularly upon organization commanders in this respect. In this connection the use of any epithet deemed insulting to a racial group should be carefully avoided. Similarly, commanders should avoid all practices that the Army makes any differentiation between him and any other soldier.[11]

To test the effect of this new policy, Hastie asked Under Secretary Robert Patterson in October (seven months later) to recommend the removal of General John A. Warden, commander of Fort Francis E. Warren, Cheyenne, Wyoming, from his command. He told Patterson that the black soldiers there were very bitter over the racist mannerisms of General Warden, and that he had heard him use the word "nigger" while visiting the camp himself. Hastie also charged that General Warden distributed 500 free football tickets to white soldiers only, when he had promised a group of Cheyenne citizens that they would be distributed among all the troops, including blacks stationed at the post. Hastie was convinced that Warden's attitude toward blacks was such that his removal from the base was essential to the well-being of both black and white soldiers.[12]

Records did not reveal if Patterson acted on Hastie's recommendation, but he was, at least, able to persuade Secretary Stimson that a prohibition against abusive language and racial epithets was in the best interest of the armed services, and that it would have a salutary effect on the morale of not only black but white soldiers as well.

However, the company executive officer of Camp Breckenridge, Kentucky, either had not been informed of the new policy, or he disregarded it because, for example, five months after the policy took effect (February 14, 1942) a black soldier at the camp claimed he had been abused. Private Clarence E. Adams said:

I drew a book from the Service Club Library to read. The title of the book is *Negro Poets and Their Poems*, by Kerlin. I had the book with me at the motor pool where I work (I am the dispatcher). I had finished up my work (Records) for the day and was just about ready to leave when the Company Executive Officer walked in the office. My paraphernalia was laying on the desk including the book, so he picked up the book and began looking through it; finally he came to this poem: "Mulatto" by Langston Hughes. He cursed and used all kinds of vile language about the author. He wanted to know who wrote it, where did I get the book; I told him, and this is his reply: "Take that damn book where you got it and I don't want to ever see anything like that around the company. The wrong person might get a hold of it and it might cause some trouble."[13]

At other military bases, despite the new policy, black soldiers continued protesting their malevolent treatment by biased white officers. For instance in Van Buren, Arkansas, three soldiers spoke of a Major Sheriden. Because he had locked a fellow black soldier "in a chain which was chained to a tree so long until his arm started to swell," and put him on a diet of "bread and water, two times a day," they called him "a rough dried, leather neck Negro hating cracker from Louisiana, who has insulted all Negroes in general, calls our women everything but women, misuse soldiers, [and] treats us as if we were in a forced labor camp or chain gang."[14]

While most of the soldiers' complaints decried the attitude of southern commanders, black soldiers viewed biased northern commanders with similar contempt. For example, a soldier stationed in Sioux Falls, South Dakota, wrote that "the City of Sioux Falls is very jim crowed and there are no decent places to go. At camp it is the same thing. It is not a strange thing to hear a Lieutenant or Major use the word N - - - - R."[15]

Samuel L. Ransom, a black major stationed at Camp McCoy in Wisconsin, echoed yet another example of name-calling and racial abuse suffered by black soldiers. He claimed that black soldiers "even stopped going to camp dances because they were subjects of racial abuse." Ransom went on to say:

On the post and off we are subjected to being called names, by both officers and enlisted men. When we report these things, they are overlooked. There is an inner tension going among the men, they feel they would just as soon as die in the guard house as in this slave camp. I think that this should be looked into as soon as possible, one man was cut in a fight the other night. Hell might break loose any minute.[16]

These are but two among many examples that illustrate that in the North black soldiers were reminded that army life there was not a "promised land." For the black troops, racial discrimination was a national phenomenon! As they wrote of these kinds of racial experiences, their *esprit de corps* was damaged. But for the first time in U.S. military history, the War Department had officially banned the use of racial epithets and insulting language. This action was another signal that the military was, however reluctantly, making some noteworthy shifts in race relations, even though the continued protest of some black soldiers after 1942 indicated that the directive was disregarded by some white officers.

Although the new policy forbidding commanding officers to use racial epithets and abusive language when addressing enlisted men provided Hastie a brief respite from the anguish of his War Department experiences, it was not long afterwards that he challenged yet another army condition that prevented black soldiers from enjoying the leisure side of their military tenure. In so doing Hastie informed the War Department in early 1941 that where there were no leisure time recreational facilities for black soldiers, he would propose their immediate construction and, where facilities existed, seek to have them opened to blacks (especially on military bases) on a nondiscriminatory basis.[17]

After weeks of meetings and moral suasion, the War Department acceded to Hastie, at least on this aspect of his recommendations in this realm of concern. In September 1941, the dedication of the first recreation camp for black soldiers took place in Washington, D.C. For the first time in military history, a complete recreational area was opened, designed and created specifically for black soldiers. Hastie delivered the principal address, which was broadcast over CBS. The War Department expected him to confine his remarks to expressions of praise for the new facility and to the efforts of the department in moving toward the elimination of discrimination and the promotion of racial harmony among black and white soldiers. Instead, Hastie seized the occasion to criticize the War Department, segregationist politicians, and the military's top brass for the maltreatment and segregation of black soldiers.[18]

By his own admission, Hastie had hoped that his address would appeal to the American conscience but believed that the un-American activities he had spoken of at the dedication ceremonies were ideologically steeped in the character of most white America and largely indicative of the discrimination black soldiers were subjected to on and off the military posts.[19]

Hastie's determination to have the War Department abandon its support of segregated recreational facilities created uneasiness in the department, but it clung to its official policy of segregation and its unofficial policy of racial discrimination. Nonetheless, Hastie continued his efforts to convince the department that the complaints of black soldiers were too numerous and too frequent for them to be mere figments of their imagination.

Because he was aware of the department's unalterable stance for maintaining the same social distinctions in the armed services that existed among blacks and whites in civilian life, Hastie once again called upon his sources of power for help. In September 1941, he and Gibson met with Walter White, executive director of the NAACP, and P. L. Prattis, editor of the *Pittsburgh Courier*. They agreed to press the War Department to use blacks as well as whites in all army camps as morale officers; that position papers be developed to aid commanding officers in dealing with black soldiers; that *Army Talk*, the Army's official news organ, stress the need of eliminating racial prejudices in all army camps; and that various race relations pamphlets be made available for all American soldiers. Before these recommendations were discussed with War Department officials, Hastie asked C. B. Crump, publicity and promotion chairman for the NAACP, to urge the editors of the major black press to run protest editorials and advertisements, dramatizing the efforts of the struggle made by his office and the NAACP against the degradation suffered by black soldiers at army camps in all parts of the country.[20]

Crump complied with Hastie's wishes and widely circulated the following protest example among the black press:

WE ARE STILL WAITING

Three weeks ago, the War Department and the President promised, after country-wide demands, to investigate the racial clashes at Fort Bragg, N.C., and Camp Robinson, Ark., and to let the public know the results. *We're still waiting to hear!*

Three weeks ago, the NAACP supported by the Negro press and aroused individuals, asked that a civilian, or civilian-military board be appointed by the President to investigate the entire military police set-up and to stop abuse of colored soldiers stationed in Southern camps. *We're still waiting for action!*

We want to know how the administration and the War Department can talk about defending democracy when Negro soldiers get Nazi-like treatment.

We want an end to discrimination and segregation in the armed forces. Help us by sending a postcard or letter to the President, the Senators from your State, representatives from your district, and Secretary of War Henry L. Stimson.[21]

Following Hastie's meeting with White and Prattis, he discussed their recommendations with Under Secretary Patterson and his assistant, Howard C. Petersen. They agreed that to formulate programs to improve the relations between black and white soldiers would increase the morale of all army personnel and, perhaps, decrease the serious racial conflicts occurring in the camps.[22]

Between Hastie's January 1942 meeting with Patterson, and Patterson's recommendations to General Frederick H. Osborn, chief of the Division of Special Services, in June 1942, a bitter campaign was carried out as a result of Hastie's request that the black press publish exposés on the discriminatory acts against black soldiers. General Osborn singled out and criticized him, White, and Prattis for this action. Although Osborn believed Hastie was chiefly responsible, he never directly confronted him. Instead Osborn attacked Hastie specifically, and also White and Prattis in an April 3 letter sent to White. White and Prattis, however, kept Hastie informed of their exchange with Osborn.[23]

The dialogue between White, Osborn, and Prattis lasted most of April. On the fourteenth, Prattis reported to Hastie and White that he had talked with Osborn about the racial troubles in the army camps. As Prattis maintained:

He even justified the Army's practice of extending social patterns based on southern prejudices to other sections of the country. He said that the War Department could only have one rule which must apply to the Army as a whole and that in as much as Negroes and Whites do not sit together in theaters in the South, it was necessary when the War Department set up a system of theaters to establish separate accommodations for Negro and white soldiers. Since the War Department could issue only one rule, it, therefore, became necessary to issue a "Jim Crow" rule which would apply to the South and North alike, although different from the ones in the South. I think he is a man of good heart, but I do not think we can depend upon him to be any help in leading us out of the wilderness.[24]

Hastie corroborated Prattis's conclusion about Osborn. He had similar feelings, which he made known to White and Prattis on April 16, 1942. Hastie informed them that "it is my present thought that there is nothing further that you can do with Osborn as an individual." Yet in his letter to White, Hastie asked him to use the influence of the NAACP to make another attempt to convince Osborn and Secretary Stimson that the use of blacks as morale officers in army camps would have a beneficial effect on the *esprit de corps* of all military personnel. Meanwhile, Hastie reminded Under Secretary Patterson of his promise to recommend his morale-building proposals to General Osborn for implementation. Patterson did as Hastie wished; however, Osborn was quick to reply three days later on June 25, 1942:

The matter of assigning Special Service Officers in the field is outside our jurisdiction, as Special Service Officers are selected by the Commanding Officers from among the officers in his command. This office, therefore, does not control their appointment. It will be our policy to encourage the selection of colored officers for this service with colored units.[25]

Osborn's attitude seemed to indicate that he was against Hastie, not his proposals, because he had told White on June 20 that the use of black morale officers was being implemented at an accelerated pace. Such heroes as Noble Sissle, a black bandleader, and Joe Louis, the black boxing champion, were two examples to substantiate Osborn's story. They became two of the first blacks to be used in army camps to help raise the morale of black soldiers in particular and to improve race relations in general throughout the armed services.[26]

In July 1943, General Osborn's stance revealed that he had accepted Hastie's recommendations without question. He sent a memo marked "confidential" to Secretary Stimson, advising him that there was a need to devise more plans for morale building among black soldiers. Osborn suggested that the Public Relations Bureau increase its flow of news about black military achievements in combat and in training; that a special effort be made to assign black soldiers to combat and other important military duties; that the enemy's racial doctrines and practices be revealed to emphasize to military and civilian blacks the importance of winning the war; that the practice of patronizing black soldiers be avoided; and that commanding officers be encouraged to protect their men from civilian abuse and exploitation.[27]

General Osborn's actions on black morale were paradoxical. It represented an enigmatic character and, to some extent, the dilemma of the War Department regarding the black personnel of the armed services; because while the general staff of the War Department hedged on implementing Hastie's recommendations to modify and/or correct the official policies of the military toward black soldiers, the soldiers themselves continued to experience debilitating conditions on and off the army posts.

At Camp Barkeley, Texas, for example, the soldiers complained that the swimming pool was off limits for them except on Mondays and Fridays. They also charged that they were not allowed inside the theater but were forced to "sit on the outside to see the picture; if it rain's [sic] there isn't [sic] any picture." The soldiers went on to say that "most of the fellows here like to play basketball we have no where to play but out on the hard ground; [yet the camp has] a field house here [but] we can't even use it to practice to play basketball." They did not like the camp's P.X. policies either. The soldiers said "we don't have a P.X. like the whites you can get only 1 bottle of beer 1 box of ice cream. Yet can't use the white P.X.'s but still they can use [ours] and get as much as they want."[28]

A black soldier from Camp Shelby, Mississippi, appealed to Hastie's assistant for help. He wrote:

In writing this letter in regards to the treatment of colored soldiers in Camp Shelby, Miss. We have no place for recreation except one place which is 3 miles away almost. We do not have anyway to get to it except to walk. We are limited duty men, and all not able to hardly do any work. When we want to go to town we can hardly get a bus. Whenever we get a bus they will only take five colored soldiers, and sometimes we have to wait about two or three hours for a bus.[29]

Blacks stationed at Camp Gordon Johnston, Florida, demonstrated another way Uncle Sam's black soldiers were treated. A soldier commented, "We cannot go to church services on the camp. We have to be told when we can go and worship God, the services clubs are off limit for us because a Staff Sgt. went over with some more of our comrades in the Co. to get a couple of sandwiches and were told by a civilian worker we don't serve colored, and Sir this is an Army Post."[30]

Like black Americans nationwide, black soldiers perceived the North as "heaven" compared to the "hell" in which they found themselves in the South. They soon realized that "jim crow" abounded, however, in and about army camps throughout the North. On these posts and in the surrounding towns, black troops were never able to forget that the "color line" more often than not determined their status even in the North. Private Bert B. Babero recalled:

Leaving the south was like coming back to God's country. You might readily understand my aversion when I discovered that as far north as Penn. segregation and discrimination is practiced in the army camps. I sometimes wish I could be indifferent but I can't. Right is right and I realize there's no such thing as half way right. Although in comparison with conditions at camp Barkeley, [Texas], these here are much more favorable but why are we segregated? Why aren't we allowed to attend but one theater out of four on the post and why can't we use any post exchange of our choice? I tried to answer these questions but I'm on the ebb of becoming neurotic.[31]

The black soldiers at Camp Adair, Oregon, voiced similar complaints. For Corporal William D. Lee, the camp had

No Day Rooms, no U.S.O. clubs, no Service Clubs, no Libraries, and no Entertainment What So-ever. We are Sure in a H - - - of a place. The camp is

Surrounded by Two Cities, one is Albany, Oregon. Second Corwallis, Oregon. Just Ten (10) miles from each to the Camp. But what good are they? If we go up and Start a conversation with the White Ladies the M-P's will Chase you in and press a charge against you The ninth Corp Area is not Suppose to be Jim Crowed its Worse out here than being way down South one thing Sure they Will have a camp Some place Where theirs plenty of Colored Ladies because they dont want you to bother theirs Also Will plan a place Somewhere for the soldiers to go after hours.[32]

Other black soldiers expressed the same sentiments as Corporal Lee. In a complaint to Hastie, a trooper stationed at Boise, Idaho, wrote:

The Jim-Crowism in this city is terrible. It is even worse than the southern cities because (1) there are no colored stores of any kind here (2) there is not more than 10 to 15 colored families in the whole city which has a population of about 26,000 to 28,000 people (3) in the whole city there is not one "not one" restaurant, beer garden, cafe or tavern which will serve a colored soldier, because we soldiers tried it last night, July 29, 1941.[33]

In contrast to Boise, black troops at La Junta Army Field, Colorado, complained they had stopped attending "the base theater on account of being discriminated against." One also claimed that "the city of La Junta, about 5 miles from the Field are two theaters where Negroes and whites attend and there is no discrimination at any one of them." He continued, "I have attended both theaters in town and have never noticed or heard of any trouble on account of Negroes and Whites sit anywhere they please. What we Negroes here can't understand is why we are discriminated in the base theater while there is no discrimination in the city's theaters. If left alone Negroes will naturally sit with one another. They have no special desire to sit beside a White Soldier. What we don't like is the discriminating policy of the War Department."[34]

At Camp George Jordan in Seattle, Washington, blacks were told that severe weather in the East had produced a coal shortage that resulted in their being asked to use wood for heating. But the soldiers became disheartened when they learned that coal was being supplied to white soldiers only two blocks away. A black trooper asserted: "This is a true fact, for I deliver coal there every day or other soldiers from this camp on that detail."[35]

The same soldier claimed "other than this un-democratic policy, there is a matter of passes and sick call. For instance, the white soldiers who work at the port, where we also work, go home from the port when quitting time comes. (I'm referring only to the married soldiers.)" He also contended that white soldiers "have class 'A' passes, which are good at any time while not on duty. The [black] married soldiers here have to return to camp when quitting time comes, make retreat at 5:00

and can't get their passes before 6:00. They must be back before reveille in the morning. The white soldiers come straight to the post in the morning. Some have told they never go to camp except to sign the pay roll and on pay day."[36]

In addition to these grievances, Gibson, responding to a soldier's charge of discrimination in post theaters at Fort Benning, Georgia, sent a memo to the adjutant general of the Army and subsequently asked for a policy decision on the matter because it was his understanding that any member of the armed forces could attend any facility on a military post. General Miller G. White, without Gibson's knowledge, sent the memo to the commanding general of Fort Benning who advised that no discrimination existed at the fort.[37]

Meanwhile, the War Department's general staff hurriedly prepared a policy statement that reflected the frame of mind of the department toward black soldiers in general and, in particular, its mood on recreational facilities on the military posts. Sergeant L. A. Guenther finalized the statement for General White. He suggested to White that Gibson

> be advised that, while the War Department's policy governing recreational facilities provides that such facilities are for the benefit of all personnel regardless of race, it does not prohibit a post commander from allocating recreational facilities on an "area" for "unit" basis if in his judgement such allocations will better serve the needs of his particular command.[38]

This new policy was characteristically indicative of Hastie's longstanding charge that post commanders were insensitive to the feelings and needs of black soldiers, and Hastie felt they, more often than not, contributed to the soldiers' low morale.[39]

Hastie of course was disappointed with the War Department's position on the usage of recreation facilities, but he welcomed its stand on two other recommendations. Hastie had suggested that the department's news organ, *Army Talk*, be used as a means for eliminating racial prejudices in the army camps. The department acceded and authorized its editors to develop such programs. In 1944, editorials such as "Prejudice! Roadblock To Progress," "How Prejudices Develop," "Errors of Generalizing," "What Is A Minority?" "Insecurity Breeds Prejudice," "Prejudice Robs Us Of Minority Talents," and "Prejudice Endangers Victory" began to appear in the magazine. The department also put into effect Hastie's recommendation that it issue position papers to commanding officers, designed to improve relations between officer and black military personnel. After 1944, position papers with titles such as "Aides To Leadership" and "The Officer-in-Charge" became a regular part of the War Department's race relations program.[40]

The one proposal that never got past the official purvey of the War

Department involved the distribution of Ruth Benedict and Gene Weltfish's *Races of Mankind*, which exposed the myth of white supremacy and suggested that churches, interracial commissions, labor unions, the federal government, and local communities enact programs aimed at the destruction of "Jim Crow" in America. The department ordered 55,000 copies, but, Representative Andrew J. May of Kentucky, Chairman of the House Military Appropriations Committee, threatened to cut off its military fund if the War Department distributed the pamphlets. Pressure from the Committee forced Secretary Stimson to ban its distribution and ordered all copies burned.[41]

Although Hastie was unaware of it, real estate broker D. W. McCoy also put pressure on Secretary Stimson to forbade the distribution of Benedict and Weltfish's *Races of Mankind*. He sent a bitter letter to the secretary purporting "to speak" for the South. McCoy made his home in Cleveland but had grown up in Texas. According to his letter, McCoy was outraged at the thought of the War Department's shortlived attempt to distribute *Races of Mankind* to military personnel. He charged that Stimson and Eleanor Roosevelt were responsible for the racial hatred in America, and that distribution of the pamphlet would be a grave insult to the dignity of the South.[42]

Although McCoy's outrage could not be viewed as representative of the total South, it reflected the racist attitude of diehard segregationists, who held firmly to the belief that whites were innately superior to blacks, who objected to military and civilian advances toward improved race relations, and who, most of all, objected to the integration of the armed forces.

Besides the political and civilian interference with Hastie's struggle to get the War Department to sponsor race relations programs unqualifiedly, General Benjamin O. Davis, Sr., a black from the Inspector General's Office, seemed to thwart Hastie's efforts. He undermined Hastie repeatedly with reports of high morale among black soldiers. From the eight surveys consulted between October 1941 and September 1943 on race relations between black and white soldiers, Davis concluded that the morale of the black soldier was excellent, and that the racial attitudes of both races in the army camps and surrounding communities were superior. According to one black soldier, this was not the case at Fort Clark, Texas. He claimed that "General Davis was down here this week to see what makes Ft. Clark tick. I and every other soldier on this post knows what this report will be. It will read something like this, 'Boys at Ft. Clark are having time of their life.' Yes, we're having a fine time of hell." Unfortunately, Davis's reports had the effect of "arming the War Department in defense against Hastie's charges" of racial discrimination and low morale among the black soldiers. His reports were even more harmful because, as the official military arm responsible for investigating soldiers' complaints, the Office of the Inspector General more often than not countered Hastie's allegations of racial impropriety.[43] This situation obviously impeded the progress toward breaking down racial discrimination and segregation on the military posts.

The protests of black soldiers who complained about their treatment off the military posts also occupied much of Hastie's attention, especially the complaints of soldiers who were stationed in the South. Hastie constantly reported these altercations to Secretary Stimson and indicated that the troops blamed southern civilians and the white military police for their troubles. According to one black soldier, the troops considered the South "worse than hell itself."[44]

Hardly a month passed that black soldiers did not complain about being in the South and suffering from the humiliation and abuse heaped upon them by white civilians and white military police. For instance, black soldiers at Jackson Air Base in Jackson, Mississippi, collectively reported that the "civilian polices have threated to kill several soldiers here. Some part of Mississippi, Negro soldiers are not allow to walk in town. Lieutenant Bromburg said all Negroes need to be beaten to death. He assist Civilian polices in the punishment of these Negro soldiers." Conditions became so intolerable that the men asked Hastie to "please help us to be transferred out of the state of Mississippi."[45]

Conflicts between black soldiers and white civilians in and about the army camps seemed never to end. At Camp Claiborne, Louisiana, a disgusted black trooper alleged that "the conditions for a Negro soldier down here is unbearable. The morale of the boys is very low. Now right at this moment the woods surrounding the camp are swarming with Louisiana boogies armed with rifles and shot guns even the little kids have 22 cal. rifles and B&B guns filled with anxiety to shoot a negro soldier." This soldier claimed the situation arose because two white women had allegedly been raped by blacks within the camp.[46]

Whether true or not, these types of racial incidents contributed to much of the civilian unrest in the South. Alarm reached such heights that white civilians began to object to the stationing of black soldiers in camps near their communities. White civilians residing near Moore Field, Texas, for example, protested vigorously. They urged their Congressman, Milton West, to do something about what they considered a blatant disregard for the welfare of their community. Congressman West responded by pressuring the War Department to do something about the situation, and the War Department sought advice from Hastie. He suggested to Lieutenant General Henry H. Arnold (Commanding General of the Army Air Forces) that the Army explore the possibility of replacing black with white troops at Moore Field. Hastie considered this the most feasible solution to a serious problem, since he believed the Army had failed to protect its black soldiers from civilian attacks.[47]

Meanwhile the situation in Texas worsened. Secretary Stimson eventually criticized the civilians for their attitudes toward black soldiers. He wrote in his diary:

Texas particularly has protested against the stationing of colored troops in that State, citing the race riots that took place in the last war at Houston and the previous outbreak of the 24th Infantry in Brownsville. We are suffering from the persistent legacy of the original crimes of slavery; the section of the country, they thought, which foisted that crime upon us is that part of the country which now protests most loudly against being subjected to any of the risks which have followed the wrongdoings of their ancestors.[48]

While Stimson and the War Department staff pondered the Army's predicament, Hastie, the black leadership and his white supporters, continued to attack the armed forces for not protecting black soldiers from civilian mistreatment. For instance, Roy Wilkins suggested to Hastie that he specifically tell Secretary Stimson: "The chief complaint against the Army, and the one which has stirred both Negro soldiers and civilians, is that the Army has surrendered completely to local prejudices and has compelled its Negro soldiers to accept brutality and discriminatory treatment in and about the camps where they are stationed."[49]

After months of indecision and Hastie's insistence on an official policy, the War Department issued a policy statement on troop stationing in May 1942. The department decided that, where feasible, black southern troops would be assigned to units in the South and black northern troops would be assigned to units in the North. Moreover, the policy called for the Planning and Liaison Branch of the War Department to station black and white troops in and about communities with commensurate civilian populations.[50]

Hastie and his staff welcomed the new policy but felt it was based on the War Department's presupposition that the uneasiness of white civilians was caused chiefly by northern soldiers who had enjoyed a semblance of unrestricted civility in northern communities, and who viewed themselves differently from their southern counterparts.[51]

On this matter, the War Department's reasoning was more right than wrong. In an incident involving a black soldier and public transportation, Private T. Nicklus confirmed the department's belief. Nicklus claimed that he was humiliated by a train conductor in Claiborne, Louisiana. In sworn testimony, Nicklus recalled how the conductor pushed and hit him. When he protested, the conductor said: "Give me the ticket, Nigger." Nicklus reportedly responded that he was not a "nigger" and the conductor replied in anger, "Yes, you are a nigger, a god-damn nigger. You are down below the Mason-Dixon Line and you are all nigger boys down here."[52]

Other affrays between black soldiers and white civilians seemed never to end, especially in the South. Hastie continued to protest their mal-treatment, but the War Department and the military's top brass were either unable to protect or less enthusiastic about protecting its black soldiers. Black trooper Latrophe F. Jenkins, as late as 1944, wrote pitifully to Hastie's ally, P. L. Prattis, "This is our last hope of receiving help from the outside world. This is the final quiet before death comes. This is the dark dreary hour before dawn, a dawn that seemed to have died for us last nite, in disillusioned expectations that we thought we'd won by our willingness and sacrifices of serving overseas for nearly two punishing years." Jenkins went on to say:

We are now in Camp Rucker, Alabama; a name that shall live in the lives of the men that live to get out of here, just as much as the memories of Saipan, Tarawa, Pearl Harbor, or any of the bloody battle fields of this war, live in the minds of the men who fought there. We are here on War Department orders. Not because we chose this theatre of war to serve in, without protection. It is the same if they had landed us on New Georgia without the support of the Navy and Air Force. Even with those great odds against us, we would rather be landed on New Georgia without protection than to be left here to die as "fatted pigs" at the mercy of the iron hearted people we are surrounded by, arms against our flesh.... Please take this call for mercy as the last whisper before we die.[53]

Private Jenkins's complaint against the South was one among many that involved the perennial prejudices of white civilians toward black soldiers.[54]

Reports of black troops being mistreated, beaten, and even hanged in uniform in the South seemed to become a weekly occurrence. Blacks in and out of uniform believed white military police were either responsible or stood by while white civilians unleashed their abusive assaults on black soldiers. While Hastie continually appealed to the War Department to take preventive action, the black leadership and concerned whites such as Eleanor Roosevelt sent resolutions and telegrams, made suggestions, and called for open and public investigations of the atrocities heaped upon black soldiers.[55]

As early as September 8, 1941, Hastie, sensing a state of urgency, had asked Secretary Stimson to issue a public statement regarding the frequent altercations between white civilians, white military police, and black soldiers. He cited incidents of violence and brutality as justification for a public announcement. Hastie also insisted that the Inspector General's investigations had failed to solve, for example, the homicides at Fort Benning, Georgia. He then reminded Stimson that nothing had been done about the shooting attack on black soldiers in the barracks at Fort Jackson, South Carolina; that the recent killings of black troops at Fort Bragg, North Carolina, had gone unsolved; and that the investigation of the civilian police attack on black soldiers in Bastrop, Louisiana, had failed to produce any substantive results. Hastie ended his memo with a strong plea for Secretary Stimson to address these matters at his next news conference.[56]

Stimson yielded to Hastie on September 27 and issued a public statement that expressed the War Department's sincere concern over the disturbances involving black soldiers, white civilians, and military police. He said, moreover, that the War Department not only was concerned in achieving justice, but that it was determined to correct the causes that led to the racial conflicts in order to raise the morale of all soldiers. Stimson also spoke of the military police as respectable soldiers who should not be feared and who should maintain law and order without unnecessary force. Finally, he maintained: "Recent affrays between colored soldiers and white civilians are also under investigation. The Army will not tolerate breaches of discipline by its personnel or assaults upon soldiers engaged in line of duty. Most soldiers and civilians will meet on a plane of mutual respect and understanding. However, wrong doers whose willful conduct is impeding the cause of the Military Program must be dealt with sternly."[57]

Hastie had hoped Stimson's announcement would at least halt the atrocities committed against blacks by white military police, but the mistreatment of black soldiers continued. In Tampa, Florida, for example, several white military policemen were reported to have severely beaten a black soldier while others and civilian authorities watched and forced a gathering crowd of black and white spectators to move on.[58]

Another incident involving white military police and black soldiers occurred at Keesler Field, Mississippi. In spite of Stimson's statement, Private Edward N. Lyles reported the event in vivid detail. He claimed:

On December 1, 1943, which was the day after payday, a number of Negro soldiers, having received the customary six hour pass from the Company Commanders of their respective organizations, went into Biloxi.

In Biloxi, about two miles distance, a Negro soldier may find a change from army routine through the medium of a U.S.O., one theatre, and a few cafes.

On this particular evening that "change" was interrupted by twenty-odd white military policemen. Note: There are Negroes policing the Negro district. The whites drove into the district in jeeps armed with .45 automatics and Thompson machine guns.

They entered the various establishments, and reprimanded the soldiers for such minor offenses as buttons not fastened, caps tilted too much, ties loosened, and others of similar nature. They were then roughly ushered into a formation and marched to the Military Police Headquarters in Biloxi.

The lieutenant in charge gave orders to take all passes, and march the men back to Keesler Field. He told the M.P.'s to use their clubs, and if that did no good they would know what to do.

When one soldier asked (while in ranks) what was going to happen to them, he was struck brutally across the face with a club. Several others were struck either with fists, or clubs, or straps.

One soldier, living in Biloxi and stationed at Keesler Field, was walking with his wife. He too, was forced into the formation leaving his wife crying as were many other colored civilians who witnessed this humiliation.

The helpless Negro M.P's took no part in this disgraceful mockery of democracy.

The soldiers were then marched back to Keesler Field, their names taken, and dismissed.

Several of the non-commissioned officers have made formal protests. What consideration non-commissioned officers, in good standing, will receive in the face of brutal inefficiency can be decided by the Commanding Officer in time only.

To date nothing has been done.[59]

Besides the cruelty of the white military police, Hastie agonized over what he considered to be the brutal and unwarranted punishment of black soldiers. In letter after letter to him and his sources of support, black soldiers complained and asked for relief from being punished when too ill to work, from having to work long hours in all kinds of weather without proper clothing, from enduring life in tents without flooring, from inadequate food and feeding facilities, from shock treatment and "blue" discharges (further described below) as punishment, and from an excessive and unusually high rate of courts-martial and sentences.[60]

The military's use of courts-martial to punish blacks became one of the most publicized grievances of black soldiers. For instance, troops from Camp Livingston, Louisiana, wrote letter after letter in which they complained about their high rate of courts-martial for minor infractions such as objecting to being called a "nigger," being A.W.O.L. for one or two days, and, as Private Lyles had expressed, other "minor offenses as buttons not fastened, caps tilted too much, ties loosened, and others of similar nature." Private Milton Adams was one soldier who complained to Hastie about the treatment. He told Hastie in a 1942 letter that "since they [white officers] can't very well hang us, they take the next steps, which is court martial, and that is better known as railroading. Now you don't stand a chance, before them. They are just like a lynch mob with a neggro to hang."[61]

Other soldiers expressed similar thoughts. For instance, Private Roy Hermitt was distraught because he was put in the camp stockade, kept for one month, and tried under a general court-martial without, as he claimed, just cause. Hermitt received five years and a dishonorable discharge from the Army because he had been accused and convicted of hitting a white lieutenant in a post exchange. He contended the crime had been "planted on me because I was from a Northern state, and the person that hit the Lt. was a tall man, and I answered the description."[62]

At Fort Bragg, North Carolina, the Army's cruel and unusual punishment for black soldiers surfaced again. This time 35 black soldiers were said to have been treated like animals and "held as garrison prisoners for eight and nine months before being tried for small cases such as two days A.W.O.L., which is supposed to be only company punishment or restrictions. Then they are tried and given six months." These same men moreover had to "sleep out doors in pup tents regardless of the weather—rain, sleet, snow, no matter how cold it is." The soldier reporting this particular incident finally said, "What I am trying to say is I don't think it is right for them to have to sleep on the ground in such weather like dogs when there is so much shelter for everyone."[63]

The rate at which blacks were discharged from the Army under Section VIII of Army Regulations, 615–360, Paragraph 10, Special Order no. 69, was indicative of another kind of cruel and discriminatory circumstance that blacks had to endure. A Section VIII dismissal from the Armed Forces was called a "blue" discharge, which was not a dishonorable discharge but one without honor and veterans benefits. For Hastie the "blue" discharge was another vestige of racial abuse in a series that he sought to have eliminated and/or modified. The records indicate that many black soldiers were given "blue" discharges without substantive provocation. For instance, Private George R. Gilbert was given a Section VIII dismissal for allegedly refusing to carry out orders when he was physically unable to do so. His letter to Hastie's office reflected the kind of grounds on which blacks were given such discharges. Gilbert contended rather disquietingly:

After I had been in the Army about 8 ½ months I started to complain about my stomach (you see I have had two operations on my stomach and they began to give me trouble). The doctors told me there wasn't anything wrong with my stomach. I also had a ureathed discharge in my penis which I had ever since I was in the Army and the doctors couldn't seem to stop it. I told my commanding officers I couldn't do any hard work so they took me before a Section VIII board. I don't think I deserve a discharge of that kind after serving (11) months of honorable service.[64]

Because of Hastie's insistence, Gilbert's case and several others were investigated by the Office of the Inspector General, but the problem of Section VIII discharges remained. Out of a total of 48,603 "blue" discharges from December 1, 1941, to June 30, 1945, 10,806 were issued to blacks. This would not have been an equitable percentage even if the ratio of blacks in the armed forces had been the same as that in the civilian population, but since the total strength of the armed forces' black personnel never rose above 6.5 percent, the inequity was even greater because blacks received 22.2 percent of the "blue" discharges issued during the period.[65]

Private Lloyd Lythcott wrote about shock treatment, another example of what he considered to be black punishment. In a letter to the editor of the Afro-American Newspaper Chain, Lythcott graphically detailed the horrors of his ordeal:

You know . . . after I came back to the States they gave me a "shock treatment." I'll tell you how they did it. First they lay you on a table, second they strap a band around your head, then they put a sponge in your mouth, and then they turn on a switch, you don't remember anything until the next day.

I ran away from the hospital. They caught me and brought me back then they put me in a locked ward and gave me the treatment more often. Now listen to this. You know . . . when I left you I was well, only headaches. They kept me locked up in a little room for three months, couldn't see nobody or write. One day I slipped away from a guard, I made up my mind that they were not going to keep me and torture me any longer.

Remember all of this is happening in "Kentucky" where nobody can help me. Anyhow . . . I couldn't get out of there this time, so I made up my mind to die. I remembered once when I was in the bathroom I saw a can of "lye" in there. I got a paper cup and poured some of the lye in it and mixed it with water. . . . I drank it, not because I was crazy, but because of the way those crackers treated me. I forgot to tell you they used to beat me up while I was unconscious under the shock treatment. The reason I know is because sometimes my jaw was swollen and hurt, and at other times I would have a mouse under my eye, you know, a lump. Now to make things worse, the lye I drank has taken all the enamel off my teeth and my eyes are ruined from the shock treatment. I try to be happy, but I can't. I have seen your wife twice so far. I tried to explain what happened to me, but I don't think she believes me. You see I know you will believe, because I have two black burns on each side of my temple from the electric shock treatment, and you know they were never there before.[66]

In spite of the fact that Lythcott's letter and some others may have been examples of mendacity and exaggeration, the soldiers' protests were overwhelmingly legitimate. Hastie believed they were genuine because the letters were written too often and too frequently for them to be mere illusions of racial abuse. He also believed the soldiers because of his own investigations of racial discrimination at various army posts and the official and unofficial reports from his nongovernmental support.[67] The War Department even legitimized the soldiers' grievances with its direct and indirect shifts in policies regarding the treatment and well-being of its black troops.

Although the controversy surrounding the use of black blood donors did not come under the official purview of the Office of the Civilian Aide, Hastie and his assistant became involved when they learned that the surgeons-general of the Army and Navy had sent a secret memo to the American Red Cross, informing them of the War Department's desire to use blood collected only from white donors for use in the military. The surgeons-general maintained that because 95 percent of the men in the armed forces were white and preferred plasma from white donors, their policy was in line with the wishes of the majority of the men in uniform. As far as black soldiers were concerned, they informed the Red Cross that "where transfusions are required for Negro servicemen, they will be given normal transfusions from Negro donors if they do not desire the use of blood or plasma from white donors."[68]

The memo implied that black soldiers were not expected to be sent to combat zones. If used there, they would be forced to accept whole blood or plasma from white donors, for how could a wounded or dying soldier hope to receive "normal" transfusions from black donors on the battlefield unless the military intended to use black soldiers themselves as the donors. The memo was even more ridiculous since the American Medical Association spoke out against the policy, graphically stating that "there is no factual basis for the discrimination against the use of Negro blood or plasma for injection into white people." The Red Cross itself went on record publicly in opposition to the department's policy. According to an article appearing in the December 28, 1941 issue of the *New York Times*, the Red Cross declared: "No soldier who is about to die is going to arise from his bed or the operating table and say, stop, doctors! Wait a minute! If you are not absolutely positive that not one single drop of Negro blood is in that blood—let me die."[69]

In spite of the Red Cross's public statement, ironically the national headquarters prepared and used the following statement to reply officially to inquiries from Hastie and Gibson regarding black blood donors:

Unfortunately, the differences of opinion on this subject are such that they cannot be reconciled by the Red Cross. Consequently, we have had no alternative but to recognize the existence of a point of view which, if disregarded, would militate against the effective use of the blood plasma.

We have a job to do for the armed forces which the Army and the Navy have asked us to do and which is being done in accordance with their desires. The Red Cross objective is the alleviation of suffering and the conservation of human life. The course pursued, however unacceptable to some, has contributed most effectively toward that end.

The controversial aspects of the problem are beyond the scope of the Red Cross and, as I have said, cannot be solved by it.[70]

Hastie viewed the Red Cross's stance with regret but continued to maintain his diametric opposition to the War Department's policy. He wondered how the armed services could practice such blatant discrimination against black people when black soldiers were fighting and dying under the battle cry of freedom and democracy. Thus in December 1941, he requested an explanation and the facts surrounding the policy from Adjutant General James A. Ulio. Ulio responded with a terse reply: "By order of the Secretary of War." Hastie was undaunted. Two days after Ulio's reply, he contacted Assistant Secretary of War Robert P. Patterson and urged him to put pressure on the surgeons-general to rescind their order to the Red Cross. One month later, the War Department circulated a new ruling on donors. The announcement was released to the press in January 1942. The department, in agreement with the Red Cross, stated:

The facilities for processing blood plasma having now been expanded considerably to meet not only the increased needs of the armed forces but those of civilian emergencies as well, the American Red Cross in agreement with the Army and Navy, is prepared hereafter to accept blood donations from colored as well as white persons. In deference to the wishes of those from whom the plasma is being provided, the blood will be processed separately so that those receiving transfusions may be given plasma from blood of their own race.[71]

Although Hastie had been successful in persuading the War Department to modify its donor policy, he was not satisfied with the new ruling. He began immediately to press for the complete elimination of the racialism inherent in the department's new policy. Shortly after the new policy was released to the public, Hastie informed Assistant Secretary Patterson that the black press and the black leadership, with his support, would wage an intensive campaign against the department if it insisted on separating and labeling black and white blood.[72]

As Hastie indicated, the black press and the black leadership reacted negatively to the new policy. For example, one person who strongly reacted was Dr. Charles Drew, Hastie's friend and a member of the black vanguard whom the War Department and the Red Cross had jointly appointed as medical supervisor of the plasma project soon after the program began in 1941. Drew stated publicly that separating and labeling black and white blood was "indefensible from any point of view." Dr. Drew had used blood, without reference to race, from both black and white donors to research and develop the methods of processing and preserving whole blood for future use. He had established a nondiscriminatory precedent while at Columbia University School of Medicine, but the War Department and the Red Cross apparently ignored Dr. Drew's position. When Hastie informed him of the department's intractable stance, Drew resigned his post.[73]

The *Philadelphia Tribune*'s comments on the "no mixing of blood" policy were indicative of the black press. "So there is to be no mixing of blood," it noted, adding, "It is perfectly all right for 'white' blood to be pumped into colored soldiers; and it continues as an American custom, wherever the white man goes to mix his blood with native women, whether in the Pacific or in Africa."⁷⁴

Even the American Association of Physical Anthropologists rejected the new policy. "It pointed to many Southern families' reliance on black wet nurses and asserted that the white infants ingested not only 'the nutritious elements in the milk of those colored women [but also] many of the same substances which were circulating in the blood stream [sic] of the women who were suckling them.' "⁷⁵

Meanwhile Hastie appealed to Secretary Stimson to rescind the policy. He, like others, argued that the policy hindered the war effort and reflected a Nazi view of race. Finally, Hastie "told Stimson that all blacks were insulted by policy made in deference to those who insist that our country treat the Negro as a loathsome being even as all non-Aryans are regarded under the ideology which we are fighting to the finish with force of arms. Even the saving of the lives of soldiers is weighed against the appeasement of the sentiments most alien to our professions, and found to be wanting."⁷⁶

Hastie also asked the Surgeon-General of the Army, Dr. Norman T. Kirk, to reconsider advising the Red Cross to discontinue its practice, with the understanding that soldiers could obtain a direct transfusion from their own race if the donors were readily available.⁷⁷

Hastie's appeals were fruitless. The Red Cross itself had come to believe that the rising tide of black protest over the War Department's new policy was an effort to undermine the effectiveness of the blood donor program. Norman H. Davis, chairman of the Red Cross National Board, in upholding the new policy, felt that it was not "the job of the Red Cross to try to settle racial controversies or take sides in such controversies." Davis eventually asked whether "under a Democracy the wishes or prejudices of those who are to receive the blood should prevail or the wishes of a relatively small percentage of those who wish to give their blood?"⁷⁸

In 1942, Davis's belief was indirectly confirmed in a letter to Hastie from Assistant Surgeon-General C. C. Hillman. General Hillman justified the War Department's new policy, basing it upon mores existing in the larger American society. He further acknowledged, agreeing with Hastie that there was absolutely no scientific basis for separating black and white whole blood and/or blood plasma but also informed him that "there is a disinclination on the part of many whites, which you of course recognize, to have Negro blood injected into their veins." Hillman continued that "it is the conviction of this office that disregard of that feeling would greatly mitigate against the successful conclusion of the program for collecting blood for plasma for the armed forces." In his closing remarks to Hastie, Hillman felt that "while this office sympathizes with the aspirations of the Negro race, it feels that it must continue its present policy in the matter of blood plasma, though it may not be the ideal solution."[79]

Hastie's assistant, Truman K. Gibson, Jr., was uncompromising on this issue. When he succeeded Hastie as Civilian Aide to the Secretary of War, he pointedly recommended to Colonel H. A. Gerhardt, executive officer in the Office of the Assistant Secretary of War, that "the War Department withdraw any and all directives issued to the Red Cross in this matter and indicate in all future correspondence that blood from all persons will be received and used as the need appears." Gibson felt his proposal would remove the War Department from an indefensible position, which it had created from the beginning when the department imposed its position on an otherwise civilian institution. On November 12, 1943, he reiterated Hastie's stand on the nonscientific nature of processing blood plasma separately and told Colonel Gerhardt: "In view of the fact that the [War Department's] position coincides with the Nazi philosophy of superior blood, it is my personal view that the present policy should be quietly abandoned." Gibson thought it was equally important for the department to end a ridiculous propagation that men dying on a battlefield would request a particular kind of plasma.[80]

In spite of the efforts of Hastie and his assistant, Surgeon-General Kirk announced publicly, as late as 1944, that he knew of no reason to change the policy of separating and labeling black and white blood for the military's donor program. Thus the practice was maintained throughout the Second World War in the face of mounting criticism from Hastie and his black and white supporters. The policy did not change until December 1, 1950. At that time, the Blood Program Committee of the Board of Governors and the Committee on Medical Policies and Procedures of the American National Red Cross, in concurrence with the Office of the Secretary of Defense, "unanimously agreed that the racial designation should be removed from the Donor Registration Card."[81]

Although Hastie admitted privately that he never expected the War Department to abandon what he considered to be an indefensible position, he vowed not to temporize with its unsavory stand. Unfortunately, it took eight years for the department and the Red Cross to implement a color-blind donor program.[82]

NOTES

1. Letter, A Loyal Negro Soldier to Truman K. Gibson, Jr., November 5, 1943, Civilian Aide to the Secretary of War Subject File, 1940–1947, NARG 107.

2. Letter, Private Charles F. Wilson to President Franklin Roosevelt, May 9, 1944, Civilian Aide to the Secretary of War Subject File, 1940–1947, NARG 107.

3. For a more detailed perspective of black soldiers see Phillip McGuire,

Taps for a Jim Crow Army: Letters from Black Soldiers in World War II (Santa Barbara, Calif.: ABC-Clio Press, 1983).

4. Letter, Eleanor Roosevelt to John J. McCloy, September 29, 1943, Civilian Aide to the Secretary of War Subject File, 1940–1947, NARG 107.

5. Letter, Corporal J. H. Becton to *Army & Navy Screen Magazine*, August 26, 1944, Civilian Aide to the Secretary of War Subject File, 1940–1947, NARG 107.

6. Quoted in Lucille B. Milner, "Jim Crow in the Army," *New Republic* 110 (March 13, 1944): 339.

7. Letter, A Group of Soldiers from Jackson Air Base to Hastie, October 11, 1943; Letter, Concerned Soldiers to Gibson, March 2, 1942; Letter, Private Carlton Shepherd to Hastie, September 30, 1942; Letter, Disgusted Soldier to P. L. Prattis, January 14, 1942, all in Civilian Aide to the Secretary of War Subject File, 1940–1947, NARG 107.

8. Letter, 328th Aviation Squadron and 908th Quartermaster Company to *Richmond Afro-American*, November 22, 1943, Civilian Aide to the Secretary of War Subject File, 1940–1947, NARG 107.

9. Letter, A Negro Soldier to the *Atlanta Daily World*, April 23, 1943, Civilian Aide to the Secretary of War Subject File, 1940–1947, NARG 107.

10. Memorandum, Howard MacC. Snyder to George C. Marshall, November 13, 1941, Army General Staff, NARG 407.

11. Memorandum, R. G. Hersey to The Commanding Generals, Field Forces, February 14, 1942, Army General Staff, NARG 407.

12. Memorandum, Hastie to Robert P. Patterson, October 23, 1942, Civilian Aide to the Secretary of War Subject File, 1940–1947, NARG 107.

13. Letter, Clarence E. Adams to Gibson, July 8, 1942, Civilian Aide to the Secretary of War Subject File, 1940–1947, NARG 107.

14. Letter, Daniel E. Williams, Sterle Wilson, and Jasper Smith to the *Pittsburgh Courier*, June 30, 1942.

15. Letter, A Soldier to the *Richmond Afro-American*, May 10, 1943, Civilian Aide to the Secretary of War Subject File, 1940–1947, NARG 107.

16. Letter, Major Samuel L. Ransom to Colonel Marcus Ray, November 12, 1946, Civilian Aide to the Secretary of War Subject File, 1940–1947, NARG 107.

17. Letter, Hastie to author, October 8, 1947; Memorandum, Truman K. Gibson, Jr. to Robert A. Lovett, October 9, 1942, Civilian Aide to the Secretary of War Subject File, 1940–1947, NARG 107.

18. Speech, "Army Dedicates First Colored Recreation Camp in Washington," September 18, 1941, Civilian Aide to the Secretary of War Subject File, 1940–1947, NARG 107.

19. Letter, Hastie to author, December 8, 1974; Judge William H. Hastie, interview with author, March 8, 1974.

20. Letter, Hastie to Walter White, March 14, 1941, Box 264, NAACP Papers; Letter, White to Hastie, September 3, 1941; Letter, Hastie to C. B. Crump, September 11, 1941; Letter, Gibson to White, November 12, 1941, all in Box 230, NAACP Papers.

21. Advertisement, "We Are Still Waiting," n.d., Office of the NAACP, Box 230, NAACP Papers.

22. Memorandum, Hastie to Patterson, January 1, 1942, Box 151, Patterson Papers.

23. Letters, White to Hastie to Prattis, and to Frederick H. Osborn, April 1, 1942; Letter, Osborn to White, April 3, 1942, all in Box 264, NAACP Papers.

24. Letters, Prattis to Hastie and White, April 14, 1942; Letter, Prattis to White, April 4, 1942; Letter, White to Osborn, April 6, 1942; Letter, Gibson to White, April 6, 1942; Letter, White to Hastie and Prattis, April 18, 1942, all in Box 264, NAACP Papers.

25. Letters, Hastie to White and Prattis, April 16, 1942; Letter, White to Hastie, June 22, 1942; Letter, White to Osborn, May 23, 1942; Letter, White to Stimson, June 13, 1942, all in Box 264, NAACP Papers; Memorandums, Patterson to Osborn, June 22, 1942, Osborn to Patterson, June 25, 1942, Box 151, Patterson Papers.

26. Letter, Noble Sissle to White, September 17, 1941; Telegram, Osborn to Sissle, May 8, 1941; Letter, Osborn to White, June 20, 1942; Telegram, Sissle to Hastie, January 7, 1943, Box 230, NAACP Papers; "Army Awards Sgt. Joe Lewis Legion of Merit," *Chicago Defender*, September 29, 1945.

27. Memorandum, Osborn to Stimson, July 31, 1943, Civilian Aide to the Secretary of War Subject File, 1940–1947, NARG 107.

28. Letter, A Group of Soldiers to P. L. Prattis, February 10, 1943, Civilian Aide to the Secretary of War Subject File, 1940–1947, NARG 107.

29. Letter, Private Norman Brittingham to Truman K. Gibson, Jr., July 17, 1943, Civilian Aide to the Secretary of War Subject File, 1940–1947, NARG 107.

30. Letter, A Negro Soldier to the *Baltimore Afro-American*, September 27, 1943, Civilian Aide to the Secretary of War Subject File, 1940–1947, NARG 107.

31. Letter, Private Bert B. Babero to Truman K. Gibson, Jr., March 13, 1944, Civilian Aide to the Secretary of War Subject File, 1940–1947, NARG 107.

32. Letter, Corporal William D. Lee to the *Pittsburgh Courier*, July 28, 1943, Civilian Aide to the Secretary of War Subject File, 1940–1947, NARG 107.

33. Letter, A Negro Soldier to Hastie, July 30, 1941, Civilian Aide to the Secretary of War Subject File, 1940–1947, NARG 107.

34. Letter, A Negro Soldier to the NAACP, March 19, 1945, Civilian Aide to the Secretary of War Subject File, 1940–1947, NARG 17.

35. Letter, A Very Dear Friend of Billy Rowe to the Managing Editor of the *Pittsburgh Courier*, February 5, 1945, Civilian Aide to the Secretary of War Subject File, 1940–1947, NARG 107.

36. Ibid.

37. Memorandum, Gibson to General Miller G. White, June 10, 20, 1944, Military Personnel Division, General Staff, NARG 165.

38. Memorandum, L. A. Guenther to White, June 24, 1944, Military Personnel Division, General Staff, NARG 165.

39. Memorandum, Hastie to Patterson, October 23, 1942, Civilian Aide to the Secretary of War Subject File, 1940–1947, NARG 107; Hastie, interview with author, March 8, 1974.

40. *Army Talk: Orientation Fact Sheet* (Washington, D.C.: War Department, 1944), 1–8; "Aides To Leadership," Prepared by The Office of the Secretary of War, April 11, 1944, Civilian Aide to the Secretary of War Subject File, 1940–1947, NARG 107; Memorandum, D. O. Van Ness, Lieutenant Commander, Naval Personnel, to Gibson, November 25, 1944, Military Personnel Division, General Staff, NARG 165.

41. James C. Evans, interview with author, July 23, 1974; Jean Byers, "A Study of the Negro in Military Service" (Washington, D.C.: Department of Defense, 1947), 79; Evelyn P. Myers, *The Case Against Our Jim Crow Army Demands Investigation by the U.S. Congress* (Washington, D.C.: United States Government Printing Office, 1947), 9; "Army To Destroy Tolerance Booklet," *Pittsburgh Courier*, March 11, 1944; Ruth Benedict and Gene Weltfish, *The Races of Mankind* (New York: Public Affairs Committee, Inc., 1943), 27–31.

42. Letter, D. W. McCoy to Stimson, March 8, 1944, Civilian Aide to the Secretary of War Subject File, 1940–1947, NARG 107.

43. Memorandums, Benjamin O. Davis, Sr. to MacC. Snyder, Inspector General, October 13, 1941 and September 9, 1943, Civilian Aide to the Secretary of War Subject File, 1940–1947, NARG 107; Lee Finkle, "Forum for Protest: The Black Press and World War II," (Ph.D. diss., New York University, 1971), 198; James C. Evans, interview with author, July 23, 1974.

44. Letter, Unsigned letter to *Philadelphia Afro-American*, April 19, 1943, Civilian Aide to the Secretary of War Subject File, 1940–1947, NARG 107.

45. Letter, A Group of Soldiers from Jackson Air Base to Hastie, October 11, 1942; Letter, Jessie W. Greene to Hastie, October 17, 1942; Letter, Eleanor Roosevelt to John J. McCloy, September 29, 1943; Letter, McCloy to Eleanor Roosevelt, October 2, 1943, all in Civilian Aide to the Secretary of War Subject File, 1940–1947, NARG 107.

46. Letter, A Disgusted Negro Trooper to the *Cleveland Call and Post* August 16, 1944, Civilian Aide to the Secretary of War Subject File, 1940–1947, NARG 107.

47. Memorandum, Henry H. Arnold to Hastie, August 15, 1942; Memorandum, Hastie to Arnold, August 18, 1942, Civilian Aide to the Secretary of War Subject File, 1940–1947, NARG 107.

48. Stimson Diary, January 17, 1942.

49. Letter, Roy Wilkins to Hastie, April 26, 1942, Box 264, NAACP Papers; Stimson Diary, January 29, 1942; Memorandum, Hastie to James A. Ulio, Adjutant General, October 21, 1941; Letter, Senator Chan Gurney to Stimson, December 17, 1942; Letter, Eleanor Roosevelt to John J. McCloy, September 30, 1943; Letter, McCloy to Eleanor Roosevelt, October 2, 1943; Letter, Matthew Thorton, Jr. to President Roosevelt, October 13, 1941, all in Civilian Aide to the Secretary of War Subject File, 1940–1947, NARG 107.

50. Memorandum, Adjutant General James A. Ulio to the Commanding General, Services and Supply, May 8, 1942, Army General Staff, NARG 407; Ulio to Senator Chan Gurney and Hastie, December 30, 1942, Civilian Aide to the Secretary of War Subject File, 1940–1947, NARG 107.

51. Hastie, interview with author, March 8, 1974; Letter, Hastie to author, October 8, 1974.

52. Affidavit, William J. Clark, Acting Adjutant General, to Headquarters Company "C" Camp Claiborne, Louisiana, October 31, 1943.

53. Letter, Latrophe F. Jenkins to P. L. Prattis, September 12, 1944, Civilian Aide to the Secretary of War Subject File, 1940–1947, NARG 107.

54. See McGuire, *Taps for a Jim Crow Army*, 183–203.

55. Resolution, Springfield Branch of the NAACP to Stimson and Franklin D. Roosevelt, September 14, 1941; "We Are Still Waiting," *Washington Afro-Amer-*

ican, October 5, 1941; Letter, Stimson to Senator Prentise M. Brown, September 16, 1941, all in Box 230, NAACP Papers; Letter, Patterson to Walter White, September 18, 1941, Robert L. Patterson Papers; Telegram, John P. Davis to Stimson, April 2, 1941; Letter, Davis to Roosevelt, September 2, 1941, John P. Davis Papers, The Schomburg Center for Research in Black Culture, New York Public Library, New York City; Letter, Congressman Arthur W. Mitchell to Stimson, February 14, 1942; Letter, Jessie W. Greene to Hastie, October 17, 1942; Letter, Eleanor Roosevelt to McCloy, September 29, 1943; Letter, McCloy to Mrs. Roosevelt, October 2, 1943, all in Civilian Aide to the Secretary of War Subject File, 1940–1947, NARG 107; Memorandum, Davis to McCloy, September 4, 1941, Army General Staff, NARG 407.

56. Memorandum, Hastie to Stimson, September 8, 1941; Memorandum, Hastie to Ulio, February 9, 1942, Civilian Aide to the Secretary of War Subject File, 1940–1947, NARG 107.

57. Policy Statement, Henry L. Stimson to the Personnel of the United States Armed Forces, September 25, 1941, Civilian Aide to the Secretary of War Subject File, 1940–1947, NARG 107.

58. "Soldiers Flogged by Military Police," *Norfolk Journal and Guide*, September 13, 1942; Memorandum, Major James S. Tatman, Acting Chief of the Analysis Branch, to the Director of the Office of War Information, June 14, 1943, Office of War Information, NARG 208.

59. Letter, Edward N. Lyles to the Editor of the *Cleveland Call and Post*, December 3, 1943, Civilian to the Secretary of War Subject File, 1940–1947, NARG 107.

60. See McGuire, *Taps for a Jim Crow Army*, 149–163; Hastie, interview with author, March 8, 1974.

61. Letter, Private Milton Adams to Hastie, May 13, 1942, Civilian Aide to the Secretary of War Subject File, 1940–1947, NARG 107.

62. Letter, Private Roy Hermitt to *The Chicago Defender*, May 16, 1942, Civilian Aide to the Secretary of War Subject File, 1940–1947, NARG 107.

63. Letter, An Unknown Soldier of the Race to the Editor of the *Baltimore Afro-American*, March 6, 1943, Civilian Aide to the Secretary of War Subject File, 1940–1947, NARG 107.

64. Letter, Private George R. Gilbert to Truman K. Gibson, Jr., March 19, 1943; Pedro E. Pla to Gibson, July 5, 1943; Nathaniel Ester to Gibson, August 14, 1943; Marshall C. Brown to Gibson, December 14, 1944; Edward C. Green, Jr. to Gibson, July 12, 1943, all in Civilian Aide to the Secretary of War Subject File, 1940–1947, NARG 107.

65. Letter, Hastie to author, October 8, 1974; Memorandum, MacC. Snyder to Gibson, August 23, 1943; Letter, Edward F. Witsell, Adjutant General, to Jesse Dedmon, Jr., Director of Veterans Affairs, NAACP, December 3, 1945, Civilian Aide to the Secretary of War Subject File, 1940–1947, NARG 107; "Blue Discharges Reach Senate; 92nd Betrayed by Leadership," *Pittsburgh Courier*, November 13, 1945.

66. Letter, Private Lloyd Lythcott to W. I. Gibson, October 25, 1945, Civilian Aide to the Secretary of War Subject File, 1940–1947, NARG 107.

67. Hastie, interview with author, March 8, 1974.

68. Memorandum, Surgeons-General of the Army and Navy to The American

National Red Cross. This document appeared in the *New York Times*, December 24, 1941; Letter, Edward H. Cavin, Assistant Administrator of the American National Red Cross to Truman K. Gibson, Jr., Assistant Civilian Aide, November 6, 1943, Civilian Aide to the Secretary of War Subject File, 1940–1947, NARG 107; Foster Rhea Dulles, *The American Red Cross, A History* (New York: Harper and Brothers, 1950), 419–420.

69. Morris Fishbein, editor, "Use of Negro Blood for Blood Banks," *Journal of the American Medical Association* 119 (May 16, 1942): 308; "Army Navy Ban on Colored Blood Downright UnAmerican and Stupid," *New York Times*, December 28, 1941.

70. Letter, Cavin to Gibson, November 6, 1943.

71. Memorandum, Hastie to General James A. Ulio, December 26, 1941; "Statement of Policy Regarding Negro Blood Donors," January 21, 1942, Civilian Aide to the Secretary of War Subject File, 1940–1947, NARG 107; Memorandum, Hastie to Patterson, December 28, 1941, Box 151, Patterson Papers.

72. Memorandum, Hastie to Patterson, January 28, 1942; Letter, Davis to Patterson, October 2, 1941, Box 151, Patterson Papers; Letter, Walter White to Stimson, December 30, 1941; Telegram, Citizens of Ohio Future Outlook League, to Hastie, January 3, 1943; Letter, T. M. Smith, president of the National Medical Association, Inc., to Hastie, August 8, 1942.

73. General Douglas B. Kendrick, *Blood Program in World War II* (Washington, D.C.: Department of the Army, 1964), 14–15, 139; Hastie, interview with author, March 6, 1974; Abridged Autobiography, Dr. Charles R. Drew, February 1944, Hastie Papers; John H. Franklin, *From Slavery to Freedom: A History of Negro Americans* (New York: Alfred A. Knopf, 1980), 443.

74. *Philadelphia Tribune*, January 3, 1943.

75. Quoted in Gilbert Ware, *William Hastie: Grace Under Pressure*, (New York: Oxford University Press, 1984), 108.

76. Letter, Hastie to Stimson, January 8, 1942, Civilian Aide to the Secretary of War File, 1940–1947, NARG 107.

77. Memorandum, Hastie to Norman T. Kirk, August 14, 1942, Civilian Aide to the Secretary of War Subject File, 1940–1947, NARG 107.

78. Quoted in Dulles, *The American Red Cross*, 420–421.

79. Letter, C. C. Hillman to Hastie, August 15, 1942, Civilian Aide to the Secretary of War Subject File, 1940–1947, NARG 107; Dulles, *The American Red Cross*, 420.

80. Memorandum, Gibson to H. A. Gerhardt, November 5, 6, 12, 1943, Civilian Aide to the Secretary of War Subject File, 1940–1947, NARG 107.

81. "Army Keeps Jim Crow Blood Banks," *Norfolk Journal and Guide*, April 8, 1944; Memorandum, Hastie to Patterson, January 28, 1942; Letter, Davis to Patterson, October 2, 1941; Letter, White to Stimson, December 30, 1941; Telegram, Citizens of Ohio to Hastie, January 2, 1942; Letter, John O. Holby, president of the Future Outlook League, to Hastie, January 3, 1943; Letter, Smith, to Hastie, August 8, 1942; Memorandum, Hastie to Kirk, August 14, 1942, all in Civilian Aide to the Secretary of War Subject File, 1940–1947, NARG 107; Dulles, *The American Red Cross*, 420; Letter, Katherine E. Kemper, Assistant Director of Donor Resources Development, to author, August 12, 1977.

82. Letter, Hastie to author, October 8, 1974; Hastie, interview with author, March 6, 1974.

4

Hastie and the Apparent End of a Painful Quest

In a real sense, Hastie's disgust with the War Department's policy concerning its blood donor program was his "last stand" against the segregationist attitude and discriminatory practices of the department. He had failed to convince Secretary of War Henry L. Stimson to abandon the racialism inherent in the program. This controversy, however, was among several that created an impasse between Hastie and the department with regard to the segregation and discrimination of black soldiers. Perhaps the most pressing issues of all involved the Army Air Corps and the Advisory Committee for Negro Troop Policy. Because of the intransigent position of Assistant Secretary of War for Air Robert A. Lovett on the use of black troops (discussed in Chapter 2) and the refusal of the Advisory Committee to invite Hastie to its regularly scheduled meetings, he resigned his post. In January 1943, Hastie told Secretary Stimson that he had decided to resign because he felt that his presence in the department was no longer effective; that the racial policies of the War Department would change only as a result of strong public indignation; that his usefulness to black soldiers would be greater as a private citizen; and that he honestly believed the department had deliberately waged a campaign to dishearten him in an effort to break his will for social justice and for the military equality sought for black soldiers.[1]

Hastie left the War Department at the end of January and returned to Howard University as a professor and Dean of the Law School. As he had implied in his letter of resignation, however, he continued to address the problems of black soldiers as president of the Washington, D.C. branch of the NAACP.[2]

Stimson was not surprised at Hastie's departure. He accepted his resignation effective January 31, 1943. He routinely expressed regret that Hastie had decided to resign, and appreciation that he and the War Department's general staff felt towards Hastie's contribution to solving the racial problems of the military. He made it clear that Hastie should feel free to make suggestions to the War Department in the future on matters affecting blacks in the armed forces. Hastie did not know how much irony was in Stimson's words. Just three months earlier Stimson had recorded in his diary that Hastie's usefulness in the War Department was limited and his ideas were unrealistic.[3]

Contrary to Stimson's assessment of Hastie, the black community and much of the liberal white public praised him for the work done in the War Department. Perhaps the most eloquent expression of public gratitude occurred in February 1943 when he was named to the "Honor Roll of Race Relations," awarded the NAACP's Spingarn Medal in March 1943, and selected one year later to the 1944 edition of *Current Biography*. These honors were bestowed upon Hastie because of his efforts to achieve full integration and equal opportunity for blacks in the military, and specifically the Army Air Corps. Hastie wrote, in a letter to Walter White, "I hope that the [Spingarn Medal] will serve to symbolize the union of a great number of Americans, white as well as colored, in their uncompromising opposition to racial bigotry, segregation and discrimination."[4]

The press and the national leadership also praised Hastie. Congressman Will Rogers, Jr., of California stated that Hastie "refused to temporize with racial bigotry, segregation, or discrimination." Walter White considered his resignation a "severe jolt to Washington complacency." The *Washington Afro-American* felt that Hastie's resignation was "quite proper." The *Pittsburgh Courier* serialized his reasons for resigning in editorials titled "The Hastie Report," *Time Magazine* published an article on his resignation, and the Associated Press found that it was a public consensus that Hastie did the right thing.[5]

Historian W. E. B. Du Bois's thoughts on Hastie perhaps best expressed the sentiments of the black leadership. They are penetrating and deserve to be quoted at length:

There are two sorts of public relations officials in Washington working on the situation of the Negro: one sort is a kind of upper clerk who transmits to the public with such apologetic airs as he can assume, the refusal of the department to follow his advice or the advice of anyone else calculated to sease [sic] the racial situation. The other kind of race relations official seeks to give advice and to get the facts and if he receives a reasonable amount of cooperation he works on hopefully. If he does not, he withdraws. It is, of course, this second type of official alone who is useful and valuable. The other is nothing. Hastie belongs to the valuable sort and will not be easily replaced.[6]

Editorially, the black press praised Hastie specifically for having the courage to protest publicly the policies and practices of the War Department. Both the northern and southern press reflected a widespread endorsement of Hastie. The *New York Age* was typical of the Northern press:

It is refreshing to realize that there is still Negro leadership with good red blood flowing through its veins—a type of leadership which is patient and cautious but which, in the final analysis, will not compromise the basic principles of democracy for the price of prestige and power. One of the grandest and greatest figures today on the horizon of Negro leadership is William H. Hastie, who recently issued a revealing statement disclosing his reasons for resigning from that position. Now we know that he never let us down. Now we know that when Tuskegee Air Field was founded on a basis of damnable segregation and maintained on a practice of equally condemnable jim-crow; that when Negro soldiers who donned the uniforms of their country to fight and were assigned to labor—now we know that William H. Hastie used every weapon at his command to combat the traditional brass hat Army tactics which are the most insurmountable bottleneck to the vigorous prosecution of this war. To him in years to come will belong an honored place in the history of the fight of the Negro to set America free from her own bigotry and selfishness. This is the hour when the nation needs such men as Hastie.[7]

The *Atlanta Daily World* represented the general opinion of the southern black press. It asserted:

We are sorry that Mr. Hastie had to resign but his action will focus effective attention on demoralizing conditions. The reasons given for his resignation would have influenced any other man of his stature and forthright convictions to have done likewise. Nevertheless, we are comforted by the fact that Mr. Hastie did the best he could under the circumstances, and that the fate he suffered was no worse nor better than any other Negro would have suffered similarly placed. But one thing we may all be certain, his courage and fortitude, smack of a new type of leadership in our group, which prefers no job at all to that of holding on to a position which not only stifles his own manhood principles but likewise, betrays the confidence and trust of his race.[8]

Of the 29 white newspapers examined, located in the northern and southern regions of the country, they either failed to comment on Hastie's resignation or merely reported in small capital letters that he had resigned from the War Department.[9]

James C. Evans, Civilian Aide 1947–1970, considered Hastie's resignation as having more impact on the War Department's racial policies than any other single factor or set of circumstances. Hastie's influence was evident when the War Department made certain immediate changes following his departure. The replacement, for example, of Colonel Frederick Kimble, who allegedly was anti-black, with Colonel Noel Parrish as commanding officer of Tuskegee Air Base, was one of the first changes made. Colonel Parrish was considered a liberal commander among the officials of the War Department and the military top brass. He was instrumental in modifying some of the racial inequalities at Tuskegee, although blacks continued to be trained in separate air force units. Nevertheless, under Parrish's leadership recreational facilities on the base were integrated, more black flight instructors were added to the staff, the officers' club was opened to black officers, the 333rd Fighter Squadron was created, blacks were trained as heavy bombardment fliers, black flight surgeons were trained in integrated facilities at Randolph Field, Howard University, and Hampton Institute were among the black schools approved to participate in the Air Force Enlistment Program, and the general morale of black soldiers and personnel was raised.[10]

Within the War Department, the relationship between Hastie's successor, Truman K. Gibson, Jr., and the Advisory Committee on Negro Troop Policy improved. Gibson and the Advisory Committee began working more closely on matters affecting the morale and the nondiscriminatory effective usage of black soldiers. By February 1944, the War Department's Public Relations Bureau had prepared and distributed three pamphlets titled *Command of Negro Troops*, *Army Talk*, and *Leadership and the Negro Soldier*. These documents acknowledged the concept of equal opportunity, something Hastie had so desperately advocated as the civilian aide. Later that year, a motion picture titled *The Negro Soldier* was created and produced by the Special Service Division of the Public Relations Bureau. Except in the South, the picture was shown to all soldiers as well as to civilian Americans in most of the theaters around the country. The NAACP had to file an *Amicus Curiae* brief in the District Court of New York against the War Activities Committee of the Motion Picture Industry before the American public in the South could see the achievements of black soldiers on film. Hastie, a private citizen, and Thurgood Marshall wrote the brief that said in essence that any interference with the distribution of the film would seriously hinder the war effort.[11]

As a private citizen, Hastie welcomed these military policy innovations. He viewed them as positive steps toward an eventual color-blind military, but to him the process and progress of equal opportunity and full military integration were not complete. Thus out of office he continued to protest the plight of black soldiers. For example, six weeks before Hastie's January 1943 resignation, he prepared a list of known black soldiers who had been turned over to civilian authorities for alleged crimes committed while in uniform as members of the armed forces. The list was sent to John P. Davis, national secretary of the National Negro Congress, who passed it on to Truman Gibson. As the new black Civilian Aide to the Secretary of War, Gibson used the list and cited several more cases of this type when he protested the action to the War Department. To support his protest, he also cited War Article 74 of the Army Regulations Codes, which prohibited the surrender of soldiers to civilian authorities during wartime. Consequently, Gibson recommended that the War Department issue a directive to all field commanders to discontinue what he considered to be a flagrant violation of the soldiers' civil rights. Besides, he said to Assistant Secretary of War John J. McCloy, "there can be no guarantee of a fair trial for Negro soldiers in most courts in the deep South. Particularly is this so where any Negro is called on to dispute the veracity of a white witness, if indeed any Negro would have the temerity to do so foolhardy an action where all the cards are stacked against him."[12]

McCloy responded to Gibson's recommendation with the War Department's usual subterfuges for correcting existing patterns of discrimination against black soldiers. In his reply to Gibson, McCloy referred Gibson to a July memo released by Major General Myron C. Cramer, Judge Advocate General, who saw no need for Secretary Stimson to issue a directive. In fact, Cramer maintained that such an order would unfairly infringe upon the legal authority of the commanding officers and render their "impartial" services ineffective. Subsequently, McCloy informed Gibson in August 1943 that a general directive was not justified inasmuch as the cases discussed were found to be handled impartially by the Office of the Judge Advocate General. Although Hastie was no longer with the War Department, to him this decision was biased and discriminatory, for he believed that "the Army's use of military and civilian Courts to keep Negroes in their place through the imposition of specially harsh and severe punishment upon men who have expressed resentment against Jim Crow practices, is a recurring evil and the cause of much bitterness among Negro members of the armed forces and civilians alike."[13]

The public indignation to which Hastie referred increased as he continued to protest the way in which black soldiers accused of crimes were treated. A case in point was the sensationalized rape incident in May 1943 that allegedly occurred in New Caledonia (a French island in Melanesia, in the Coral Sea). Two black soldiers received life sentences because they allegedly raped a white prostitute when in fact it was reasonably proven by Hastie and Congressman Vito Marcantonio, attorneys for the soldiers, that the woman willingly consented to accept a fee for her services. Hastie and Marcantonio built their case upon the following facts: the investigating officer had concluded that the evidence did not warrant a charge of rape; that the woman's testimony contained serious improprieties; that the woman was an admitted prostitute; and that her medical history made her story invalid. In that regard, Dr. Ginieys, examining physician, stated categorically that since Fisher and Loury, the accused black soldiers, did not have gonorrhea, "it would have been a medical impossibility for her gonorrhea condition to have been due to intercourse with Fisher and Loury since the lesions at the neck of the uterus found by me within 24 hours of the alleged rape could not have been caused by any contact had with any person during the previous 24-hour period."[14]

In their plea for clemency, Hastie and Marcantonio pointed out to Secretary Stimson the unjustifiable severity of the life sentences since military justice was supposed to bear a reasonable relationship to the penal law of the community where the crime was committed. They insisted that rapists were, according to Section 332 of the French Penal Code for New Caledonia, subject to five but not more than twenty years at hard labor. Hastie and Marcantonio finally appealed to Stimson to consider all of the evidence surrounding the case before making a decision on their plea for clemency for the black soldiers. They were also resolute in their belief that the sentences represented the "Scottsboro Case" of the U.S. Army. (The Scottsboro Case involved nine young black boys—ages twelve to nineteen—who were arrested in Scottsboro, Alabama, in 1931 for allegedly raping two white prostitutes on a freight train. One boy was freed, and the others were sentenced to die in the electric chair. The case received national and international news coverage before all eight were eventually freed by 1955.)[15]

Hastie was particularly concerned with the fate of these soldiers because, as civilian aide, he had been aware of the racial discrimination and physical abuse blacks endured as members of the armed services. Then, too, his first-hand knowledge of the unequal justice the "Scottsboro Boys" were subjected to made him more sensitive and keenly aware of white perceptions (whether legal or illegal) of black men involved sexually with white women. Thus Hastie pleaded with Stimson to let the facts of the case guide his decision.[16]

Secretary Stimson refused to grant Fisher and Loury a full pardon, but he reduced their life sentences to eight and ten years respectively.[17]

Hastie was pleased with Stimson's decision, but several other heavy rape sentences handed down to black soldiers disturbed him. There was some basis for his belief. For example, in a black anti-aircraft company stationed in the South, the white officer in charge of the unit posted a notice to the effect that any type of association with white women would be considered rape, the penalty for which was death. This may have been a scare tactic; nevertheless, it dampened the morale of the black troops. It was not until February 1, 1948, however, that the War Department repealed the automatic death sentence for murder and rape.[18]

In addition to the rape cases, other incidents involving deadly and humiliating attacks on black soldiers had increased at such an alarming rate by June 1943 that Hastie released a rather long and exacting statement to the New York *Daily News*. Acting as a private citizen on behalf of black soldiers, he criticized the War Department and the military in general for their indecisiveness in formulating effective policies designed to prevent racial confrontations. He declared:

At Camp Stewart, Georgia, Negro soldiers and military policemen engage in a fatal gun battle. In Centerville, Mississippi, a sheriff kills a Negro soldier. At Camp Shelby, Mississippi, two Negro soldiers lie in a hospital, wounded in an affray with highway patrolmen. The environs of Camp Shelby are more than familiar to the military authorities who have surveyed and studied that very area because of the acute problems of racial relations which confront the Army there. It is only the sensational cases of shootings, killing and rioting which attract public attention. But day by day the Negro soldier faces abuse and humiliation. In such a climate resentments, hatreds and fears and misunderstandings mount until they erupt in sensational violence. Yet, both the administration and the military authorities persist in trying to muddle through, without plan or program, hoping that somehow things will come out all right. The Army, long wedded to the mores of the South and immobilized by its traditional methods of procedure, pursues a course of dealing with each incident as it occurs. Formal investigations and reports, an occasional court-martial, the removal of some individual from his command, the shifting of a troublesome regiment to another station—these are the Army's customary and familiar devices. It sticks to them doggedly. The Army cannot check the increasing wave of violence by ponderous investigation of each case as it occurs. The Army itself is busy with booklets, lectures and various devices of indoctrination, teaching our soldiers how to treat the peoples of India, the South Sea Islanders, the Arabs, everyone but their fellow American soldiers. It is time that similar efforts and techniques be employed in the business of building comradeship within our own military and civilian communities.[19]

The continued confrontation between black soldiers, white military police, and civilian communities was one of several concerns that attracted Hastie's attention as a private citizen. Another issue involved Secretary Stimson's decision to convert the black Second Cavalry Division into a service corps. When Hastie learned of this action, he was outraged, because as Civilian Aide he had attempted to get the War Department to avoid repeating what he called the "tragedy of World War I."[20]

As early as 1942, Hastie realized that 75 percent of the Army's black personnel were being used in service and supply units. He considered this situation one of his biggest headaches, (because of the War Department's intransigence on the utilization of blacks in combat, pressure from the black leadership and the black press, and the desire of black soldiers themselves to fight) but he attempted to get information on the number and percentage of blacks who were utilized in these units in World War I to compare them to similar usage in World War II. But Under Secretary of War Robert P. Patterson denied him access to the records on grounds that the Adjutant General's office could supply the answers to all questions regarding blacks who served in these units during World War I. Patterson's denial was a major setback for Hastie. The issue was never resolved while he was in office, but the protest to force the military to put more black troops into combat continued.[21]

That the military needed more combat troops was indisputable. In response to this need and the growing controversy over whether black soldiers would be used in combat zones overseas, the Advisory Committee on Negro Troop Policies recommended to Secretary Stimson in 1943 that "Negro combat troops be dispatched to an active theatre of operations at an early date," because, "in the opinion of the committee, such action would be the most effective means of reducing tension among Negro troops."[22]

Rather than act on the Committee's recommendation, Secretary Stimson chose to accept a recommendation from his staff; he announced on January 28, 1944, that, in spite of the Army's urgent need for more seasoned combat troops, the black Second Cavalry Division would be converted into various service units. This action was taken, though not made public, to release white soldiers for combat and more technical duties, and because black soldiers were more acceptable as service units than as combat units to American commanders overseas. Also, Stimson's staff had suggested that the War Department "quit catering to the Negroes' desire for a proportionate share of combat units. Put them where they will best aid the war effort."[23]

Although the War Department felt the vast majority of black soldiers would be more useful in service units, the conversion policy was an affront to Hastie, and to black soldiers, as well as to black and white national leaders. Interestingly, Secretary Stimson was aware of the impending black protest, for he had written in his diary a day earlier:

The Staff had just recommended the transformation of the Second Cavalry Division which is our only remaining cavalry division into a service corps and that aroused melancholy feelings in the minds of McCloy and myself and others in my civilian staff because it means the wiping out of the two famous old colored regiments, the Ninth and Tenth Cavalry. These gentlemen came today and laid

The Apparent End of a Painful Quest   91

out the whole situation before me and it appeared that there was nothing else to be done; our manpower is so short and the emergency requirements are so immediate that we had to take a division which has trained as this one has and put it to use. It was to go to France to take part there and while not a combatant division it will be in vigorous use and vigorous peril. The talk led to a discussion of what we should do with our colored inductees. I told them I had come to the conclusion that we must face the situation more seriously and courageously. We have got to use the colored race to help us in the fight and we have got to officer it with white men in my opinion and although it injures their sensibilities, it is better to do that than to have them massacred under incompetent colored officers.[24]

The irony of Stimson's rationale was that the Second Cavalry had trained for combat duty since the War Department's announcement in 1940 that black troops would be utilized in combat; moreover, some of the officers had fought and won battle medals in World War I. Hence, the decision to convert this particular division to service units left many black and white Americans angry. New York Congressman Hamilton Fish (white), for example, asked Stimson to submit to his office the plans for utilizing black troops in combat. Instead, Stimson submitted a detailed letter in which he explained that prior to 1942 the Second Cavalry had been defensive corps, but after that date not only it but some white defensive units were being converted into service units because the possibility of an enemy attack in the United States no longer existed. Then, too, he claimed that several units of the Second Cavalry had not mastered the techniques of modern weaponry due to their inferior educational status. Never once did Stimson address the question of why the most experienced and most useful black combat units were being relegated to service and supply units when manpower shortages of ground forces were urgent, and when no black units to date had been committed to overseas combat duty, despite the War Department's 1940 promise to do so.[25]

Hastie went further than Congressman Fish, but rather than attack Stimson publicly, he accused him and the War Department staff privately of deliberately devising plans to keep black soldiers out of combat. Hastie maintained that of the five infantry regiments, and the five anti-aircraft artillery units mobilized in 1941 for combat duty, not a single outfit had been used in overseas combat. Moreover, he called Stimson's attention to the fact that the Ninth and Tenth Cavalry had been created by law for combat duty; yet, they were being converted into a service corps. Hastie also emphasized that the defensive unit and poor educational qualification explanation to Congressman Fish confirmed the beliefs of many black and white citizens that the War Department never intended to use black soldiers in overseas combat. Finally, Hastie challenged Stimson to repudiate the following statement:

The truth of the matter is that these original Negro combat units have been the problem children of the Army for more than two years, not because they were incompetent, but because no one wanted them. Nurtured on the myth that Negro troops cannot be relied upon in combat and fearing to add a 'racial problem' to other headaches in the theatre of war, field commanders and the Operations Branch of the War Department turned thumbs down on the utilization of the great majority of the Negro combat units. Anti-Aircraft Artillery was in a special category. Such a unit could be given a separate and more or less permanent defensive station in the theatre of operations. It need not be integrated with other combat forces. So the utilization of Negro Anti-Aircraft units in the theatre of operations was adopted as a device best calculated to confound the critics of any policy as to Negro combat troops without basically changing that policy. It is respectfully submitted that it is time and past time that the matter of utilization of Negro combat units pass out of the hands of those who deal with this matter as a distasteful search for compromise born of political necessity, and into the hands of those who have the will and the understanding to exploit the great combat potential of the Negro soldier as a valuable asset in the winning of the war.[26]

Secretary Stimson's reply to Hastie was essentially what he had written to Congressman Fish, except that he introduced the matter of the Army General Classification Tests as the major reason preventing the usage of black soldiers overseas in combat zones. Hastie, however, never knew that the classification tests were, according to Stimson's diary, deliberately manipulated to minimize the number of blacks in the armed services.[27]

Unlike Hastie, the black press, other black leaders, and national black protest groups publicly ridiculed Stimson for his decision to convert the Second Cavalry into service units. They believed the conversion policy was racially motivated. It was ironic to them that the War Department could justify converting trained combat troops to service and supply units when field commanders were calling for more combat personnel. Roy Wilkins noted particularly the inconsistency in Stimson's thinking. He was anxious to know how the military could be satisfied with the Second Cavalry as a defensive unit to protect the leaders of the United States when it could not master the techniques of modern weaponry to fight in the combat zones of Europe.[28]

Black soldiers themselves also questioned the wisdom of Secretary Stimson. Those of the Second Cavalry who wanted to participate in combat reportedly commented on this issue and believed that the breakup of the cavalry was a deliberate attempt by the War Department to claim in the future that black troops did not measure up and thus failed to do their part in combat. Their attitude was echoed in such representative statements as: "Someone had to be a stevedore, longshoreman, etc. It was a simple matter—give it to the colored man. After the war is over demands couldn't be so great; didn't his white brother(?) die on the front line, while he was comparatively safe in the rear echelon; that's right, isn't it?" And, "The reason why I prefer combat is because we all are suppose to be American citizens and there aren't any of us Negro people fighting in this war. Since we are citizens we should be granted the privilege that the rest are getting because we are just as good as the next man. Under the condition it will better our status after the war."[29]

Whether the status of black soldiers improved after the war due to their limited combat duty is a matter of conjecture. That Hastie worked toward an improved status for black soldiers, however, is indisputable. Thus he must be viewed as their spokesman, one who, as a loyal and patriotic public servant, accepted the responsibility "to work effectively toward the integration of the Negro into the Army and to facilitate his placement, training, and promotion."[30] Hastie must also be remembered as the man whose recommendations and activities as civilian aide and as private citizen bespoke of his intent to safeguard the future well-being of blacks in the armed services. He devoted two years and two months of his public life to improving opportunities for black soldiers, and constantly reminded Secretary of War Henry L. Stimson, his department staff, the Army's top brass as well as all of America that the treatment of black soldiers ran counter to professed democratic and egalitarian rhetoric and to the basic tenets of the American liberal tradition.

After vigorously protesting Secretary Stimson's 1944 decision to separate wounded and battle weary black and white soldiers returning from the war in separate and unequal rehabilitative facilities, Hastie joined Thurgood Marshall (the current Associate Justice of the U.S. Supreme Court) and other NAACP attorneys as they concentrated on and worked within the legal system to break down racial barriers in all segments of American life, but especially in educational and public accommodation institutions. Hastie served in this capacity and as dean of Howard University Law School until 1946, when President Harry S. Truman appointed him governor of the Virgin Islands. After vigorously campaigning for Truman's 1948 reelection, Hastie was appointed in 1949 to his last federal post as circuit judge of the Third Appellate Court of the United States. He rose to chief judge in 1970; he died as senior judge of the court in April 1976.[31]

NOTES

1. Memorandum, William H. Hastie to Robert A. Lovett, April 29, 1942; Memorandum, Hastie to Henry L. Stimson, January 5, 1943, Civilian Aide to the Secretary of War Subject File, 1940–1947, NARG 107; Stimson Diary, November 2, 1942; James C. Evans, interview with author, August 6, 1974; "Air

Force Policy Forced Me To Resign," *Pittsburgh Courier*, February 6, 1943; Hastie, interview with author, March 8, 1974; A. Russell Buchanan, *Black Americans in World War II* (Santa Barbara, Calif.: ABC-Clio Press, 1977), 70.

2. Hastie, interview with author, March 6, 1974.

3. Memorandum, Hastie to Stimson, January 6, 1943; Memorandum, Stimson to Hastie, January 29, 1943, Civilian Aide to the Secretary of War Subject File, 1940–1947, NARG 107; Stimson Diary, October 19, 1942.

4. Letter, Hastie to Walter White, March 31, 1943; Letter, John H. Holmes, pastor of the Community Church of New York, to White, February 9, 1943; Letter, A. Philip Randolph, executive secretary of the Union of Sleeping Car Porters and Maids, to White, February 11, 1943; "Report of the Spingarn Medal Award Committee," March 8, 1943; Letter, George W. Lattimore president of the International Theatrical Agency, to Hastie, March 22, 1943; John H. Owens, Sr., corresponding secretary of the Los Angeles Forum, to White, April 14, 1943, all in box 274, NAACP Papers; Letter, Robert P. Patterson to C. A. Franklin, editor of the *Cleveland Call and Post*, January 25, 1943, Box 151, Patterson Papers; Anna Rothe, editor, *Current Biography* (New York: H. W. Wilson Company, 1944), 277–279.

5. "Text of the Award of the Twenty-eighth Spingarn Medal to Judge Hastie," March 1943, Box 274, NAACP Papers; Walter White, *A Man Called White* (New York: The Viking Press, 1948), 223; *Washington Afro-American*, February 6, 1943, "The Hastie Report," *Pittsburgh Courier*, February 6, 1943; Letter, Hastie to the *Time* Editorial Office, February 5, 1943, Civilian Aide to the Secretary of War Subject File, 1940–1947, NARG 107.

6. Editorial, *New York Amsterdam Star-News*, February 6, 1943.

7. Editorial, *New York Age*, February 13, 1943; Editorial, *Philadelphia Tribune*, February 6, 1943; Editorial, "Wanted: A Military New Deal," *Pittsburgh Courier*, February 6, 1943; Editorial, *California Eagle*, February 17, 1943.

8. Editorial, *Atlanta Daily World*, February 3, 1943; Editorial, "Hastie Gains in Stature by Resigning War Post," *Baltimore Afro-American*, February 6, 1943; Editorial, *Norfolk Journal and Guide*, February 20, 1943.

9. "Hastie Resigns," *New York Times*, February 1, 1943; "Hastie Resigns," *Washington Post*, February 1, 1943; "Negro Resigns as Stimson Aide," *Los Angeles Times*, February 1, 1943; "Aide to Stimson Quits, Saying Negro Flyers Are Treated Badly," *Denver Post*, February 1, 1943; "Negro Quits Post with Stimson in Protest at Bias," *Philadelphia Record*, February 1, 1943; "Hastie Says He Quit Over Racial Bias," *New York Post*, February 1, 1943; "Negro Aide in Stimson's Office Quits Charging Discrimination," *Montgomery Advertiser*, February 1, 1943; "Negro Assistant to Stimson Quits," *Atlanta Constitution*, February 1, 1943; "Discrimination Laid to Army By Resigned Stimson Aide," *Baltimore Sun*, February 1, 1943; "Discrimination Against Negro Air Force Charged," *Greensboro Daily*, February 1, 1943; "Stimson's Negro Civilian Aide Quits in Protest of Policy," *Richmond-Times Dispatch*, February, 1, 1943; "Negro Aide to Stimson Quits, Hits Segregation of Airmen," *Houston Post*, February 1, 1943. None of these papers wrote editorial comments on Hastie's resignation.

10. Evans, interview with author, July 23, 1974; Letter, Patterson to La Roe, March 23, 1943; Memorandum, Gibson to John J. McCloy, February 3, 1943; Memorandum, Gibson to General Edgar P. Sorensen, Assistant Chief of Air

Intelligence, September 14, 1943; Letter, McCarthy to Colonel Noel Parrish, December 2, 1944; Letter, Parrish to McCarthy and McCloy, December 27, 1944, all in civilian Aide to the Secretary of War Subject File, 1940–1947, NARG 107; "Army to Expand its Program for Training Negro Fliers," *New York Age*, February 6, 1943; "Air Force Policy Thwarts War Effort," *California Eagle*, February 17, 1943; "Army To Expand its Program for Training Negro Fliers," *Atlanta Daily World*, February 2, 1943; Ulysses Lee, *United States Army in World War II: Special Studies: The Employment of Negro Troops* (Washington, D.C.: United States Government Printing Office, 1966), 175–178.

11. Lee, *The Employment of Negro Troops*, 175–178; United States War Department Pamphlet, *Command of Negro Troops* (Washington, D.C.: United States Government Printing Office, 1944); *Army Talk: Orientation Fact Sheet* (Washington, D.C.: United States Government Printing Office, 1945); Headquarters, Army Service Forces, *Leadership and the Negro Soldier* (Washington, D.C.: United States Government Printing Office, 1944); Negro Marches On, Incorporated, Plaintiff-Against-War Activities Committee of the Motion Picture Industry; Defendants, 1944, Civilian Aide to the Secretary of War Subject File, 1940–1947, NARG 107.

12. Letter, Hastie to John P. Davis, December 16, 1942; Memorandum, Gibson to McCloy, June 1, 1943; Memorandum, Gibson to McCloy, July 20, 1943, all in Civilian Aide to the Secretary of War Subject File, 1940–1947, NARG 107.

13. Memorandum, General Myron C. Cramer to McCloy, July 27, 1943; Memorandum, McCloy to Gibson, August 5, 1943, Civilian Aide to the Secretary of War Subject File, 1940–1947, NARG 107; Letter, Hastie to Margaret C. McCulloch, Department of Social Science, Fisk University, July 28, 1944, Hastie Papers.

14. William H. Hastie and Vito Marcantonio, Petition For Clemency and Brief In Support Thereof to Secretary of War Henry L. Stimson, Army General Staff, NARG 407, 1–17.

15. Ibid., 18–23; see Dan T. Carter, *Scottsboro: A Tragedy of the American South* (Baton Rouge: Louisiana State University Press, 1969).

16. Hastie, interview with author, March 6, 1974.

17. Hastie and Marcantonio, Petition, 18–23.

18. Hastie, interview with author, March 6, 1974; Editorials, "Black and White Rape," April 1944, Civilian Aide to the Secretary of War Subject File, 1940–1947, NARG 107; "Army Ends Death Sentence for Murder and Rape in New Code Effective February 1," *New York Times*, July 15, 1948.

19. Soldiers Flogged by Military Police," *Norfolk Journal and Guide*, September 13, 1942; Memorandum, Major James S. Tatman, Acting Chief of the Analysis Branch, to Director of the Office of War Information, June 4, 1943, Office of War Information, NARG 208.

20. Hastie, interview with author, March 6, 1974.

21. Memorandum, Hastie to Patterson, February 3, 1942; Patterson to Hastie, February 10, 1942, Box 151, Patterson Papers; Hastie, interview with author, March 6, 1974.

22. Bernard C. Nalty and Morris J. MacGregor, eds., *Blacks in the Military: Essential Documents* (Wilmington, Del.: Scholarly Resources, 1981), 123.

23. Lee, *The Employment of Negro Troops*, 415, 413–423.

24. Stimson Diary, January 27, 1944.

25. Letters, Hamilton Fish to Stimson, February 1, 1944; Stimson to Fish,

February 19, 1944, Civilian Aide to the Secretary of War Subject File, 1940–1947, NARG 107.

26. Letter, Hastie to Stimson, February 29, 1944, William H. Hastie Papers, Howard University Law School Library, Washington, D.C.

27. Letter, Stimson to Hastie, March 31, 1944, Civilian Aide to the Secretary of War Subject File, 1940–1947, NARG 107; Stimson Diary, May 12, 1942; Phillip McGuire, "Black Civilian Aides and the Problems of Racism and Segregation in the United States Armed Forces, 1940–1950" (Ph.D. diss., Howard University, 1975), 45–48.

28. "Many Negro Combat Units Being Broken Up," *Pittsburgh Courier*, October 30, 1943; "Fish Protests Breaking Up of Negro Cavalry," *Chicago Defender*, April 2, 1944; "Secretary of War Attacks Record of Race Combat Units," *Pittsburgh Courier*, March 4, 1944; Letter, Wilkins to Stimson, March 2, 1944; Letter, Adelaide C. Hill, executive secretary of the Englewood Urban League, Inc., to Stimson, March 15, 1944; Letter, Theodore D. McNeal, St. Louis Unit Director of the March-on-Washington Movement, to Stimson, March 9, 1944; Letter, Colonel Harrison Gerhardt to Theodore D. McNeal, March 13, 1944, all in Civilian Aide to the Secretary of War Subject File, 1940–1947, NARG 107.

29. Samuel A. Stouffer et al., *The American Soldier: Adjustment During Army Life* (Princeton, N.J.: Princeton University Press, 1949), 527–535.

30. Hastie, interview with author, March 6, 1974; "Colonel Eugene Householder's Remarks at the Conference of Negro Newspapers Representatives," December 8 and 9, 1941, NARG 107; *New York Amsterdam Star-News*, November 2, 1940; *Norfolk Journal and Guide*, November 2, 1940.

31. "Opening Statement of Judge William H. Hastie on the Wink Forum," July 29, 1944, Hastie Papers; Letter, White to Gibson, September 15, 1944, Box 279, NAACP Papers; Hastie, interview with author, March 6, 1974; "Hastie Appointed Governor of Virgin Island," *Pittsburgh Courier*, January 6, 1946; Anna Rothe, editor, *Current Biography* (New York: H. W. Wilson Company, 1944), 277–279; John H. Franklin, *From Slavery to Freedom: A History of Negro Americans* (New York: Alfred A. Knopf, 1974), 468; Bernard C. Nalty, *Strength for the Fight: A History of Black Americans in the Military* (New York: The Free Press, 1986), 204–207.

5

The Conclusion: Shifts in Military Policy

When World War II ended in 1945, a legacy of racial discrimination and segregation plagued the armed services, black soldiers, and the black community. Hastie's experiences, both as private citizen and as Civilian Aide to the Secretary of War, supported this assessment. The complaints of black soldiers, black and white national protest leadership, and the charges of the black press also sustained the claim of widespread racial discrimination and segregation in the armed services. In addition, the policy changes affecting black soldiers that were put into effect while the war was in progress and thereafter also forged a living testimony to the fact that racial discrimination and the segregation of white and black military personnel were practiced and maintained through the war. However, important shifts in military policies affecting blacks and the changing status of black Americans in the larger society suggested the beginning of an end to an old order of restrictive outlooks and actions toward black soldiers in the "armed forces of democracy."

That Hastie played a significant role in occasioning the beginning of this new socio-military attitude is indisputable. His diametric opposition to jim crow and his successes in the War Department beg to be acknowledged, and must be attributed to his sources of power, his previous career as public servant and civil rights activist, and his crusade as a private citizen speaking out for American democracy. Drawing upon his capacity to articulate facts underscoring the immorality of racism and segregation, he was always supported by the black community, black soldiers, significant and influential black leaders, the major black press, all of the black national pressure organizations, many white liberals, and, to some degree, white national pressure organizations and some elements of the white press. As black military personnel and nongovernmental opponents of racism and segregation, these elements were instrumental in aiding Hastie as he and they exposed the discriminatory policies and practices of the armed services.[1]

Hastie used this power base to launch a crusade aimed to destroy a past that barred black soldiers from receiving the optimum benefit of army life and that denied them the moral right to function as citizens in a democratic republic. He was not protesting personal but institutional racism based upon the "color line"; he hoped moral suasion would destroy the personal prejudices that rankled the military. Hastie wanted black soldiers accorded their rights within a context of military efficiency and on an integrated basis. The War Department and the military's top brass, on the other hand, believed that efficiency would be best achieved by maintaining segregated services irrespective of the rights and morale of black personnel.

Hastie's failures as civilian aide can be attributed to his inability—in spite of the overwhelming moral and empirical evidence—to convince the War Department and the military's top brass that the injustices of racial discrimination and segregation retarded rather than improved the efficiency of the armed services.

In spite of his formidable opponents both within and outside the War Department, Hastie's activities for change kept the "American dream" alive in the hearts and minds of black soldiers. To them, as well as to black Americans and to some white Americans, he represented the "cutting edge" of American democracy. Unfortunately to the War Department, his actions and appeals for policy modifications were viewed as hopelessly visionary.

Although Hastie, black soldiers, the black community, and segments of the white community had not achieved their foremost objective—integration of the armed forces—the Army Air Forces, for example, began training black pilots in 1941, and in 1942 the Navy began enlisting blacks other than for messman duty.[2]

Other significant changes affecting black soldiers also occurred: an increasing number of blacks were attending officer candidate schools; the War Department banned the use of racial epithets by commanding officers; a film on black contributions to the war effort was made and distributed throughout the country; more blacks were enrolled in and graduated from the Army's special training schools on an integrated basis (although they were returned to segregated Army units in the Regular Army); black schools participated in the Air Force Enlistment Program; with the establishment of two black medical facilities at Fort Huachuca, Arizona, and Tuskegee Air Base, more black medical personnel were commissioned; the Army and Navy, in conjunction with the Red Cross, agreed to accept blood donations from blacks; the Army Air Forces allowed blacks to fly combat missions over North Africa; and in 1944 fatigued black and white soldiers returning from Europe were assigned to the same redistribution centers.[3]

With the aim of eliminating racial prejudices in all camps, the Army also published and distributed magazines such as *Army Talk*, and made available to black and white soldiers alike pamphlets on race relations. Moreover, as previously mentioned, notables such as boxing champion Joe Louis and black bandleader Noble Sissle appeared at army camps in an effort to raise the level of morale among black troops.[4]

The military was not alone in relaxing major restrictions and racial attitudes toward black soldiers. Race relations in the larger society also changed. The Second World War had created a new social and political climate in which black Americans could forge ahead in their determination to eliminate discrimination and racial segregation. Wider use of the ballot gave them new political power, and black migration from the South provided new economic and educational opportunities. Such was the racial climate that encouraged Hastie, black soldiers, black pressure organizations (notably the NAACP), the black leadership, the black press, and segments of the white community to work even more vigorously to obtain racial equality for blacks in the armed services.

Other segments of society also provided new opportunities for black Americans. Blacks took full advantage of the persuasive powers of liberal politicians, of major civil rights decisions in the federal courts—decisions in which Hastie played a significant role—and of the liberal civil rights policies of President Harry S. Truman. These forces aided blacks and helped to produce new attitudes in the War Department. The new Secretary of War, Robert P. Patterson, took special note, and in 1945 directed a three-member board under Lieutenant General Alvin C. Gillem, Jr. to prepare a comprehensive policy on black manpower in the postwar period.[5]

In March 1946, this board of officers, known as the Gillem Board, issued its report (see the appendix following this chapter). It concluded that black manpower was poorly utilized in World War II (a conclusion that Hastie had voiced six years prior to the Gillem findings but was unfortunately disavowed and ignored then by the War Department); however, the report did not explicitly address the question of segregation. On the other hand, the report recommended that segregated educational and recreational facilities, mess halls, and the officers' clubs be continued where blacks were stationed; that postwar black units be stationed near communities where their presence would not be offensive; that black manpower should make up only 10 percent of the Regular Army; and that small black units should be integrated into larger composite white divisions. Nonetheless, the report recommended the elimination of all forms of segregation and racial discrimination against black officers. Aside from this ironic contradiction and from the idea of experimenting with small integrated units, the Gillem Report represented no significant breakthrough for black soldiers. The military still refused to implement any recommendations that would have the effect of creating an integrated and nondiscriminatory armed forces.[6]

Hastie did not comment on the Gillem Report. He probably remained silent on this issue because President Truman had nominated him to succeed Charles Harwood as governor of the Virgin Islands. Then, too, Hastie was in the midst of his Senate confirmation hearings, which were controversial and somewhat hostile because of his unflinching commitment to a "color-blind" society, and his past legal activities as a NAACP civil rights attorney.[7]

Several War Department officials, however, commented on the Gillem Report. Among them were Assistant Secretary of War John J. McCloy and Civilian Aide to the Secretary of War Truman K. Gibson, Jr. McCloy applauded the report as a step in the right direction but condemned the board for failing to address the central issue of military segregation. He also criticized the board for its recommendation that the military adopt a quota on black enlistments, "pointing out that a fixed percentage would arbitrarily exclude potential recruits regardless of their education or aptitude (an issue Hastie had constantly voiced but to no avail). McCloy also failed to see "any place for a quota in a policy that looks to the utilization of Negroes on the basis of ability."[8]

Like McCloy, Gibson objected to racial quotas and suggested that the Board make a firm statement in support of the eventual and total elimination of segregation in the armed services. Yet Gibson believed the Gillem Report represented a modification of the War Department's racial policies, and he saw this modification as the beginning to an end of an old order of restrictive policies toward black soldiers. In a real sense, Gibson viewed the reformist recommendations of the Gillem Board as a military watershed in much the same way as he saw that "the federal courts were undermining the barriers that denied blacks equal access to higher education, interstate buses and trains, [public accommodations], and the ballot box in elections for federal office." In short, Gibson was quick to link together the decisions of the federal judiciary and the recommendations of the Gillem Board as sparks to ignite the armed services and the American people in their eventual acceptance of racial equality.[9]

When the War Department released the Gillem Report publicly, black leaders and the black press rejected the new policy because it failed to recommend an end to segregation. Roy Wilkins of the NAACP and Lester Granger (successor to Eugene Jones as executive secretary of the National Urban League) branded the report a jim crow document. The *Chicago Defender* stated: "The Negro's position is that, if conscription is maintained, it must be strictly along democratic lines with no Jim Crowism or segregation in any forms." The *Philadelphia Tribune* asserted that the Gillem Report was "by no means integration and will not answer legitimate complaints of Negro officers and enlisted men who served in the last war." The *New York Age* maintained that "the policy is still a little foggy and falls far short of its advanced advertising that it would abolish segregation in the Army." And the black Publishers' Association reported that the recommendation that called for mixed units had not been implemented among the residual forces in Europe.[10]

Some members of the Publishers' Association, however, supported the Gillem Report. For example, the *Norfolk Journal and Guide* stated: "It appears that the War Department has definitely turned the corner in policy." The *Baltimore Afro-American* declared: "We believe that the Army is headed in the right direction and recommend that its sister services also get in step." And the *New York Amsterdam Star-News* found the Gillem Report "Still some distance from the elimination of a jim crow army; but it represents advance and progress. As such, we say hurray and good deal."[11]

The new black Civilian Aide to the Secretary of War, Colonel Marcus H. Ray, also endorsed the Gillem Report but, following a tour of European forces, stated in a December 1946 report to the new Secretary of War Robert P. Patterson that the recommendation to integrate the structure and function of small army units had not taken place. Colonel Ray maintained further that "to accept the racial prejudices of the German people as a reason for non-utilization of the American soldiers who happen to be non-white is to negate the very ideas we have made part of our re-education program in Germany."[12]

Although Colonel Ray questioned the Army's failure to implement the European phase of the Gillem Report, he and Assistant Civilian Aide James C. Evans supported other recommendations of the new policy. For example, they approved of the one-to-ten ratio for intermingling black troops with large white divisions, the plan to deny re-enlistment to all soldiers who failed to meet the Army's minimum standards, and the policy of freezing black volunteer enlistment in order to ensure the 10 percent black quota, which represented no change from the 1940 policy.[13] To ensure that black strength did not rise above the 10 percent quota, Colonel Ray sent a proposal to Secretary of War Patterson that if carried out would have honorably discharged all soldiers (blacks) in the Regular Army who did not meet minimum army standards.[14]

There was other evidence that Colonel Ray supported the quota concept. In a federal suit to enjoin the U.S. Army and the Selective Service System from banning black volunteer enlistment, Colonel Ray proposed a compromise to NAACP attorneys Charles H. Houston and Joseph C. Waddy that would have permitted black I-A registrants to volunteer only for the Army Ground Forces. Houston and Waddy rejected Ray's compromise, and rather than go through a court trial and perhaps face the possibility of having to explain and justify a racial quota in peacetime, the War Department amended the Gillem recommendation and directed the Selective Service to accept additional blacks in the Ground Forces as well as in the Army Air Forces but on an unassigned basis.[15]

This new directive caused more black protest. Black leaders berated the policy because it did not answer such basic questions as: What did "unassigned" mean? What would the new volunteers do? Did unassigned mean assignment to labor and supply units? Because they viewed Evans as an adjuster of racial discrimination and segregation rather than as a voice of black protest, black leaders could not rely on the new civilian aide (who replaced Colonel Ray in October 1947), for answers to their questions. Instead they criticized him for his gradual approach to solving racial problems in the armed services. Their view of him was probably justified because Evans himself said that "neither the War Department nor Walter White and his group were ever able to pin me down." In fact, he told White, Roy Wilkins, Thurgood Marshall, A. Philip Randolph, and Lester Granger, "You go your way and I'll go mine. We'll see who gets there quickest." "I was," stated Evans, "not about to dictate their policy to the War Department."[16]

Moreover, though this was unknown to black leaders, Evans approved of a memo sent to Secretary of the Army Kenneth Royall in which Director of Personnel Major General Willard S. Paul defined the Army's position on "unassigned" black volunteers. In the 1947 memo, General Paul said, "My observations have led me to the conclusion that a more usable Negro soldier can be developed under a system of rigid training with carefully controlled conditions which insure, insofar as possible, the development of pride in self and organization. The eliminations must be accomplished before the *misfits* are assigned to units for duty."[17]

This memo was important because Secretary Royall would prove to be the last major military official to oppose the integration of the armed services, and he would use the contents of such memos and special reports to buttress his position.[18]

In spite of the support Secretary Royall received from Civilian Aide Evans, conservatives, diehard politicians, military and white civilian leaders, the issue of armed forces integration gained momentum during the latter half of 1947 and early 1948. Several significant developments accounted for this unprecedented upsurge: A. Philip Randolph's National Committee Against Jim Crow in Military Service and Training threatened civil disobedience if segregation in the armed services was not ended; discussions of the claim that mixed units had good fighting records during the war began to surface in Congress and at the White House; reports of the success of the Navy's policy of integrating its training and fighting forces were prepared for Secretary of Defense James V. Forrestal;[19] Chief of Staff Omar N. Bradley publicly criticized segregation in the armed services; the Armed Forces Radio Service began to broadcast programs fostering racial equality; civilian resolutions sent to the White House demanded integration, and meetings between President Truman and the black leadership were held; the black press demanded an immediate end to segregation and racial discrimination in all branches of the armed services; and Secretary Forrestal convened a conference of black and white military and civilian leaders to discuss and propose ideas for integrating all branches of the armed services.[20]

National and state politicians were also active in the drive to integrate the armed forces. For instance, President Truman made resounding civil rights speeches to regular and special sessions of Congress, and spoke at the 39th Annual Meeting of the NAACP, where he promised to end segregation. His Commission on Civil Rights and the Advisory Commission on Universal Military Training (UMT) recommended the integration of the armed forces in their 1947 and 1948 reports. Influential black and white Congressmen, such as Senators Henry Cabot Lodge, Jr., Robert A. Taft, and William Langer; Speaker of the House Joseph Martin; and Congressmen Adam C. Powell, Jr., Vito Marcantonio, William Dawson, and Jacob Javits introduced antidiscrimination amendments to the 1948 draft bill. The governors of Minnesota, New York, and New Jersey urged President Truman to use this executive authority to end segregation so that they could begin nondiscriminatory programs in their National Guard units. And, with respect to the armed forces, both Republican and Democratic National Platform Committees adopted antidiscrimination planks in 1948.[21]

These developments spurred the black community to push even harder for integration. For example, A. Philip Randolph and Reverend Grant Reynolds (a Harlem civic leader) organized the Committee Against Jim Crow in Military and Training. On March 22, 1948, along with several other prominent black leaders, they met with President Truman to solicit his support for the antidiscrimination amendments to the proposed draft bill. Randolph in particular wanted the President to know that "Negroes are in no mood to shoulder guns for democracy abroad, while they are denied democracy here at home." He then told Truman that he would counsel civil disobedience if Truman did not end segregation in the armed services.[22]

At a New York meeting on March 27, the NAACP and several other black organizations also called for the immediate end to segregation in the armed forces. By this time, however, presidential politics had become a major topic of discussion among the conferees. Subsequently, they passed resolutions and released a public statement declaring black support in exchange for the elimination of segregation and racial discrimination in the armed services.[23]

Meanwhile, on March 30, Randolph and Reynolds appeared before the Senate Armed Services Committee. There, they repeated their threats to encourage young blacks to boycott the draft unless segregation and racial discrimination were ended.[24]

The black community, however, was divided on this issue. At the hearing, former Civilian Aide Truman K. Gibson, Jr. and Reynolds almost clashed physically. Gibson was so angry that he threatened to knock Reynolds's teeth out. However, the main reason for Gibson's behavior probably stemmed from an incident that had occurred earlier when Gibson was at the War Department. Reynolds had written him to protest discrimination against black soldiers in a local bar near Fort Huachuca (Arizona) in which Gibson's father had business interests. Moreover, Reynolds and Randolph had publicly called Gibson a "Negro Judas Iscariot" and accused him of being a mouthpiece for the War Department because Gibson had publicly reported in 1945 that troops in the all-black 92nd Division were "melting away" in combat.[25]

Gibson's contempt for Reynolds and Randolph prompted him to say in an April conversation with his friend, White House Assistant on Minority Affairs Philleo Nash, "Randolph and Reynolds did not represent the opinion of the majority of American Negroes when they told the President that Negroes would not fight unless the Army's racial policy was changed."[26]

Contrary to Gibson's views, black leaders such as Walter White, Lester Granger, and Congressman Adam C. Powell, Jr., supported Randolph and Reynolds for voicing black grievances, however, these leaders cautioned their black community against the idea of civil disobedience. The black press also backed Randolph and Reynolds, but it, too, opposed civil disobedience.[27]

In the meantime, Secretary of Defense Forrestal finalized plans for a National Defense Conference on Negro Affairs. On April 26, 1948, sixteen prominent blacks met with defense officials and voiced strong opposition to the racial policies of the armed services. The blacks insisted on immediate integration rather than supporting the gradual approach encouraged by Secretary Forrestal. Interestingly, conference member Truman K. Gibson, Jr., had written in a letter to Nash on April 15 that "the Forrestal Conference is dangerous because of the opportunity it will afford to call for some oversimplified solution like the issuance of an Executive Order abolishing segregation in the Army. The President should be on the offensive in this area."[28]

By the middle of 1948, President Truman had joined the forces for integration. He was determined to carry on the principal, solidified with Franklin D. Roosevelt New Deal Administrations, of positive government action to rehabilitate and preserve the dignity and human resources of the United States. Secretary of the Army Royall, his successors, and the advocates of segregation continued, however, to maintain that integration would impair military efficiency and damage the morale of American troops, but the forces of integration were too strong to be overlooked. Secretary of Defense Forrestal, Secretary of the Navy John L. Sullivan, Secretary of the Air Force W. Stuart Symington, black and white political and civic leaders, powerful civil rights organizations, presidential politics, and the black press put increasing pressure on the White House. On July 26, 1948, President Truman acted. He issued Executive Order 9981, which called for "equality of treatment and opportunity for all persons in the armed services, without regard to race, color, religion, or national origin." The order also established the President's Committee on Equality of Treatment and Opportunity in the Armed Services; the committee was authorized to examine race relations in the armed services and to determine how best to implement the new policy. The committee was known as the Fahy Committee after its white liberal chairman, Charles Fahy. In 1950, after having worked with all branches of the military, the committee issued its report, which recommended an end to segregation in the armed services.[29]

Hastie welcomed Executive Order 9981. He was so pleased with Truman's bold action that he took leave from the governorship of the Virgin Islands from September to November and campaigned vigorously for the president's 1948 re-election. He did so because he had come to respect and laud Truman as a champion of human rights. Hastie said privately that "with the stroke of a pen, Truman's action signaled the official end of discrimination and racial segregation in the armed forces of this country. Truman deserved to be re-elected."[30]

The black leadership also applauded President Truman's bold step. With Hastie's previous appointment to the War Department, they had believed, as Roy Wilkins had exclaimed in 1940: "Through Hastie we can fight toward the objective [integration of the armed services] we want. We have cracked the toughest department in the whole government. If anything should happen now to put Hastie out, we would have to begin the long, weary fight all over again—and we would not have the advantage of an election campaign in our favor."[31] Thus, both within and outside the War Department, Hastie, along with his black and white sources of strength—had orchestrated a protracted attack on the wrongheadedness and inherent bigotry of a segregated armed services.[32]

Finally, eight years after 1940, the objective Hastie and the black community had sought as they "cracked" the War Department was delivered by President Truman's Executive Order 9981. Perhaps as gratitude for Truman's having officially destroyed the "age-old monster" of prejudice and racial segregation within the military, once again (as they had done in Roosevelt's 1940 presidential campaign), Hastie, the black leadership, and the black vote played a significant role in Truman's 1948 re-election. As Hastie's only biographer, Gilbert Ware, put it: "It is certain that Truman did not win on black votes alone. It is equally certain that he would not have won without them."[33] And President Truman personally thanked Hastie in particular for a job well-done: he said, "Governor, I haven't seen you for several months now, but I know where you've been and I know what you've been doing. I just want to say thank you."[34]

Although segments of the military, especially the Army, were slow, to comply with the new policy, significant changes took place when the U.S. entered the Korean Conflict. For example, the U.S. Army and Air Force abolished racial quotas; black soldiers were used as replacements in white combat units; eyewitness accounts of mixed units in combat resulted in recommendations to integrate the American forces; white officers who had experience with racially mixed combat units suggested integration as the most effective way to utilize black troops; and Korean commanders such as General Matthew B. Ridgway asked the Pentagon for permission to integrate all units under their command. Moreover, the Army itself had commissioned Johns Hopkins University to study the effects of both segregation and integration on its forces. Known as "Project Clear," the study concluded that "racially segregated units limited overall Army effectiveness." The study also determined that integration in the Army "was feasible and that a quota on black participation was unnecessary." Furthermore, liberal white politicians such as Senators Hubert H. Humphrey of Minnesota and Herbert H. Lehman of New York called for an immediate end to segregated armed services. And black leaders and the black press continued their protests for an integrated military.[35]

By 1954 integration in the armed services was a reality. The Pentagon accepted this fact and would use its authority to see that it was effectively implemented throughout the services. Major General Anthony C. McAuliffe said it best when he summed up why the armed forces integrated: "I should say that integration of the Negro in the Armed Forces has worked very well and that we are getting greater usefulness from the available manpower than we ever did under segregation. It was merely a matter of getting the best out of the military personnel that was available."[36]

But to black Americans, military integration meant "taps" for an old order of restrictive outlooks and actions toward black soldiers. To them, as Sergeant First Class John Lawrence stated, "The young Negro in uniform feels big in it. It shows he's an American and that he's as good as anyone else." Or, as Deputy Assistant Secretary of Defense for Civil Rights and Industrial Relations Jack Moskowits put it in 1966: "That uniform gives prestige and status to a guy who's been 100 years on the back burner."[37]

Some vestiges of military segregation and racial discrimination continued into the 1960s. For example, some army facilities on and off military posts were still closed to black soldiers; black promotions continued to be disproportionately low; off-post discrimination hindered blacks educationally and impeded their economic growth; the military justice system continued to be disproportionately hard on black troops; low black morale continued on some military posts; the National Guard continued to segregate and practice racial discrimination; and black soldiers often found it difficult to obtain decent housing in surrounding communities. In 1963 Captain Sylvain Wailes, who had been transferred to Fort Bragg, recalled: "When I was at Fort Belvoir, Virginia there was no decent place to live unless you went into Washington. Housing is segregated around Fayetteville. I stay on the base for athletics and movies, sometimes go to Raleigh, an hour's drive, for a stage play."[38]

The military, after dragging its feet during the Eisenhower administration, began to address the remaining racial problems of black servicemen in 1961 when President John F. Kennedy entered the White House. Kennedy appointed the President's Committee on Equal Opportunity in the Armed Forces. Known as the Gesell Committee (after its chairman, Gerhard A. Gesell), the committee issued its initial report on June 13, 1963. The committee praised the military for "significant progress in eliminating discrimination among those serving in defense of the nation" but concluded that "much remains to be done, especially in eliminating practices that cause inconvenience and embarrassment to servicemen and their families in communities adjoining military bases."[39]

Reacting to the Gesell Committee report and other internal investigations, Secretary of Defense Robert S. McNamara issued a far-reaching directive: "Every military commander has the responsibility to oppose discriminatory practices affecting his men and their dependents and to foster equal opportunity for them, not only in areas under his immediate control but also in nearby communities where they may live or gather in off-duty hours."[40]

In 1964, the Gesell Committee issued its final report. The report focused on segregation and racial discrimination against black soldiers overseas and concluded that base commanders should make vigorous attempts to prevent segregation and racial discrimination against black servicemen in public accommodations and nearby communities. Moreover, the Committee emphasized, "it is particularly urgent to do this where the discrimination reflects attitudes of some of our own military personnel and is not generally practiced by nationals of the host country involved."[41]

Meanwhile, changing conditions for black Americans in the larger society kept pace with changes for black soldiers in the military. Since the 1950s, black Americans had made significant progress in redressing their grievances. The social and political climate that allowed them to do so was facilitated largely by the 1954 Brown Decision, in which the U.S. Supreme Court overturned the 1896 "separate-but-equal" doctrine, declaring that separate facilities were inherently unequal and that racial segregation violated the Fourteenth Amendment to the U.S. Constitution. This decision destroyed the legal basis for institutional racism and racial segregation in America. It also laid the basis for the civil rights movement of the 1960s and 1970s, which revolutionized black/white relations in the United States.

The major civil rights issues of the 1960s and 1970s were the struggles by blacks, aided by white Americans, to vote, to obtain decent housing and equal educational opportunities, and to secure themselves economically in decision-making jobs.

The efforts of black Americans proved beneficial. By executive order, President Kennedy banned racial and religious discrimination in federally aided housing, and Congress passed the far-reaching and comprehensive Civil Rights Act of 1964 and the Voting Rights Act of 1965. The U.S. Supreme Court handed down decisions enforcing civil rights for blacks. Some public schools and universities opened doors to blacks for the first time, and public accommodations were integrated. In 1967 Thurgood Marshall was the first black to be named to the U.S. Supreme Court; Robert C. Weaver, as Secretary of Housing and Urban Development, was the first black appointed to a Cabinet post; Carl B. Stokes of Cleveland, Ohio was the first black to be elected mayor of a major American city; Leontyne Price opened the Metropolitan Opera in 1966; in 1963 Sidney Poitier was the first black male to win an Oscar for best actor; Reverend Doctor Martin Luther King, Jr., won the Nobel Peace Prize in 1964 for civil rights leadership; Patricia Harris and other blacks were appointed U.S. ambassadors; and fifteen black representatives and one senator were serving in Congress.

These were but a few of the gains made by stateside black Americans during the era of the Vietnam War. When it ended in 1973, black soldiers, too, had distinguished themselves with honor in America's "first truly integrated war."[42]

During the years following the war, some old problems of segregation and racial discrimination remained in the armed services. However, since the 1970s the Department of Defense has instituted human race relations education programs, established affirmative action programs, and created equal opportunity programs in off-base housing. All segments of the military are required to make progress reports on recruiting, assignment, evaluation, training, promotion, discipline, separation, recognition, utilization of skills, and discrimination complaints.[43]

When the decade of the 1980s began, integration of the armed forces was an accomplished fact. Civil rights issues were no longer of major concern to the military or to black America. For blacks had achieved much to be proud of: twenty-five general officers were on active duty in the Army, five in the Navy and Marine Corps, twelve in the Air Force, and four in the Army and Air National Guard. Moreover, 24 black civilians held executive and senior executive positions in the Defense Department. But the most fitting tribute to black America, both in and out of uniform, was President Jimmy Carter's 1976 appointment of Clifford A. Alexander as Secretary of the Army.

However, in the light of newly raised questions about black soldiers' reliability, one wonders if the remaining years of the decade will be a period of calm and continued progress or one of regression for black soldiers. At present no one can predict the outcome precisely but the reliability of black soldiers has always been a major issue in the minds of white America. For blacks who have fought and died in defense of this country, a recent Brookings Institution study, *Blacks and the Military* by Martin Binkin and Mark J. Eitelberg, with Alvin J. Schnexnider and Marvin M. Smith, has created suspicions of "white racism" and unwarranted concern among black Americans in and out of uniform. Vietnam War veteran Ted Bagley put it best in a recent letter to the editor of a southern newspaper. Graphically, Bagley asked:

Why is it that black soldiers' credibility, dedication and mental capacity are constantly being challenged by "new and old" studies. I am a black ex-G.I. who has a college degree, went to Vietnam, represented this country in a battle like many other black and Hispanic soldiers did. Why is it that white soldiers' integrity is never challenged? Why not write about the many black, white, and Hispanic Americans who died defending the flag instead of whether black soldiers can be reliable or if there are too many blacks in the services? It is of little consolation to me that Martin Binkin and Mark Eitelberg made the statement that we no longer, as black soldiers, have to prove ourselves. The fact that these types of articles are printed is reason to believe that we will always have to prove something to someone.[44]

The Binkin and Eitelberg study suggests that the day has yet to come when the "color line" will no longer be an issue in the military experience of black soldiers but the day when it was an overriding factor has passed! And Hastie, often misrepresented by American historians as unrealistic and ineffective in the War Department during the early 1940s, played, more than any other individual, a decisive role in creating the environment that would result in the eventual democratization of a "color-blind" military. His activities, democratic rhetoric, and moral suasion, and his uncompromising commitment to a totally integrated armed services fostered a reformist spirit, however reluctant, within the War Department that revolutionized the perceptions of Uncle Sam's black soldiers. Hastie was a catalyst: within two, sometimes painful, years, he and his sources of strength had occasioned more changes in the placement, promotion, and egalitarian treatment of black soldiers than during all of the periods of American military history combined prior to the Second World War.

NOTES

1. For examples and detailed discussions of Hastie's private and public career, see Phillip McGuire, "Black Civilian Aides and the Problems of Racism and Segregation in the United States Armed Forces, 1940–1950" (Ph.D. diss., Howard University, 1975); Phillip McGuire, *Taps for a Jim Crow Army: Letters from Black Soldiers in World War II* (Santa Barbara, Calif.: ABC-Clio Press, 1983).

2. For detailed discussions of blacks in the U.S. Navy and Army Air Forces during World War II, see Dennis D. Nelson, *The Integration of the Negro into the U.S. Navy* (New York: Farrar, Straus and Young, 1951); Alan M. Osur, *Blacks in the Army Air Forces During World War II* (Washington, D.C.: United States Government Printing Office, 1977); Frederick S. Harrod, "Integration of the Navy (1941–1978)," *United States Naval Institute Proceedings* 105 (October 1979): 41–47; McGuire, "Black Civilian Aides," 119–127.

3. McGuire, "Black Civilian Aides"; Bernard C. Nalty, *Strength for the Fight: A History of Black Americans in the Military* (New York: The Free Press, 1986), 204–217.

4. McGuire, "Black Civilian Aides," 101–119.

5. General Alvin C. Gillem, Jr. stated in the Gillem Report: "In accordance with verbal instructions from the Secretary of War, a board of three general officers met on 1 October 1945 and subsequent dates to conduct a broad investigation into utilization of Negro manpower in the military establishment," November 17, 1945, Military Personnel Division, General Staff, NARG 165. For discussions of Hastie's legal struggles and successes against racial discrimination and segregation in the American courts, see Gilbert Ware, *William Hastie: Grace Under Pressure* (New York: Oxford University Press, 1984), 35–174.

6. "Report of Board of Officers on Utilization of Negro Manpower in the Post-War Army," Alvin C. Gillem, Jr. to George Marshall, March 4, 1946, Military Personnel Division, General Staff, NARG 165; Bernard C. Nalty and Morris J. MacGregor, eds., *Blacks in the Military: Essential Documents* (Wilmington, Del.: Scholarly Resources, 1981), 207–244; Nalty, *Strength for the Fight*, 214–234. See appendix for Gillem Report.

7. Hastie, interview with author, March 8, 1974.

8. Nalty, *Strength for the Fight*, 215.

9. Ibid., 215–216.

10. "Raps Gillem Report; Still Jim Crow Army, Roy Wilkins and Granger Decide," *Pittsburgh Courier*, April 26, 1946; Editorial, *Chicago Defender*, March 9, 1946; "New Army Policy Fails to Abolish Segregation," *Philadelphia Tribune*,

March 16, 1946; Editorial, *New York Age*, March 9, 1946; Report, "The Negro Newspapers Publishers' Association on Troops and Conditions in Europe," to Robert P. Patterson, July 18, 1946, Army General Staff, NARG 407; "General McNarney Ignores Gillem Report, Isolates GI's," *Pittsburgh Courier*, October 26, 1946; "More on the Gillem Report," *Pittsburgh Courier*, May 4, 1946.

11. Editorial, *Norfolk Journal and Guide*, March 9, 1946; Editorial, *Baltimore Afro-American*, March 9, 1946; Editorial, *New York Amsterdam Star-News*, March 9, 1946.

12. Nalty and MacGregor, *Blacks in the Military*, 217.

13. "Army Adopts 1–10 Ratio for Negroes," *Pittsburgh Courier*, May 11, 1946; Letter, Marcus H. Ray to Charles R. Lawrence, Jr., Social Science Institute of Fisk University, November 6, 1946, Civilian Aide to the Secretary of War Subject File, 1940–1947, NARG 107; Nalty and MacGregor, *Blacks in the Military*, 224–226.

14. "Ray Proposes Plan to Discharge Men in Army below Standards," *Norfolk Journal and Guide*, August 10, 1946.

15. "War Department Tries Compromise To Halt Test on Race Quota." *Pittsburgh Courier*, October 5, 1946; "A $64 Question: Army Drops Induction?" *Pittsburgh Courier*, October 19, 1946; James C. Evans, private interview with author, November 30, 1974.

16. Evans, interview with author, October 6, 1974.

17. Memorandum, Through Civilian Aide—James C. Evans, General Willard S. Paul to Secretary of the Army Kenneth Royall, December 2, 1947, Military Personnel Division, General Staff, NARG 165.

18. For detailed discussions of Secretary Royall's position on integration, see Richard M. Dalfiume, *Desegregation of the U.S. Armed Forces: Fighting on Two Fronts, 1939–1953* (Columbia, Mo.: University of Missouri Press, 1969), 158–219.

19. In 1947 the military establishment was reorganized under the Department of Defense with James V. Forrestal as its first secretary. Forrestal supported a gradual approach to integration.

20. "Calls UMT Bill Public Enemy No. 1, " December 27, 1947; "Randolph Urges Army Advisers To Denounce Jim Crow Policy," *Chicago Defender*, November 22, 1947; "Drive Seeks To Ban Segregation in Bill for Universal Training," *New York Post*, December 2, 1947; "General Bradley Lashes Bias in Armed Services," *Pittsburgh Courier*, January 24, 1948; Letter, Walter White to James V. Forrestal, February 17, 1948; Letter, Lester Granger to Marx Leva, May 14, 1948; Report, Lieutenant Dennis D. Nelson, United States Naval Reserve, to Marx Leva, May 24, 1948, all in Secretary and Assistant Secretary of Defense Files, NARG 330; "Threats of Treason Resented," *Norfolk Journal and Guide*, April 10, 1948; "Hurl New Blow at Army Bias; Randolph Opens Up," *Pittsburgh Courier*, July 3, 1948; Letter, Grant Reynolds, National Chairman of the Committee against Jim Crow in Military Service and Training and New York Alderman, and A. Philip Randolph, National Treasurer, to President Harry S. Truman, July 15, 1948; "Resolutions Adopted by 39th Annual Conference of the NAACP," June 26, 1948, both in Secretary and Assistant Secretary of the Army Files, NARG 335.

21. "Draft Bill Faces New Hurdles as Civil Rights Riders Loom, *New York Times*, May 27, 1948; "Taft Pledges Jim Crow End for Military," *New York Am-*

sterdam Star-News, January 3, 1948; "UMT Has Not Been Bias-Proof Negro Segregation Apparently Slated," New York Post, January 16, 1948; "Martin Says He Will Fight Jim Crowism in UMT Measure," New York Post, February 5, 1948; "GOP Leaders Condemn Bias in Army Training," Pittsburgh Courier, February 14, 1948; "Calls South's War Our Civil Rights Pressure Battle," Pittsburgh Courier, July 17, 1948; Congressional Record, 80th Congress, 2nd Session (1948), 3714, 4543, 8390–8394, 8691–8694; "Truman's Speech on Civil Rights," June 29, 1947, Harry S. Truman Papers, Harry S. Truman Library, Independence, Missouri; Letter, Luther W. Youngdahl, Governor of Minnesota, to James V. Forrestal, March 6, 1948; Memorandum, Marx Leva, special assistant to the Secretary of Defense, to James V. Forrestal, March 8, 1948; Newspaper Clipping, "Attention Minnesota Democrats," April 16, 1948; Letter, Henry C. Lodge, Jr., to James V. Forrestal, April 19, 1948; Letter, Hubert H. Humphrey, Mayor of St. Paul, to James V. Forrestal, April 26, 1948; Telegram, Youngdahl to President Truman, July 19, 1948, all in Secretary and Assistant Secretary of Defense Files, NARG 330; *Public Papers of the Presidents of the United States, Harry S. Truman 1945–1953* (Washington, D.C.: United States Government Printing Office), 311–315; The President's Committee on Civil Rights, *To Secure These Rights* (Washington, D.C.: United States Government Printing Office, 1947), 41–43, 82–87. For detailed discussions of President Truman and Civil Rights during this period, see William C. Berman, *The Politics of Civil Rights in the Truman Administration* (Columbus, Ohio: Ohio State University Press, 1970); Donald R. McCoy and Richard T. Ruetten, Quest and Response; Minority Rights and the Truman Administration (Laurence: University of Kansas Press, 1973).

22. Quoted in Berman, *The Politics of Civil Rights in the Truman Administration*, 97–98.

23. "Declaration of Negro Votes," Box 376, NAACP Papers.

24. United States Senate, Armed Services Committee, *Hearings on Universal Military Training* (Washington, D.C.: United States Government Printing Office, 1948), 644–689; Berman, *The Politics of Civil Rights in the Truman Administration*, 98–99; Dalfiume, *Desegregation of the U.S. Armed Forces*; 164–169; Nalty and MacGregor, *Blacks in the Military*, 237–239.

25. United States Senate, Armed Services Committee, *Hearings on Universal Military Training*, 644–689; "Civil Disobedience Movement Urged; Gibson and Reynolds Nearly Swap Blows," *Pittsburgh Courier*, April 3, 1948; Evans, interview with author, August 6, 1974.

26. Letter, David K. Niles, special assistant to President Truman on minority affairs, to Matthew J. Connelly, President Truman's secretary, April 5, 1948, Truman Papers. Gibson's conversation with Nash was reported in the April letter from Niles to Connelly.

27. *Pittsburgh Courier*, April 10, 1948; Hastie, interview with author, March 8, 1974; Berman, *The Politics of Civil Rights in the Truman Administration*, 99–100.

28. Letter, Truman K. Gibson, Jr., to Philleo Nash, April 15, 1948, Truman Papers; Nalty and MacGregor, *Blacks in the Military*, 241–242. Blacks attending the National Defense Conference on Negro Affairs included: Sadie T. M. Alexander, John W. Davis, Truman K. Gibson, Jr., J. W. Gregg, Charles H. Houston, John H. Johnson, Mordecai Johnson, P. B. Young, Ira F. Lewis, Benjamin E.

Mays, Loren Miller, Hobson E. Reynolds, Channing H. Tobias, George L. P. Weaver, Roy Wilkins, and Lester B. Granger.

29. Joint Army and Air Force Bulletin No. 32, *Executive Order 9981* (Washington, D.C.: Department of the Army and the Air Force, August 2, 1948), 2–3; Letter, Bayard Rustin, Secretary of the Campaign To Resist Military Segregation, to James V. Forrestal, August 20, 1948; Press Release, "Negro Leaders Submit Report and Recommendations on Segregation," Ssptember 18, 1948; Memorandum, James V. Forrestal to Secretaries of Army, Navy, and Air Force, October 21, 1948, all in Secretary and Assistant Secretary of Defense Files, NARG 330; Memorandum, Representative Lyndon B. Johnson to Kenneth Royall, March 22, 1948; "General Eisenhower's Testimony on the Race Issue in the Army," April 5, 1948; Memorandum, Brigadier General John J. O'Hare, Chief of the Personnel Management Group, to Kenneth Royall, March 9, 1948; "Department of the Army Statement Regarding Utilization of Negro Manpower," July 21, 1948; Letter, Major William H. Ramsey to General Omar Bradley, July 30, 1948; Memorandum, Kenneth Royall to James Forrestal, November 18, 1948; Memorandum, W. Stuart Symington to James V. Forrestal, December 17, 1948; "Truman Orders End of Bias in Forces and Federal Jobs; Addresses Congress Today," *New York Times*, July 27, 1948; "Army Segregation To Go, Says Truman," *New York Times*, July 30, 1948; "Secretary Royall Insists Present Pattern Will Not Now Be Modified," *Norfolk Journal and Guide*, May 1, 1948; "Jim Crow Has No Place in the U.S. Army," *Pittsburgh Courier*, January 10, 1948; "Truman Executive Order 9981," *Pittsburgh Courier*, July 31, 1948; "The Order Mr. Truman Did Not Issue," *Pittsburgh Courier*, August 7, 1948; "Senator Allen J. Ellender On Executive Order 9981," *Baltimore Sun*, July 27, 1948; "Truman's Army Program Is Repugnant," *Montgomery Advertiser*, July 29, 1948; "President Truman Is Grandstanding," *Shreveport Times*, August 1, 1948; "Proposed Policy for the National Military Establishment Office of the Secretary of Defense," March 17, 1949; Memorandum, Lieutenant General Edward A. Brooks, Director of Personnel and Administration, to Deputy Chief of Staff For Administration, March 30, 1949, Army General Staff, NARG 407; "Meeting of the President and the Four Service Secretaries with the President's Committee on Equality of Treatment and Opportunity in the Armed Services," January 13, 1949; Memorandum, Gordon Gray, Secretary of the Army, to Louis Johnson, September 30, 1949, both in Secretary and Assistant Secretary of Defense Files, NARG 330; Letter, Louis Johnson to Senator Carl Vinson, July 7, 1949; Memorandum, Charles Fahy to President Truman, December 14, 1949, all in Secretary and Assistant Secretary of the Army Files, NARG 335; Memorandum, Gordon Gray to Louis Johnson, May 26, 1949, Military Personnel Division, General Staff, NARG 165; *Congressional Record*, 81st Congress, 1st Session (1949), 6135; "Johnson Approves Air Force Plan To Distribute Negroes Among Units," *New York Times*, May 12, 1949; Jacob Javits, "Address Delivered on Floor of House Thursday," *Pittsburgh Courier*, January 12 1950; Letter, Jacob Javits to Louis Johnson, January 24, 1950, Civilian Aide to the Secretary of War Subject File, 1940–1947, NARG 107; Memorandum, "Discontinuance of Racial Enlistment Quotas," March 190, 1950; "Policy On Integration Program," March 31, 1950; "Data Pertaining to the Comments of the Navy and Air Force," April 5, 1950; Letter, Roy Wilkins to Frank Pace, Jr., July 21, 1950; Letter, Pace to Wilkins, August 8, 1950, all in Military Personnel Di-

vision, General Staff, NARG 165, *Congressional Record*, 81st Congress, 2nd Session (1950), 9078, 12852, 131183–13184; "Senate Strikes Out Segregation Plan in Its Bill on Draft," *New York Times*, June 22, 1950; The President's Committee on Equality of Treatment and Opportunity in the Armed Services, *Freedom To Serve* (Washington, D.C.: United States Government Printing Office, 1950). For detailed discussions of the Fahy Committee, see Dalfiume, *Desegregation of the U.S. Armed Forces*, 175–200; Nalty and MacGregor, *Blacks in the Military*, 243–294.

30. Hastie, interview with author, March 8, 1974; Ware, *William Hastie: Grace Under Pressure*, 213–224.

31. Editorial, *New York Amsterdam Star-News*, November 2, 1940; Letter, Mary McLeod Bethune to Eleanor Roosevelt, November 1, 1940, Box 151, Patterson Papers; Finkle, "Forum for Protest: The Black Press and World War II." 197–198; Letter, T. Arnold Hill to Roosevelt, October 31, 1940, Roosevelt Papers; *New York Age*, November 2, 1940; Editorial, *Baltimore Afro-American*, November 2, 1940; Editorial, *Pittsburgh Courier*, November 2, 1941 "Truman Executive Order 9981," *Pittsburgh Courier*, July 31, 1948; Grant Reynolds, "A Triumph for Civil Disobedience," *The Nation*, 147 (August 28, 1948): 228–29; *Pittsburgh Courier*, August 28, 1948.

32. See McGuire, "Black Civilian Aides."

33. Ware, *William Hastie: Grace Under Pressure*, 220.

34. Ibid., 222.

35. "White GIs Join All Negro Unit," *Pittsburgh Courier*, September 9, 1950; "Racial Gains Speed by War, Army Says," *New York Times*, March 19, 1951; "Bias Rules Army Courts Says Lawyer," *Norfolk Journal and Guide*, March 3, 1951; "Officials Maintain Strict Segregation of Soldiers," *Norfolk Journal and Guide*, July 28, 1951; "Says Allies Not Blind to U.S. Racial Hypocrisy," *Pittsburgh Courier*, March 31, 1951; "Torpedoes Army Bias in Pending House Bill," *Pittsburgh Courier*, April 21, 1951; "Camp McCoy Race Policy Vilest in U.S.," *Pittsburgh Courier*, June 9, 1951; "Negro GI Wins Medal of Honor," *Pittsburgh Courier*, June 23, 1951; "Courier Articles Influenced Army," *Pittsburgh Courier*, August 4, 1951; "Army Sees End of Segregation," *Pittsburgh Courier*, March 15, 1952; "Truman Speaking," *New York Times*, June 14, 1952; "Army Sets Deadline for Segregation End," *New York Times*, October 13, 1953. For detailed discussions of integration efforts during the Korean Conflict, see Dalfiume, *Desegregation of the U.S. Armed Forces*, 201–219; Nalty and MacGregor, *Blacks in the Military*, 295–323; Nalty, *Strength for the Fight*, 255–269.

36. Quoted in Richard Stillman, "Negroes in the Armed Forces," *Phylon: A Review of Race and Culture* 30 (Summer 1969): 142.

37. Ibid.

38. Quoted in Stillman, "Negroes in the Armed Forces," 159; Nalty and MacGregor, *Blacks in the Military*, 327–343; Dalfiume, *Desegregation of the U.S. Armed Forces*, 220–222.

39. Nalty and MacGregor, *Blacks in the Military*, 327–330; Nalty, *Strength for the Fight*, 270–286. The Gesell Committee included Gerhard A. Gesell, Nathaniel S. Colley, Abe Fortas, Louis J. Hector, Benjamin Muse, John H. Sengstacke, and Whitney M. Young, Jr.

40. Nalty and MacGregor, *Blacks in the Military*, 336; Dalfiume, *Desegregation of the U.S. Armed Forces*, 222; Nalty, *Strength for the Fight*, 282–302.

41. Nalty and MacGregor, *Blacks in the Military*, 331–332; Nalty, *Strength for the Fight*, 303–317.

42. Department of Defense, *Black Americans in Defense of Our Nation* (Washington, D.C.: Office of Deputy Assistant Secretary of Defense for Equal Opportunity, 1981), 38–64; Whitney M. Young, Jr., "When the Negroes in Vietnam Come Home," *Harper's Magazine* 234 (June 1967): 63–69.

43. For detailed discussions of segregation and racial discrimination, and of the equal opportunity programs established in the military after the Vietnam War, see Nalty and MacGregor, *Blacks in the Military*, 332–352; Department of Defense, *Black Americans in Defense of Our Nation*, 64–74; Nalty, *Strength for the Fight*, 318–332.

44. "New Study Questions Reliability of Black GIs," *Wilmington Morning News*, June 28, 1982; Letter to the Editor, *Wilmington Morning News*, July 7, 1982.

Appendix

The Gillem Report (March 4, 1946): Report of Board of Officers on Utilization of Negro Manpower in the Post-War Army

I. PURPOSE

A. *Statement of the Problem*: The Board was directed in a memorandum dated 4 October 1945 to prepare a broad policy for utilization of Negro manpower in the military establishment, including the development of means required in the event of a national emergency.

The proposed policy and means will cover:

1. Broadening the professional base of Negro personnel in the Regular Army.
2. Organization of Negro units.
3. Implementation and revision of policies by a Staff Group.
4. Induction and training of Negro personnel.
5. Indoctrination of all ranks throughout the Service in the policy promulgated.

The plan proposed is based upon the lessons of experience and envisions maximum efficiency in the use of all authorized manpower in the event of another emergency straining every resource of the nation.

B. *Plan of Investigation*: The Board has concerned itself with an examination of past and present War Department policies, their effectiveness during the period between World Wars and in World War II, and the advisability of continuing these policies during the post-war period. In the course of its proceedings, the Board has obtained a free expression of the view of representative military and civilian leaders.

Essentially the problem has resolved itself into the following questions:

1. How shall Negro personnel be utilized in the Army in the event of another national emergency?
2. What basis of Negro personnel is necessary in the post-war Army in order to provide for rapid expansion in time of war?
3. What shall be the scope of the War Department General Staff and of subordinate commanders in implementing any policy adopted?
4. How shall authorized Negro personnel be selected, processed, trained and assigned?
5. Shall changes in policy be adopted and promulgated immediately?

II. FACTS BEARING ON THE PROBLEM

GENERAL ASPECTS OF NEGRO MANPOWER POTENTIAL

The United States of America has just successfully concluded a global war which strained her manpower, industry and material resources to the utmost. Every citizen of the democracy was called upon to exert the utmost effort as part of the National team. That every citizen did so, to the limit of his and her ability, is history.

The natural and artificial resources of any nation are dependent upon and reflect the vigor of her manpower. An intelligent patriotism is imperative, if the nation is to vindicate the past, maintain the present, and rise to its future destiny.

LESSONS GAINED FROM WORLD WAR II

Lessons of primary military interest gained from the experience of the last five years are:

> That there is a limit to the amount of manpower available in the nation to form a modern military organization capable of prosecuting a major war;
>
> That the manpower available, of itself, varies in quality.

The principle of economy of forces clearly indicates, therefore, that every effort must be expended to utilize efficiently every qualified available individual in a position in the military structure for which he is best suited. It follows logically that we must always strive for improvement in the quality of the whole.

THE NEGRO MANPOWER POTENTIAL

The Negro constitutes approximately 10% of the civilian population of the country and thus becomes no small part of the manpower reservoir available for use in time of peace or in the event of a National Emergency.

An impartial review and analysis of the progress made by the Negro citizen between World War I and World War II, particularly in the last five years, has led this Board to the conclusion that comprehensive study involving the Negro manpower of the nation in the military establishment is timely.

The Negro is a bona fide citizen enjoying the privileges conferred by citizenship under the constitution. By the same token, he must defend his country in time of national peril. Testimony presented to this Board has indicated that the Negro is ready and eager to accept his full responsibility as a citizen.

It follows therefore:

> That the Negro, desiring to accept his legal and moral responsibility as charged by the constitution, should be given every opportunity and aid to prepare himself for effective military service in company with every other citizen who is called.

> That those charged with the utilization of manpower in the military establishment have an equal legal and moral obligation under the constitution to take all steps necessary to prepare the qualified manpower of the nation so that it will function efficiently and effectively under the stress of modern battle conditions.

ASSIGNMENT DIFFICULTIES IN WORLD WAR II

During the national emergency just concluded, approximately 909,000 Negroes, including reserves and volunteers, were selected for use in the Army. These men were obtained from a reservoir of approximately 2,463,000 Negroes who registered for service. In the placement of the men who were accepted, the Army encountered considerable difficulty. Leadership qualities had not been developed among the Negroes, due principally to environment and lack of opportunity. These factors had also affected his development in the various skills and crafts.

CORRECTIVE MEASURES

In the opinion of the Board, many of these difficulties can be overcome by forward planning, and by the development of a broader base of trained personnel, both officer and enlisted, than that which existed prior to World War II. This nucleus can assimilate a much larger proportion of the available Negro manpower than was done heretofore.

EFFECTS OF THE WAR

No study would be complete that failed to evaluate the collateral education gained by every Negro man and woman during the war years. The imprints of travel, of bettered living and health conditions, plus the increased financial resources, have left a mental stamp which will persist and continue to become more articulate.

During the last few years, many of the concepts pertaining to the Negro have shown changing trends. They are pointing toward a more complete acceptance of the Negro in all the diversified fields of endeavor. This trend has been noticeable to a greater extent in the Northern and Western sections of the country. The Negro to a greater extent has been accepted in industry, and in administrative and scientific fields, both as individuals and groups, with good results. This acceptance has resulted in better wages which automatically raised his standard of living. Of more importance from a military viewpoint, however, are the opportunities which have been afforded the Negro to expand his knowledge of the trades and skills. The latter have a ready market in the intricacies of a modern military machine.

Many Negroes who, before the war, were laborers, are now craftsmen, capable in many instances of competing with the white man on an equal basis. This change in the industrial status has, further, allowed the Negro to give his children more and better education. In many colleges and universities of the North and West, the Negro student is accepted solely on the basis of his individual merit and ability. This rise in the technical and cultural level of the Negro has, in turn, given him a more articulate voice in government.

RELATED PERTINENT DATA

The Negroes' increasing capability for participation in society and government is evident from consideration of the facts below:

Growth in Educational Attainments

	All Negroes, World War I	Negroes of 12 Southern States, World War II	Other Negroes, World War II	Whites of U.S., World War II
1–8 Years Grade School	95%	64%	40%	26%
1–4 Years High School	5%	32%	53%	62%
1 or more yrs College	few	4%	7%	12%

Rate of Negro Emigration from the South

	World War I	World War II
Ratio of Negroes who came from North of Mason-Dixon Line:	1 to 5	1 to 3

Increase in Negro Participation in Government

	1938	1944
Percent of all persons employed by Federal Government in Washington who were Negroes	8.4	19.2
Percent of above Negroes whose jobs were custodial	90	40

Increase in Industrial Experience

The great expansion of industry during the war gave the Negro greater opportunity to gain industrial experience than ever before. The War Manpower Board reports that Negro participation in defense industries increased from 3% in 1942 to 8.3% in 1944, or over 100%. This increase in industrial experience is an important factor when considering manpower from the standpoint of national defense.

FACTORS AFFECTING FUTURE UTILIZATION

These three factors of education, craftsmanship and governmental participation have enhanced the military value of the Negro. A broader selectivity is now available than was heretofore possible, with a resultant beneficial effect on military efficiency.

SCOPE AND NATURE OF POLICY

While the lessons learned from the service of the Negro in the war just concluded are still fresh in our minds, and while the people as a whole are still military minded, it is the considered opinion of this Board that a progressive policy for greater utilization of the Negro manpower be formulated and implemented now, if the nation is to establish its military structure on the experiences of the past. The nation should not fail to use the assets developed through a closer relationship of the races during the years of war.

The policies prepared by the War Department should be progressively flexible. They should envision the continued mental and physical improvement of all citizens. They should be implemented *promptly*. They *must* be objective in nature. They *must* eliminate, at the earliest practicable moment, any special consideration based on race. They should point towards the immediate objective of an evaluation of the Negro on the basis of individual merit and ability. They should point towards a long-range objective which visualizes, over a period of time, a still greater utilization of this manpower potential in the military machine of the nation.

REQUIRED ACTION

Courageous leadership in implementing the program is imperative. All ranks must be imbued with the necessity for a straightforward, unequivocating attitude towards the maintenance and preservation of a forward-thinking policy.

Vacillation or weak implementation of a strong policy will adversely affect the

Army. The policy which is advocated is consistent with the democratic ideals upon which the nation and its representative army are based.

SUMMARY OF EVALUATION OF COMBAT PERFORMANCE— WORLD WAR II

1. General

A careful analysis of the combat service performed by the Negro in World War II indicates clearly that:

The participation of the Negro in World War II was in many instances creditable, and definitely contributed to the success attained by our military forces.

No analysis would be complete, however, that fails to evaluate the disadvantages under which the Negro entered the conflict and which militated against his success.

2. Disadvantages Accrued to the Negro

The records and testimony indicate that:

(1) Although it was definitely known that the Negro manpower would amount to approximately 10% of the manpower available for war, plans were not prepared prior to World War II for mobilization and employment of major units of all arms. This resulted in some instances in a disproportionate allocation of lower bracket personnel to combat elements.

(2) Likewise, no provisions were made initially for utilizing the Negro manpower in supporting type combat units. These eventually embraced all categories. This latter condition apparently resulted from the pressure initiated by the Negroes themselves.

(3) The initial lack of plans for the organization and utilization of the wide variety of combat units was reflected in frequent reorganization, re-grouping and shifting from one type of training to another. For example, some engineers and artillery were thus affected.

(4) Evidence indicates that in some instances units were organized without definite T. of O. and E. [Training of Operation and Experience] and without a general prescription as to the missions for which organized. This was an expediency to off-set the lack of plans when manpower was suddenly made available in large numbers.

(5) The above factors, when added to the definite lack of information as to ultimate time and place of assignment and mission to be assigned the various units, was undoubtedly confusing to the Negro mind and may have become a contributing cause for some of the reported failures in combat.

(6) Official reports on Negro units do not reflect many factors which may have been contributing causes of the sub-standard performance in combat.

An over-all far-reaching factor which affected adversely the efficiency of combat units of all types was the shortage of trained subordinate leaders. This shortage stemmed directly from limitations for which the Army was only partially at fault. Environment and lack of administrative and educational advantages in pre-war days greatly handicapped the Negro in the performance of his war-time duties.

3. Advantages Accrued to the Negro

Likewise in estimating the combat record of performance, careful scrutiny must be given to the advantages which accrued to the units formed from the Negro manpower and the resultant benefits derived therefrom. Consideration must be given to the facts that:

(1) First-class equipment and material, and ample munitions for training purposes, were made available.

(2) Favorable training areas and aids were placed at the disposal of commanders and in many cases, especially in combat units, normal training periods were extended to insure adequately trained units.

(3) Experienced white commanders were assigned to direct training and to lead the major elements into action.

(4) The combat units were carefully staged into the theater of operations and all echelons of command were briefed meticulously prior to entry into action.

(5) Reorganization and re-grouping were practiced with the objective of enhancing the changes of success of the units involved.

4. Deductions of Facts

Certain facts were deduced from a careful check of the records and the testimony of commanders, observers and participants in the war just terminated, and arrived at after weighing the advantages and disadvantages previously outlined.

These are:

(1) There is substantial evidence to indicate that the least proficient performance has been derived from combat units which were required to close with the enemy to accomplish a prescribed mission.

(2) In general, relatively slight losses were experienced by Negro Infantry units.

(3) There was ample evidence to show that in certain instances small infantry composite units, Negro platoons in white companies, when ably led were eminently successful even though relatively heavy casualties were suffered.

(4) The Board likewise was convinced from evidence that the Negro soldier will execute in satisfactory manner combat duties in a supporting type unit, for example, an artillery battalion.

(5) Evidence definitely indicated that the largest use of Negro manpower

was in the service type units, and that in this field they demonstrated their highest degree of efficiency. However, some service units functioned directly in support of combat units, being to all intents and purposes a part of them. Many of these elements performed most creditably.

5. Summary

From the evidence presented by the most experienced commanders, the Board cannot fail to conclude that the results obtained by all units are in direct proportion to the leadership demonstrated. The failures of Negro units have in almost every case been attributed to the lack of leadership qualities of junior officers and non-commissioned officers. Leadership, therefore, must be stressed and the development of all attributes which contribute to this end must be the prime objective of those responsible for the training of the post-war Army. In this endeavor, much benefit will be derived from the broader scope of activities which have been opened to the Negro during five years of war.

A corollary to this first objective is clearly defined, for it leads directly toward the second objective.

Infantry must be made more effective. When the quality of the close combat elements composed either wholly or in part from the Negro component is raised to the level desired and expected, the Army of this nation will be immeasurably improved.

In implementing the recommended program, all types of Negro units should be included in the peace-time Army. These units should eventually be officered by Negro officers. [In organizing units, especially infanty units, in which the Negro has demonstrated the least degree of efficiency.] The training of these units should stress initiative and command ability on the part of the Negro soldier in order to improve his character and confidence, educate him to assume responsibility, raise his morale, and better prepare him to assume the duties of a combat soldier.

After weighing the evidence carefully and objectively, it seems evident that certain remedial action can and must be taken. By so doing, the War Department will enhance the military value of this potential and thereby increase the efficiency of the armed forces of the nation.

III. CONCLUSIONS

Having considered the factual and other official materials made available by the War Department and the oral testimony of 52 military and civilian witnesses, this Board has arrived unanimously at the following conclusions:

1. A comparison of the Selective Service Records in two wars indicates that the Negro manpower which may be expected to become available to the Army in case of another national emergency will no doubt exceed that of World War II.

2. The relative advancement of the Negro in education, skills and crafts and resultant economic betterment definitely indicates that if prompt and ad-

equate steps are taken at this time, a greater and more efficient use can be realized from this manpower in the military establishment of the future.

3. Considering the advances made by the Negro civilian during the period between World War I and World War II and the increase in numbers available for military service, it is concluded that adequate plans were not prepared for the ultimate utilization of this manpower.

4. In the light of past experiences, it is believed that many of the difficulties and much of the confusion encountered in the placement of the Negro manpower during the Selective Service period of World War II could have been eliminated had War Department policies been fully implemented.

5. The experiences gained in the utilization of the Negro manpower in two major wars lead to the definite conclusion that if remedial action is taken by the War Department at this time, many of the apparent deficiencies of the Negro soldier can be eliminated and more efficient results derived from this manpower in the future.

6. Many of the deficiencies of leadership attributed to the Negro soldier in the past can be eliminated by creating in the post-war Army, for purposes of expansion, a broader Negro base of both officers and enlisted men, to assist in the training of the peace-time Army and to provide cadres and leaders to meet more efficiently the requirements of the Army in the event of a national emergency.

7. Creation of a broader Negro base in the post-war Army logically includes organization of appropriate elements of any female component.

8. In World War II some types of Negro units demonstrated greater proficiency than others. In general, service units have performed in a more satisfactory manner than combat units. Likewise, some units have consistently better combat records than others. In organizing or activating Negro units to create a broader base in the post-war Army, it is concluded that preference should be given to combat units.

9. For efficient results, the implementation and progressive development of a general policy in preparation for full utilization of Negro manpower in a national emergency will require the closest cooperation and coordination within the War Department, between the War Department and field commanders, and between local commanders and local civil officials.

10. Creation of a War Department General Staff Group of selected officers, experienced in command, who can devote their entire time to problems involving minority racial elements in the military establishment is necessary to insure adequate and continuous coordination and cooperation in implementing policy. Creation for the same purpose of a similar group on the staff of each major command is necessary.

11. The *War Department policy* announced for the administration and utilization of minority groups in the *post-war Army* should be carefully *coordinated* with *policies of the sister services* to avoid conflicting undertakings and to insure uniformity of purpose.

12. Testimony before this Board has indicated that units composed largely of personnel classified in the two lowest grades on the A.G.C.T. [Army General Classification Tests] scale require more officer supervision in training and in the field than units composed of personnel of normal distribution. It is concluded,

therefore, that attachment of officers to units including abnormal proportions of personnel in Grades IV and V on the A.G.C.T. scale is necessary when time is the critical factor, as it will be under war conditions or under a system of universal military training. This procedure is not necessary in the Regular Army in peace-time.

13. The training advantages accruing from a favorable climatic or terrain condition should be evaluated against the factor of unfavorable community attitude with its resultant effect on both training and morale. Troop locations should be selected after a consideration of these opposing factors, due regard being given in all cases to the fact that small civilian communities are incapable of absorbing large numbers of military personnel regardless of race.

14. Regardless of source of procurement and of racial antecedents, all officers of the regular establishment should be accorded equal privileges and opportunities for advancement as prescribed by law and regulations.

15. The sources of potential officer material can be extended and fostered through the medium of a more comprehensive ROTC and an Army leadership school program.

16. Processing of all personnel entering the Army, whether volunteers or selectees, through reception and training centers will help to maintain the efficiency of the Army and to insure proper assignment of individuals.

17. The high re-enlistment rate of professional privates in Negro units has in the past denied entry into the service to much potential officer and non-commissioned officer material. Economy and efficiency require that men of low intelligence and education who have been proven incapable of developing into specialists or leaders be eliminated from the service at termination of the first enlistment. Any policy implemented should include all races.

18. There are many places in the framework of the overhead units at Army installations where Negro personnel with special skills can be utilized to advantage as individuals. Periodic surveys of the installations are necessary to determine such positions.

19. Experience, education and tolerance on the part of personnel of the Army will serve to rectify many of the difficulties inherent in a mixed or composite unit.

20. Present War Department policies pertaining to the administration of educational, recreational and messing facilities and of officers clubs at posts, camps and stations where racial minority elements are located are considered adequate for the present and should be continued in effect.

21. The adoption and promulgation without delay of a broad, comprehensive, and progressive policy for the utilization of Negro manpower in the post-war Army will stimulate the Negro's interest, eliminate some of the frustrations, improve morale, and facilitate the development of individual ability and leadership.

22. The adoption and promulgation of a policy for utilization of Negro manpower in the military establishment will not in itself achieve the desired result. Steps must be taken concurrently to inform and indoctrinate all ranks of the military establishment concerning the importance to the national security of the successful accomplishment of the program.

23. The approval and promulgation of a constructive and progressive policy

involving the utilization of this manpower potential should be effected without delay. By such procedure the War Department will indicate clearly an endeavor to capitalize on and benefit from the lessons learned in the school of war.

24. Existing laws, regulations and official publications should be examined for determination of any conflict with the proposed policy envisioning a greater utilization of Negro manpower.

25. Publication of the approved policy by the War Department will facilitate an understanding attitude insofar as the press of the nation is concerned and thereby indicate that a progressive program aimed directly at the objective of more effective manpower utilization is being implemented.

IV. RECOMMENDATIONS

A. POLICY

In order that authorized Negro manpower may be utilized with maximum efficiency during the post-war period, this Board recommends that the War Department adopt, promulgate and implement the following policy:

> Within proportions corresponding to those in the civil population, to utilize the Negro manpower in the post-war Army on a broader professional scale than has obtained heretofore and, through the medium of installations and organizations, to facilitate the development of leaders and specialists to meet effectively the requirements of an expanded war Army. (See Facts Bearing on the Problems and Conclusions 1–5.)

B. IMPLEMENTATION OF POLICY

In order to develop the means required for maximum utilization of the authorized manpower of the nation in the event of a national emergency, it is further recommended:

1. That combat and service units be organized and activated from the Negro manpower available in the post-war Army to meet the requirements of training and expansion and in addition qualified individuals be utilized in appropriate special and overhead units; that the overall proportion not exceed the ratio that existed in World War II. (See Conclusions 6–8 and Tabs GI-II.*)

2. That Negro units organized or activated for the post-war Army conform in general to other units of the post-war Army. (See Conclusions 8 and Tab G III.)

3. That in the event of universal military training in peace-time, additional officer supervision be supplied to units which have a greater than normal per-

---

*"Tabs" referred to supplementary materials provided for the Gillem Board that were not contained in the report.

centage of personnel falling into A.G.C.T. classification IV and V. (See Conclusion 12 and Tab G IV.)

4. That a staff group of selected officers whose background has included command of troops be formed as an integral part of the G–1 or G–3 Division of the staffs of the War Department and each major command of the Army to assist in the planning, promulgation, implementation and revision of policies affecting all racial minorities. (See Conclusions 9–11 and Tab G-V.)

5. That there be accepted into the Regular Army an unspecified number of qualified Negro officers; and that officers initially selected for appointment in the regular establishment be taken from those with experience in World War II. (See Conclusions 6 and 21 and Tab G VI.)

6. That all officers be accorded the same rights, privileges and opportunities for advancement. (See Conclusion 14 and Tab G XI.)

7. That Negro officers to meet requirements for expansion of the regular establishment and for replacements be procured from the following sources:

(a) Reserve officers, including ROTC graduates, who shall be eligible for active duty training and service in accordance with any program established for officers of like component and status.
(b) Candidates from the ranks.
(c) Graduates of the United States Military Academy.
(d) Other sources utilized by the Army.
   (See Conclusion 15 and Tab G VI.)

8. That all enlisted men, whether volunteers or selectees, be routed through reception centers and training centers. (See Conclusion 16 and Tabs G VII-VIII.)

9. That re-enlistment be denied to Regular Army soldiers who meet only the minimum standards. (See Conclusion 17 and Tab G VII.)

10. That surveys of manpower requirements conducted by the War Department include recommendations covering the positions in each installation of the Army which could be filled by Negro military personnel. (See Conclusion 18 and Tab G VII.)

11. That experimental groupings of Negro units with white units in composite organizations be continued in the post-war Army. (See Conclusion 19 and Tab G IX.)

12. That initially Negro units of the post-war Army be stationed in localities where community attitudes are most favorable and in such strength as will not constitute an undue burden to the local civilian population. (See Conclusion 13 and Tab G X.)

13. That at posts, camps, and stations where both Negro and white soldiers are assigned for duty, the War Department policies (Tabs J and K) regarding use of recreational facilities and membership in officers' clubs, messes or similar social organizations be continued in effect and made applicable to the post-war Army. (See Conclusion 20 and Tabs G XI-XII.)

14. That the commanders of organizations, installations, and stations containing Negro personnel be made fully cognizant of their responsibilities in the execution of the overall War Department policy; and conversely that they be permitted maximum latitude in the solution of purely local problems. (See Conclusion 22 and Tab G XII.)

15. That the War Department, concurrently with promulgation of the ap-

proved policy, take steps to insure the indoctrination of all ranks throughout the Service as to the necessity for a unreserved acceptance of the provisions of the policy. (See Conclusion 22 and Tabs G XII-XIII.)

16. That approval and promulgation of a policy for utilization of Negro manpower in the post-war Army be accomplished with the least practicable delay. (See Conclusions 21 and 23 and Tab G XIII.)

17. That upon approval of this policy steps be initiated within the War Department to amend or rescind such laws and official publications as are in conflict therewith. (See Conclusion 24.)

18. That the approved War Department policy with reference to the utilization of the Negro manpower in the post-war Army be unrestricted and made public. (See Conclusion 25 and Tab G XIII.)

Bibliography

MANUSCRIPT COLLECTIONS

Army General Staff Papers. National Archives Record Group 407, National Archives Building, Washington, D.C.

Brotherhood of Sleeping Car Porters Papers. Manuscript Division, Library of Congress, Washington, D.C.

Civilian Aide to the Secretary of War Subject File Papers, 1940–1947. National Archives Record Group 107, National Archives Building, Washington, D.C.

Colonel Campbell C. Johnson Papers. Moorland-Spingarn Research Center, Howard University, Washington, D.C.

Franklin D. Roosevelt Papers. Franklin D. Roosevelt Library, Hyde Park, N.Y.

Harry S Truman Papers. Harry S Truman Library, Independence, Mo.

Henry L. Stimson Diary. Yale University Library, New Haven, Conn.

Henry L. Stimson Papers. Yale University Library, New Haven, Conn.

James C. Evans Papers. Personal Collection, Washington, D.C.

John P. Davis Papers. The Schomburg Center for Research in Black Literature and Culture, New York Public Library, New York, N.Y.

Judge Felix Frankfurter Papers. Manuscript Collection, Library of Congress, Washington, D.C.

Judge Robert P. Patterson Papers. Manuscript Collection, Library of Congress, Washington, D.C.

Judge William H. Hastie Papers. Howard University Law School, Washington, D.C.
Lester Granger Papers. Manuscript Collection, Library of Congress, Washington, D.C.
Military Personnel Division, General Staff Papers. National Archives Record Group 165, National Archives Building, Washington, D.C.
National Association for the Advancement of Colored People (NAACP) Papers. Manuscript Collection, Library of Congress, Washington, D.C.
National Urban League Papers. Manuscript Collection, Library of Congress, Washington, D.C.
Office of War Information Papers. National Archives Record Group 208, National Archives Building, Washington, D.C.
Secretary and Assistant Secretary of the Army Papers. National Archives Record Group 335, National Archives Building, Washington, D.C.
Secretary and Assistant Secretary of Defense Papers. National Archives Record Group 330, National Archives Building, Washington, D.C.
United States Senate Papers. National Archives Record Group 46, National Archives Building, Washington, D.C.
Walter White Papers. Yale University Library, New Haven, Conn.
Women's Army Corps General and Special Staff Personnel Papers, 1942–1946. National Archives Record Group 115, National Archives Building, Washington, D.C.

PUBLIC DOCUMENTS

Army Talk: Orientation Fact Sheet. Washington, D.C.: War Department, 1945.
Department of Defense, *Black Americans in Defense of Our Nation*. Washington, D.C.: Office of Deputy Assistant Secretary of Defense for Equal Opportunity, 1981.
Geis, Margaret L. *Negro Personnel in the European Command: 1 January 1946 to 30 June 1950*. Historical Division: European Command, 1952.
Headquarters, Army Service Forces. *Leadership and the Negro Soldier*. Washington, D.C.: United States Government Printing Office, 1944.
Johnson, Campbell C. *Selective Service System Special Groups: Special Monograph No. 10*. Washington, D.C.: United States Government Printing Office, 1953.
Lee, Ulysses. *United States Army in World War II: Special Studies: The Employment of Negro Troops*. Washington, D.C.: United States Government Printing Office, 1966.
Meyers, Evelyn P. *The Case Against Our Jim Crow Army Demands Investigation by the U.S. Congress*. Washington, D.C.: United States Government Printing Office, 1947.
The President's Committee on Civil Rights. *To Secure These Rights*. Washington, D.C.: United States Government Printing Office, 1947.
The President's Committee on Equal Opportunity in the Armed Forces. *Initial Report*. Mimeographed, June 13, 1963.
The President's Committee on Equality of Treatment and Opportunity in the

Armed Services. *Freedom To Serve*. Washington, D.C.: United States Government Printing Office, 1950.
Public Papers of the Presidents of the United States, Harry S. Truman, 1945–1953. Washington, D.C.: United States Government Printing Office, 1961.
Rosenman, Samuel I. *Public Papers of the Presidents of the United States, Franklin D. Roosevelt, 1933–1945*. Washington, D.C.: United States Government Printing Office, 1950.
Sher, Ronald. *Integration of Negro and White Personnel in the United States Army, 1952–1954*. Historical Division, Headquarters: United States Army, Europe, 1956.
Strickland, Patricia. *The Putt-Putt Air Force: The Story of the Civilian Pilot and the War Training Service, 1939–44*. Washington, D.C.: Department of Transportation, 1950.
Treadwell, Mattie E. *The United States Army in World War II: Special Studies: The Women's Army Corps*. Washington, D.C.: United States Government Printing Office, 1954.
United States Army. *Basic Training Talk No. 7, Negro Manpower in the Army*. Washington, D.C.: Department of the Army, 1949.
United States Assistant Secretary of Defense. *Integration and the Negro Officer in the Armed Forces of the United States of America*. Washington, D.C.: United States Government Printing Office, 1962.
United States Commission on Civil Rights. *Employment: 1961 Report*. Washington, D.C.: United States Government Printing Office, 1961.
———. *Report*. Washington, D.C.: United States Government Printing Office, 1961.
———. *Report*. Washington, D.C.: United States Government Printing Office, 1963.
United States. *Congressional Record*. 76th Congress, 1st Session, 1939.
———. *Congressional Record*. 76th Congress, 3rd Session, 1940.
———. *Congressional Record*. 77th Congress, 1st Session, 1941.
———. *Congressional Record*. 77th Congress, 2nd Session, 1942.
———. *Congressional Record*. 78th Congress, 1st Session, 1943.
———. *Congressional Record*. 78th Congress, 2nd Session, 1944.
———. *Congressional Record*. 79th Congress, 1st Session, 1945.
———. *Congressional Record*. 79th Congress, 2nd Session, 1946.
———. *Congressional Record*. 80th Congress, 1st Session, 1947.
———. *Congressional Record*. 80th Congress, 2nd Session, 1948.
———. *Congressional Record*. 81st Congress, 1st Session, 1949.
———. *Congressional Record*. 81st Congress, 2nd Session, 1950.
United States Secretary of Defense. *Advances in the Utilization of Negro Manpower: Under Ten Years of Unification of the Armed Services—Official Report, 1947–1957*. Washington, D.C.: United States Government Printing Office, 1958.
United States Senate, Armed Services Committee. *Hearings on Universal Military Training*. Washington, D.C.: United States Government Printing Office, 1948.
United States War Department. *The Army of the United States*. Washington, D.C.: United States Government Printing Office, 1940.

United States War Department Pamphlet. *Command of Negro Troops*. Washington, D.C.: United States Government Printing Office, 1944.

NEWSPAPERS

Arkansas Democrat
Atlanta Constitution
Atlanta Daily World
Baltimore Afro-American
Baltimore Sun
Birmingham News
Boston Daily Globe
California Eagle
Chicago Daily News
Chicago Defender
Cleveland Call and Post
Cleveland Gazette
Detroit News
Denver Post
Greensboro Daily News
Houston Post
Indianapolis News
Kansas City Star
Los Angeles Times
Miami Herald
Montgomery Advertiser
New Orleans Times-Picayune
News and Courier (Charleston, S.C.)
New York Age
New York Amsterdam Star-News
New York Post
New York Times
Norfolk Journal and Guide
Oregon Statesman
People's Voice
Philadelphia Record
Philadelphia Tribune
Pittsburgh Courier
Richmond Times-Dispatch
Savannah Morning News
Shreveport Times
Vicksburg Herald
Washington Afro-American
Washington Evening Star
Washington Post

PERSONAL CORRESPONDENCE

James C. Evans, Former Civilian Aide to the Secretary of the Army and Counselor to the Secretary of Defense, to the author, June 26, 1974; July 20, 1974; November 24, 1974.

Judge William H. Hastie, Former Civilian Aide to the Secretary of War and Senior United States Circuit Judge for the Third Circuit, to the author, October 8, 1974.

Katherine E. Kemper, Assistant Director of Donor Resources Development, to the author, August 12, 1977.

Philip D. Lagerquist, Chief Archivist, Harry S. Truman Library, to the author, October 26, 1973; June 26, 1974.

William J. Stewart, Acting Director, Franklin D. Roosevelt Library, to the author, October 31, 1973; June 27, 1974.

INTERVIEWS

James C. Evans, interview with author, July 23, 1974; August 6, 1974; October 6, 1974; November 30, 1974; December 17, 1974.

Judge William H. Hastie, interview with author, March 6, 1974; March 8, 1974.

UNPUBLISHED STUDIES

Avery, Sheldon B. "Up from Washington: William Pickens and the Negro Struggle for Equality, 1900–1954." Ph.D. diss., University of Oregon, 1970.

Berman, William C. "The Politics of Civil Rights in the Truman Administration." Ph.D. diss., Ohio State University, 1963.

Byers, Jean. "A Study of the Negro in Military Service." Washington, D.C.: Department of Defense, 1947.

Finkle, Lee. "Forum for Protest: The Black Press and World War II." Ph.D. diss., New York University, 1971.

Gill, Gerald R. "Religious, Constitutional, and Racial Objections to United States Involvement in World War II, 1939–1945." M. A. thesis, Howard University, 1974.

Gillem, Alvan C. "Report of Board of Officers on Utilization of Negro Manpower in the Post-War Army." Military Personnel Division, General Staff, National Archives Record Group 165, National Archives Building, Washington, D.C.

McGuire, Phillip. "Black Civilian Aides and the Problems of Racism and Segregation in the United States Armed Forces, 1940–1950." Ph.D. diss., Howard University, 1975.

Parrish, Noel F. "The Segregation of Negroes in the Army Air Forces." M.A. thesis, Air University, 1947.

BOOKS

Adams, Leonard P. *Wartime Manpower Mobilization*. New York: Cornell University Press, 1951.
Anderson, Jervis, and Peter Stone. *A. Philip Randolph: A Biographical Portrait*. New York: Harcourt Brace Jovanovich, 1973.
Appleman, Roy E. *United States Army in the Korean War: South to the Naktong, North to the Yalu*. Washington, D.C.: United States Government Printing Office, 1961.
Baldwin, James. *The Fire Next Time*. New York: The Dial Press, 1963.
Barbeau, Arthur E., and Florette Henri. *The Unknown Soldiers: Black American Troops in World War I*. Philadelphia: Temple University Press, 1974.
Bardolph, Richard. *The Negro Vanguard*. New York: Vintage Books, 1959.
Benedict, Ruth, and Gene Weltfish. *The Races of Mankind*. New York: Public Affairs Committee, 1943.
Berman, William C. *The Politics of Civil Rights in the Truman Administration*. Columbus, Ohio: Ohio State University Press, 1970.
Binkin, Martin, and Mark J. Eitelberg, with Alvin J. Schnexnider and Marvin M. Smith. *Blacks and the Military*. Washington, D.C.: Brookings Institution, 1982.
Blaustein, Albert P., and Robert L. Z. angrando. *Civil Rights and the American Negro: A Documentary History*. New York: Trident Press, 1968.
Blumer, Herbert. "Morale," in *American Society During Wartime*. Edited by William F. Ogburn. Chicago: University of Chicago Press, 1943.
Bogart, Leo. *Social Research and the Desegregation of the United States Armed Forces*. Chicago: Markam Press, 1969.
Bradley, Omar N. *A Soldier's Story*. New York: Holt, 1951.
Brink, William, and Louis Harris. *Black and White: A Study of U.S. Racial Attitudes Today*. New York: Simon and Schuster, 1967.
———. *The Negro Revolution in America*. New York: Simon and Schuster, 1964.
Brock, Clifton. *Americans for Democratic Action: Its Role in National Politics*. Washington, D.C.: Public Affairs Press, 1962.
Broderick, Francis L. *W.E.B. DuBois: Negro Leader in a Time of Crisis*. Stanford: Stanford University Press, 1959.
Broom, Leonard and Norval D. Glenn. *Transformation of the Negro American*. New York: Harper and Row, 1965.
Buchanan, A. Russell. *Black Americans in World War II*. Santa Barbara, Calif.: ABC-Clio Press, 1977.
Bullard, Robert L. *Personalities and Reminiscences of the War*. Garden City, N.Y.: Doubleday, Page and Compay, 1925.
Burns, James M. *Roosevelt, The Soldier of Freedom, 1940–1945*. New York, Harcourt Brace Jovanovich, 1970.
Bush, Noel F. *Adlai E. Stevenson of Illinois: A Portrait*. New York: Alfred A. Knopf, 1947.
Carr, Robert K. *Federal Protection of Civil Rights*. Ithaca: Cornell University Press, 1947.
Carter, Dan T. *Scottsboro: A Tragedy of the American South*. Baton Rouge: Louisiana State University Press, 1969.

Clark, Kenneth B. "Morale Among Negroes," in *Civilian Morale*. Edited by Goodwin Watson. Boston: Houghton Mifflin, 1942.
Clark, Mark W. *Calculated Risk*. New York: Harper and Brothers, 1950.
Compere, Tom, ed. *The Army Blue Book*. New YorkL: Bobbs-Merrill, 1960.
Coser, Lewis. *The Functions of Social Conflict*. Glencoe, Ill.: The Free Press of Glencoe, 1956.
Current, Richard N. *Secretary Stimson, A Study in Statecraft*. New Brunswick, N.J.: Rutgers University Press, 1954.
Curtis, Mary. *The Black Soldiers of the United States Army*. Washington, D.C.: O. D. Morris, 1915.
Dalfiume, Richard M. *Desegregation of the U.S. Armed Forces: Fighting on Two Fronts, 1939–1953*, Columbia, Mo.: University of Missouri Press, 1969.
Daniels, Jonathan. *The Man of Independence*. Philadelphia: J. B. Lippincott Company, 1963.
Davis, John P. "The Negro in the Armed Forces of America," in *The American Negro Reference Book*. Edited by John P. Davis. Englewood Cliffs, N.J.: Prentice-Hall, 1966.
Drake, St. Clair, and Horace R. Cayton. *Black Metropolis*. New York: Harcourt, Brace and Company, 1945.
Dulles, Foster Rhea. *The American Red Cross, A History*. New York: Harper and Brothers, 1950.
Evans, James C. *Counselor to the Secretary of Defense*. Washington, D.C.: Department of Defense, 1970.
―――. *Integration in the Armed Forces: Pertinent Readings and Related Background Information*. Washington, D.C.: Office of the Assistant Secretary of Defense, 1955.
Foner, Jack D. *Blacks and the Military in American History: A New Perspective*. New York: Praeger Publishers, 1974.
Francis, Charles E. *The Tuskegee Airmen: The Story of the Negro in the United States Air Force*. Boston: Bruce Humphries, 1955.
Franklin, John H. *From Slavery to Freedom: A History of Negro Americans*. New York: Alfred A. Knopf, 1974.
Frazier, E. Franklin. *The Negro in the United States*. New York: The MacMillan Company, 1957.
Friedel, Frank. *F.D.R. and the South*. Baton Rouge: Louisiana State University Press, 1965.
Garfinkel, Herbert. *When Negroes March: The March on Washington Movement in the Organizational Politics of FEPC*. Glencoe, Ill.: The Free Press of Glencoe, 1959.
Ginzberg, Eli, and Douglas W. Bray. *The Uneducated*. New York: Columbia University Press, 1959.
Ginzberg, Eli et al. *The Ineffective Soldier: Lessons for Management and the Nation*. New York: Columbia University Press, 1959.
―――. "The Negro Soldier," in *The Negro Potential*. Edited by Eli Ginzberg. New York: Columbia University Press, 1956.
Greenberg, Jack. *Race Relations and American Law*. New York: Columbia University Press, 1959.

Hastie, William H. "No Royal Road," in *Many Shades of Black*. Edited by Stanton L. Wormley and Lewis H. Henderson. New York: Morrow, 1969.
———. *On Clipped Wings: The Story of Jim Crow in the Army Air Corps*. New York: NAACP, 1943.
Hillman, William, and Alfred Wagg. *Mr. President: The First Publication from the Personal Diaries, Private Letters, Papers, and Revealing Interviews of Harry S. Truman, Thirty-second President of the United States of America*. New York: Farrar, Straus, and Young, 1952.
Holt, Rackham. *Mary McLeod Bethune*. New York: Doubleday and Company, 1964.
Horton, David S., ed. *Freedom and Equality: Addresses by Harry S. Truman*. Columbia, Mo: University of Missouri Press, 1960.
Issacs, Harold R. *The New World of Negro Americans*. New York: The John Day Company, 1963.
Jernagin, William H. *Christ at the Battlefront: Servicemen Accept the Challenge*. Washington, D.C.: Murray Brothers, 1946.
Johnson, Campbell C. *Fifty Years of Progress in the Armed Forces*. Pittsburgh: Pittsburgh Courier Publishing Company, 1950.
Johnson, Charles S. *To Stem This Tide: A Survey of Racial Tension Areas in the United States*. Boston: The Pilgrim Press, 1943.
Johnson, Jesse J. *Black Armed Forces Officers, 1736–1971*. Hampton, Va: J. J. Johnson, 1971.
———. *Ebony Brass: An Autobiography of Negro Frustrations Amid Aspiration*. New York: William Frederick Press, 1967.
Kendrick, Douglas B. *Blood Program in World War II*. Washington, D.C.: Department of the Army, 1974.
Killian, Lewis M., and Charles Grigg. *Racial Crisis in America: Leadership in Conflict*. Englewood Cliffs, N.J.: Prentice-Hall, 1964.
Knowles, Louis L., and Kenneth Prewitt. *Institutional Racism in America*. Englewood Cliffs, N.J.: Prentice-Hall, 1969.
Lippman, Walter. *United States War Aims*. Boston: Little, Brown, and Company, 1944.
Little, Arthur W. *From Harlem to the Rhine: The Story of New York's Colored Volunteers*. New York: Covici, Friede, 1936.
Logan, Rayford W., ed. *What the Negro Wants*. Chapel Hill: University of North Carolina Press, 1944.
Lomax, Louis E. *The Negro Revolt*. New York: Harper and Row, 1962.
McCoy, Donald R., and Richard T. Ruetten. *Quest and Response: Minority Rights and the Truman Administration*. Laurence: University of Kansas Press, 1973.
MacDonald, Dwight. *The War's Greatest Scandal: The Story of Jim Crow in Uniform*. New York: March on Washington Movement, n.d.
MacGregor, Morris J. *Defense Studies: Integration of the Armed Forces*. Washington, D.C.: Center of Military History, 1981.
McGuire, Phillip. *Taps for a Jim Crow Army: Letters from Black Soldiers in World War II*. Santa Barbara, Calif.: ABC-Clio Press, 1983.
Mandelbaum, David G. *Soldiers Groups and Negros Groups*. Berkeley: University of California Press, 1952.

Mangum, Charles S. *The Legal Status of the Negro*. Chapel Hill: University of North Carolina Press, 1940.
Marshall, Thurgood. *Report on Korea: The Shameful Story of the Court Martial of Negro GIs*. New York: NAACP, 1951.
Matloff, Maurice, ed. *American Military History*. Washington, D.C.: United States Government Printing Office, 1973.
Millett, Alan R., and Peter Maslowski. *For the Common Defense: A Military History of the United States of America*. New York: The Free Press, 1984.
Millis, Walter, ed. *The Forrestal Diaries*. New York: The Viking Press, 1951.
Milton, H. S., ed. *The Utilization of Negro Manpower in the Army*. Chevy Chase, Md.: Operations Research Office, The Johns Hopkins University, 1955.
Moon, Henry L. *Balance of Power: The Negro Vote*. Garden City, N.Y.: Doubleday and Company, 1948.
Moskos, Charles C. "Minority Groups in Military Organization," in *Handbook of Military Institutions*. Edited by Roger W. Little, Beverly Hills: Sage Press, 1971.
Mullen, Robert W. *Blacks in America's Wars: Shift in Attitudes from the Revolutionary War to Vietnam*. New York: Monad Press, 1973.
Munson, Edward L., Jr. *Leadership for American Army Leaders*, Washington, D.C.: The Infantry Journal, 1942.
Myrdal, Gunnar. *An American Dilemma: The Negro Problem and Modern Democracy*. New York: Harper and Brothers, 1944.
Nalty, Bernard C. *Strength for the Fight: A History of Black Americans in the Military*. New York: The Free Press, 1986.
Nalty, Bernard C., and Morris J. MacGregor, eds. *Blacks in the Military: Essential Documents*. Wilmington, Del.: Scholarly Resources, 1981.
National Urban League. *Racial Aspects of Reconversion: A Memorandum Prepared for the President of the United States*. New York: National Urban League, 1945.
Nelson, Dennis D. *The Integration of the Negro into the United States Navy*. New York: Farrar, Straus and Young, 1951.
Nichols, Lee. *Breakthrough on the Color Front*. New York: Random House, 1954.
Odum, Howard W. *Race and Rumors of Race: Challenge to American Crisis*. Chapel Hill: University of North Carolina Press, 1943.
Osur, Alan M. *Blacks in the Army Air Forces During World War II*. Washington, D.C.: United States Government Printing Office, 1977.
Ottley, Roi. *'New World A-Coming': Inside Black America*. Boston: Houghton Mifflin Company, 1943.
Park, Robert E. "Racial Ideologies," in *American Society During Wartime*. Edited by William F. Ogburn. Chicago: University of Chicago Press, 1943.
Patton, Gerald W. *War and Race: The Black Officer in the American Military, 1915–1941*. Westport, Conn.: Greenwood Press, 1981.
Quarles, Benjamin, and Leslie H. Fishel. *The Black American: A Documentary History*. New York: Scott, Foresman and Company, 1970.
Rose, Arnold M. *The Negro's Morale: Group Identification and Protest*. Minneapolis: University of Minnesota Press, 1949.
Rothe, Anna, ed. *Current Biography*. New York: H. W. Wilson Company, 1944.

Schoenfield, Seymour J. *The Negro in the Armed Forces*. Washington, D.C.: The Associated Publishers, 1945.
Scott, Emmett J. *The American Negro in the World War*. Chicago: Homewood Press, 1919.
Silberman, Charles E. *Crisis in Black and White*. New York: Random House, 1964.
Silvera, John D. *The Negro in World War II*. Washington, D.C.: Army War Department, 1955.
Smith, Lillian. *Killers of the Dream*. New York: W. W. Norton and Company, 1961.
Stillman, Richard J. *Integration of the Negro in the United States Armed Forces*. New York: Praeger, 1968.
Stimson, Henry L., and McGeorge Bundy. *On Active Service in Peace and War*. New York: Harper, 1948.
Stouffer, Samuel A. "Social Science and the Soldier," in *American Society During Wartime*. Edited by William F. Ogburn. Chicago: Chicago University Press, 1943.
Stouffer, Samuel A. et al. *The American Soldier: Adjustment During Army Life*. Vol. 1. Princeton, N.J.: Princeton University Press, 1949.
Tatum, Elbert L. *The Changed Political Thought of the Negro, 1915–1940*. New York: Exposition Press, 1951.
Taylor, Esther M. "Segregation, Desegregaton, and Integration in a Social Agency," in *Minority Groups: Segregation and Integration*. Edited by National Conference of Social Work, 1955.
Thompson, Edgar T. *Race Relations and the Problem: A Definition and an Analysis*. New York: Greenwood Press, 1968.
Tumin, Melvin M. *Desegregation: Resistance and Readiness*. Princeton, N.J.: Princeton University Press, 1958.
Ware, Gilbert. *William Hastie: Grace Under Pressure*. New York: Oxford University Press, 1984.
Wedlock, Lunnabelle. *The Reaction of Negro Publications and Organizations to German Anti-Semitism*. Washington, D.C.: Howard University Press, 1942.
Wesley, Charles H. *The Quest for Equality*. New York: Publishers Company, 1968.
White, Walter. *A Man Called White: The Autobiography of Walter White*. New York: The Viking Press, 1948.
Wiley, Bell I. *The Training of Negro Troops*. Washington, D.C.: Historical Section, Army Ground Forces, 1946.
Yarmolinksy, Adam. *The Military Establishment: Its Impacts on American Society*. New York: Harper Colophon, 1971.
Yinger, J. Milton. *A Minority Group in American Society*. New York: McGraw-Hill, 1965.

ARTICLES

"The Air Force Goes Interracial." *Ebony* (September 1949): 15–18.
Aptheker, Herbert. 'The Negro in the Union Navy." *The Journal of Negro History* 32 (April 1947): 169–200.
Berger, Monroe. "Law and Custom in the Army." *Social Forces* 25 (October 1946): 82–87.

Berkman, Paul. "Life Abroad an Armed Guardship." *American Journal of Sociology* 51 (March 1946): 380–387.

Bethune, Mary McLeod. "My Secret Talks with F.D.R." *Ebony* 4 (April 1949): 42–51.

Birnie, William A. H. "Black Brain Trust." *American Magazine* 135 (January 1943): 37–94, 95.

Blumenthal, Henry, "Woodrow Wilson and the Race Question." *The Journal of Negro History* 48 (January 1963): 1–21.

Bogart, Leo. "The Army and Its Negro Soldiers." *The Reporter* 11 (December 30, 1954): 8–11.

Bond, Horace M. "The Negro in the Armed Forces of the United States Prior to World War I." *The Journal of Negro Education* 12 (Summer 1943): 268–287.

———. "Should the Negro Care Who Wins the War?" *The Annals of the American Academy of Social and Political Science* 223 (September 1942): 81–84.

Brearley, H. C. "The Negro's New Belligerency." *Phylon* 5 (Winter 1944): 339–345.

Brecher, Ruth and Edward. "The Military's Limited War Against Segregation." *Harper's Magazine* 217 (September 1963): 79–92.

Breckingridge, S. P. "The Winfred Lynn Case Again: Segregation in the Armed Forces." *Social Service Review* 18 (September 1944): 369–371.

Brotz, Howard, and Everett Wilson. "Characteristics of Military Society." *American Journal of Sociology* 51 (March 1946): 371–375.

Brown, Earl. "American Negroes and the War." *Harper's Magazine* 184 (April 1942): 545–552.

Brown, Warren H. "A Negro Looks at The Negro Press." *Saturday Review of Literature* 25 (December 19, 1942): 5.

Brunson, Sergeant Warren T. "What a Negro Soldier Thinks About." *Social Service Review* 18 (December 1944): 534–535.

Bunche, Ralph J. "The Negro in the Political Life of the United States." *The Journal of Negro Education* 10 (July 1941): 567–584.

Carter, Elmer A. "The Fate of Democracy." *Opportunity* 19 (January 1942): 2.

———. "The Negro and Nazism." *Opportunity* 17 (July 1940): 194–195.

———. "The 369th Departs." *Opportunity* 19 (February 1942): 35.

———. "Where the Negro Stands." *Opportunity* 18 (April 1941): 98.

Cayton, Horace R. "Fighting for White Folks." *The Nation* 45 (September 26, 1942): 267–270.

———. "Negro Morale." *Opportunity* 18 (December 1941): 371–375.

Clark, Kenneth B. "Morale of the Negro on the Front: World Wars I and II." *The Journal of Negro Education* 12 (Summer 1943): 417–428.

Clement, Rufus E. "Problems of Demobilization and Rehabilitation of the Negro Soldier After World Wars I and II." *The Journal of Negro Education* 12 (Summer 1943): 533–542.

Cohne, Robert A. "Military Groups Psychotherapy." *Mental Hygiene* 31 (January 1947): 94–102.

Coleman, J. V. "The Group Factor in Military Psychiatry." *American Journal of Orthopsychiatry* 16 (April 1946): 222–225.

Collier, John, and Saul K. Padover. "An Institute for Ethnic Democracy." *Common Ground* 4 (Autumn 1943): 3–7.
Coon, Carleton S. "The Universality of Natural Grouping in Human Societies." *The Journal of Educational Sociology* 20 (November 1946): 163–168.
Cornish, Dudley T. "The Union Army as a School For Negroes." *The Journal of Negro History* 37 (October 1952): 368–382.
"Crisis in the Making." *Newsweek* 31 (June 7, 1948): 28–29.
Cushman, Robert E. "Our Civil Rights Become a World Issue." *The New York Times Magazine* (January 11, 1948): 12; 22–24.
Dabney, Virginius. "Nearer and Nearer the Precipice." *The Atlantic Monthly* 171 (January 1943): 94–100.
Dahrendorf, Ralf. "Our Utopia: Toward a Reorientation of Sociological Analysis." *American Journal of Sociology* 44 (September 1958): 115–128.
Davis, Arthur K. "Bureaucratic Patterns in the Navy Officer Corps." *Social Forces* 27 (December 1948): 143–153.
Davis, John W. "The Negro in the United States Navy, Marine Corps and Coast Guard." *The Journal of Negro Education* 12 (Summer 1943): 345–349.
Davis, Ralph N. "The Negro Newspaper and the War." *Sociology and Social Research* 27 (May 1943): 373–380.
Dollard, Charles, and Donald Young. "In the Armed Forces." *Survey Graphic* 36 (January 1947): 66–68, 111–116.
Du Bois, W.E.B. "The Black Man in the Revolution of 1914–1918." *The Crisis* 17 (March 1919): 218–223.
———. "Close Ranks." *The Crisis* 16 (July 1918): 111.
———. "Documents of the War." *The Crisis* 18 (May 1919): 16–21,
———. "An Essay Toward a History of the Black Man in the Great War." *The Crisis* 18 (June 1919): 63–87.
———. "The Negro Soldier in Service Abroad During the First World War." *The Journal of Negro Education* 12 (Summer 1943): 324–334.
———. "A Philosophy in Time of War." *The Crisis* 16 (August 1918): 164.
———. "Returning Soldiers." *The Crisis* 18 (May 1919): 13–14.
———. "The Turning of the Tide." *The Crisis* 15 (December 1917): 77.
Dwyer, Robert J. "The Negro in the United States Army: His Changing Role and Status." *Sociology and Social Research* 38 (November 1953): 103–112.
Elkin, Frederick. "The Soldier's Language." *American Journal of Sociology* 51 (March 1946): 414–422.
Fairchild, Henry P. "The Truth About Race." *Harper's Magazine* 184 (October 1944): 418–425.
Finkle, Lee. "The Conservative Aims of Militant Rhetoric: Black Protest During World War II." *Journal of American History* 60 (December 1973): 692–713.
Fishbein, Morris, ed. "Use of Negro Blood for Blood Banks." *Journal of the American Medical Association* 119 (May 16, 1942): 233–308.
Foreman, Clark. "Race Tension in the South." *New Republic* 107 (September 21, 1942): 340–342.
Frazier, E. Franklin. "Ethnic and Minority Groups in Wartime." *American Journal of Sociology* 48 (November 1942): 369–377.
Freeman, Felton D. "The Army As A Social Structure." *Social Forces* 27 (October 1948): 78–83.

Garvin, Charles H. "The Negro in the Special Services of the United States Army: Medical Corps, Dental Corps, and Nurses Corps." *The Journal of Negro Education* 12 (Summer 1943): 335–344.
"Georgia's Vinson: Battling the Pentagon." *United States News and World Report* 55 (September 30, 1963): 16.
Golightly, Cornelius L. "Negro Higher Education and Democratic Negro Morale." *The Journal of Negro Education* 11 (July 1942): 322–328.
Goodman, George W. "The Englishman Meets the Negro." *Common Ground* 5 (Autumn 1944): 3–11.
Granger, Lester. "Racial Democracy—The Navy War." *Common Ground* 7 (Winter 1946), 61–68.
Graves, John T. "The Southern Negro and the War Crisis." *Virginia Quarterly Review* 18 (Autumn 1942): 500–517.
Greene, Lorenzo J. "Some Observations on the Black Regiment of Rhode Island in the American Revolution." *The Journal of Negro History* 37 (April 1952): 142–172.
Griffin, Ronald C. "A Black Perspective of the Military." *Negro History Bulletin* 26 (October 1973): 34.
Hall. E. T., Jr. "Prejudice and Negro-White Relations in the Army." *American Journal of Sociology* 52 (March 1947): 401–409.
Hastie, William H. "A Look At The NAACP." *The Crisis* 46 (September 1939): 263–264, 274.
———. "The Negro in the Army Today." *The Annals of the American Academy of Political and Social Science* 223 (September 1942): 55–59.
———. "Negro Officers in Two World Wars." *The Journal of Negro Education* 12 (Summer 1943): 316–323.
Hausrath, Alfred H. "Utilization of Negro Manpower in the Army." *Journal of the Operations Research Society of America* 2 (February 1954): 17–30.
Henderson, Donald. "Minority Response and the Conflict Model." *Phylon* 25 (Spring 1964): 18–26.
High, Stanley. "How the Negro Fights for Freedom." *Reader's Digest* 41 (July 1942): 113–118.
Hoffman, Edwin D. "The Genesis of the Modern Movement for Equal Rights in South Carolina, 1930–1939." *The Journal of Negro History* 44 (October 1959): 346–369.
Homans, George C. "The Small Warship." *American Sociological Review* 11 (June 1946): 294–300.
Houston, Charles H. "Critical Summary: The Negro in the United States Armed Forces in World Wars I and II." *The Journal of Negro Education* 12 (Summer 1943): 364–366.
Hughes, Everett C. "Race Relations and the Sociological Imagination." *American Sociological Review* 28 (December 1963): 879–890.
"Informal Social Organization in the Army." *American Journal of Sociology* 51 (March 1946): 365–370.
Jackson, Luther P. "Virginia Negro Soldiers and Seamen in the American Revolution." *The Journal of Negro History* 27 (July 1942): 247–287.
Jenkins, William Q. "A Review of Leadership Studies with Particular Reference to Military Problems." *Psychological Bulletin* 44 (January 1947): 54–59.

Johnson, Campbell C. "The Mobilization of Negro Manpower for the Armed Forces." *The Journal of Negro Education* 12 (Summer 1943): 298–306.

Johnson, Charles S. "The Negro and the Present Crisis." *The Journal of Negro Education* 10 (July 1941): 585–596.

———, ed. "The Social Front: Armed Forces." *A Monthly Summary of Trends and Events in Race Relations* 2 (April 1945): 248–280.

Johnson, Guion G. "The Impact of War Upon the Negro." *The Journal of Negro Education* 10 (July 1941): 596–611.

Jones, Lester M. "The Editorial Policy of the Negro Newspapers 1917–1918 as Compared with that of 1941–42." *The Journal of Negro History* 29 (January 1944): 24–31.

Julian, Joseph. "Jim Crow Goes Abroad." *The Nation* 155 (December 5, 1942): 610–612.

Kenworthy, E. W. "The Case Against Army Segregation." *The Annals of the American Academy of Political and Social Science* 275 (May 1951): 27–34.

———. "Taps for Jim Crow in the Services." *The New York Times Magazine* (June 11, 1950): 12, 24–27.

Klineberg, Otto. "Race Prejudice and the War." *The Annals of the American Academy of Political and Social Science* 222 (September 1942): 190–198.

Krogman, Wilton M. "What We Do Not Know About Race." *The Scientific Monthly* 57 (August 1943): 97–104.

Lee, Alfred M. "Subversive Individuals of Minority Status." *The Annals of the American Academy of Political and Social Science* 223 (September 1942): 162–172.

Leiser, Ernest. "For Negroes It's a New Army Now." *The Saturday Evening Post* 225 (December 13, 1952): 26–27, 108, 110–112.

Lewis, Roscoe E. "The Role of Pressure Groups in Maintaining Morale Among Negroes." *The Journal of Negro Education* 12 (Summer 1943): 464–473.

Logan, Frenise A. "Paradox." *Opportunity* 22 (Summer 1944): 121.

Lohman, Joseph D. and Dietrich C. Reitzes. "Note on Race Relations in a Mass Society." *American Journal of Sociology* 68 (November 1957): 240–246.

Long, Howard H. "The Negro Soldier in the Army of the United States." *The Journal of Negro Education* 12 (Summer 1943): 307–315.

MacDonald, Dwight. "The Novel Case of Winfred Lynn." *The Nation* 46 (February 20, 1943): 263–270.

———. "The Supreme Court's New Moot Suit." *The Nation* 159 (July 1, 1944): 13–14.

McGuire, Phillip, "Desegregation of the Armed Forces: Black Leadership, Protest and World War II." *Journal of Negro History* 68 (Spring 1983): 147–158.

———. "Judge Hastie, World War II, And Army Racism." *The Journal of Negro History* 61 (October 1977): 351–362.

———. "Judge Hastie, World War II, and the Army Air Corps." *Phylon* 42 (June 1981): 157–167.

———. "Judge Hastie, World War II, and the Army's Fear of Black Blood." *Review of Afro-American Issues and Culture* 1 (Summer 1979): 134–149.

———. "Judge William Hastie: Confronting the Socio-Military Status of Blacks in the U.S. Army, 1940–42." *The Oracle* 62 (Spring 1977): 86–89.

———. "Judge William H. Hastie and Army Recruitment, 1940–1943." *Military*

Affairs: The Journal of Military History, Including Theory and Technology 42 (April 1978): 75–79.

———. "Judge William H. Hastie, Civilian Aide to the Secretary of War, 1940–1943." *Negro History Bulletin* 40 (May-June 1977): 712–713.

———. "Military Hemophobia." *The Researchers: A Journal Of Interdisciplinary Studies* 11 (Spring 1985): 1–7.

Mack, Raymond W. "The Components of Social Conflict." *Social Problems* 12 (Spring 1965): 388–397.

MacLeish, Archibald. "The American Cause." *Survey Graphic* 30 (January 1941): 21–23.

McWhirter, William A. "The National Guard—Awake or Asleep?" *Life* 63 (October 27, 1967): 85–98.

McWilliams, Carey. "Race Tensions: Second Phase." *Common Ground* 4 (Autumn 1943): 7–12.

"The Making of the Infantrymen." *American Journal of Sociology* 51 (March 1946): 376–379.

Martin, Harold H. "How Do Our Negro Troops Measure Up?" *The Saturday Evening Post* 223 (June 16, 1951): 30–31, 139, 141.

Miller, Carroll L. "The Negro and Volunteer War Agencies." *The Journal of Negro Education* 12 (Summer 1943): 438–451.

Milner, Lucille B. "Jim Crow in the Army." *New Republic* 110 (March 13, 1944): 339–342.

Morrow, E. Frederic. "Southern Exposure." *The Crisis* 46 (July 1939): 202–210.

Moskos, Charles C. "The American Dilemma in Uniform: Race in the Armed Forces." *The Annals of the American Academy of Political and Social Science* 406 (March 1973): 94–106.

———. "Racial Integration in the Armed Forces." *American Journal of Sociology* 72 (September 1966): 132–148.

Morton, Mary A. "The Federal Government and Negro Morale." *The Journal of Negro Education* 12 (Summer 1943): 452–463.

Mueller, William R. "The Negro in the Navy." *Social Forces* 24 (October 1945): 110–115.

"The Negro's War." *Fortune* 25 (June 1942): 77–80, 157–158, 160, 162.

Newton, Isham G. "The Negro in the National Guard." *Phylon* 23 (Spring 1962): 18–28.

Oak, V. V. "What About the Negro Press?" *Saturday Review of Literature* 26 (March 6, 1943): 4.

Ottley, Roi. "Negro Morale." *New Republic* 105 (November 10, 1941): 613–615.

———. "The Negro Press." *Common Ground* 3 (Spring 1943): 11–15.

———. "A White Folk's War." *Common Ground* 2 (Spring 1942): 28–31.

Page, Charles H. "Bureaucracy's Other Face." *Social Forces* 25 (October 1946): 88–94.

Peck, James L. H. "When Do We Fly?" *The Crisis* 47 (December 1940): 376–378, 388.

"The Pentagon Jumps into the Race Flight." *United States News and World Report* 55 (August 19, 1963): 49–50.

Pfautz, Harold W. "The New Negro: Emerging American." *Phylon* 24 (Fourth Quarter, 1963): 360–368.

"Pioneers in the Struggle Against Segregation." *Survey Graphic* 36 (January 1947): 91.
Powell, Adam C., Jr. "Is This a White Man's War?" *Common Ground* 2 (April 1942): 111–113.
Prattis, P. L. "The Morale of the Negro in the Armed Services of the United States." *The Journal of Negro Education* 12 (Summer 1943): 355–363.
Quarles, Benjamin. "The Colonial Militia and Negro Manpower." *Mississippi Valley Historical Review* 45 (March 1959): 643–652.
Reddick, L. D. "The Negro Policy of the American Army Since World War II." *The Journal of Negro History* 38 (April 1953): 194–215.
———. "The Negro Policy of the United States Army, 1775–1945." *The Journal of Negro History* 34 (January 1949): 9–29.
———. "What Should the American Negro Reasonably Expect as the Outcome of a Real Peace?" *The Journal of Negro Education* 12 (Summer 1943): 568–578.
Reid, Ira De A. "A Critical Summary: The Negro on the Home Front in World Wars I and II." *The Journal of Negro Education* 12 (Summer 1943): 511–520.
Reitzes, Dietrich C. "Institutional Structure and Race Relations." *Phylon* 20 (Spring 1959): 48–66.
Reynolds, Grant. "A Triumph for Civil Disobedience." *The Nation* 147 (August 28, 1948): 228–229.
Roberts, Thomas N. "The Negro in Government War Agencies." *The Journal of Negro Education* 12 (Summer 1943): 367–375.
Rose, Arnold M. "Bases of American Military Morale in World War II." *Public Opinion Quarterly* 9 (Winter 1945): 411–417.
———. "The Social Structure of the Army." *American Journal of Sociology* 51 (March 1946): 261–264.
Rutherford, William A. "Jim Crow: A Problem in Diplomacy." *The Nation* 175 (November 8, 1943): 428–429.
Sanction, Thomas. "Something's Happened to the Negro." *New Republic* 108 (February 8, 1943): 175–179.
Schuyler, George S. "A Long War Will Aid the Negro." *The Crisis* 50 (November 1943): 328–344.
Shannon, Fred A., "The Federal Government and the Negro Soldier, 1861–1865." *The Journal of Negro History* 11 (October 1926): 563–583.
Smythe, Hugh H. "The Concept of Jim Crow." *Social Forces* 27 (October 1948): 45–48.
Spindler, G. D. "The Military—A Systematic Analysis." *Social Forces* 27 (October 1948): 83–88.
Stillman, Richard. "Negroes in the Armed Forces." *Phylon: A Review of Race and Culture* 30 (Summer 1969): 142.
Stone, Robert C. "Status and Leadership in a Combat Fighter Squadron." *American Journal of Sociology* 51 (March 1946): 388–394.
Thompson, Charles H. "The American Negro and National Defense." *The Journal of Negro Education* 9 (October 1940): 547–552.
———. "The American Negro in World War I and World War II." *The Journal of Negro Education* 12 (Summer 1943): 263–267.

———. "Negro Morale and World War II." *The Journal of Negro Education* 11 (January 1942): 1–3.
Thornbrough, Emma L. "The Brownsville Episode and the Negro Vote." *Mississippi Valley Historical Review* 44 (December 1957): 469–493.
Tindall, George B. "The Significance of Howard W. Odum to Southern History: A Preliminary Estimate." *The Journal of Southern History* 24 (August 1958): 285–307.
Toppin, Edgar A. "Humbly They Served: The Black Brigade in the Defense of Cincinnati." *The Journal of Negro History* 48 (April 1963): 75–97.
Tumin, Melvin. "The Functionalist Approach to Social Problems." *Social Problems* 12 (Spring 1965): 379–388.
Weil, Frank E. G. "The Negro in the Armed Forces." *Social Forces* 26 (October 1947): 95–98.
Weeliver, Warman. "Report on the Negro Soldier." *Harper's Magazine* 192 (April 1946): 333–339.
White, Howard B. "Military Morality." *Social Research* 13 (Winter 1946): 410–440.
White, Walter. "It's Our Country, Too: The Negro Demands the Right to be Allowed to Fight for It." *The Saturday Evening Post* 213 (December 14, 1940): 27, 61, 63, 66, 68.
———. "Race Relations in the Armed Services of the United States." *The Journal of Negro Education* 12 (Summer 1943): 350–354.
———. "What The Negro Thinks of the Army." *The Annals of the American Academy of Political and Social Science* 222 (September 1942): 67–71.
White, William L. "The Negro in the Army." *Reader's Digest* 41 (April 1942): 51–54.
———. "Negro Officers, 1917 and Now." *Survey Graphic* 31 (April 1942): 192–194.
Wilkins, Roy. "Air Pilots, But Segregated." *The Crisis* 48 (February 1941): 39.
———. "Army Air Corps." *The Crisis* 47 (November 1940): 358.
———. "Army Air Corps Smoke Screen." *The Crisis* 48 (April 1941): 103.
———. "Army Can Have Jim Crow in Selective Service Act." *The Crisis* 48 (January 1941): 22.
———. "Fighting the Jim Crow Army." *The Crisis* 55 (May 1948): 136.
———. "Government Blesses Separatism." *The Crisis* 50 (April 1943): 105.
———. "National Defense and Negroes." *The Crisis* 46 (February 1939): 49.
———. "Nazi Plan for Negroes Copies Southern U.S.A." *The Crisis* 48 (March 1941): 71.
———. "A Negro Enlisted Man: Jim Crow in the Army Corps." *The Crisis* 47 (December 1940): 385.
———. "The Negro in the United States Army." *The Crisis* 48 (February 1942): 47.
———. "The Negro Soldier Betrayed." *The Crisis* 62 (April 1945): 97.
———. "No Negro Draft Board Members in Many States, Says N.A.A.C.P. Survey." *The Crisis* 48 (January 1941): 22.
———. "Now Is the Time Not To Be Silent." *The Crisis* 49 (January 1942): 7.
———. "The Roosevelt Record." *The Crisis* 47 (September 1940): 343.
———. "Snow Clearers, Cotton Pickers." *The Crisis* 50 (March 1943): 72.
———. "Still a Jim Crow Army." *The Crisis* 53 (April 1946): 106–109, 125.

———. "Too Dark for Army Air Corps." *The Crisis* 47 (September 1940): 279.
———. "U.S.A. Needs a Sharp Break with the Past." *The Crisis* 49 (May 1942): 151.
———. "Wallace's Southern Tour." *The Crisis* 55 (October 1948): 297.
Williams, Charles. "Harlem at War." *The Nation* 156 (January 16, 1943): 86–88.
Williams, Mae Smith. "Army Airport." *Opportunity* 22 (Summer 1944): 119.
Williams, Robin M. "Social Change and Social Conflict: Race Relations in the United States, 1944–1964." *Sociological Inquiry* 35 (Winter 1965): 8–25.
Wilson, Walter. "Old Jim Crow in Uniform." *The Crisis* 46 (February 1939): 42–44; (March 1939): 71–73, 82, 93.
Wirth, Louis. "Morale and Minority Groups." *American Journal of Sociology* 47 (November 1941): 415–433.
Young, Whitney M., Jr. "When the Negroes in Vietnam Come Home." *Harper's Magazine* 234 (June 1967): 63–69.

Index

Adams, Emory S., 5
Adams, Clarence E., 58
Adams, Milton, 71
Advisory Commission on Universal Military Training, 103
Advisory Committee on Negro Troop Policy, 46–47, 83, 86
Air Command, 45–47
Air Corps, 43–47
Air Force Enlistment Program, 46
Alexander, Clifford A., 109
Alexander, Will W., 9
American Association of Physical Anthropologists, 76
"American Dream," 1, 98
American Medical Association, 74
American Red Cross, 74–77
American Youth for Democracy, 34
Amicus Curiae, 37, 86
Anti-integrationists, 33
Appeasement, 10–11
Armed Forces Radio Service, 103

Army. *See* Regular Army
Army Air Corps, 26, 43–47, 83–84
Army Air Forces, 45, 98
Army Classification Tests, 7, 45, 92
Army Ground Forces, 102
Army Medical Corps, 41–42
Army Nurses Corps, 42
Army Talk, 36–37, 60, 65, 86
Army's Top Brass, 55, 59, 69, 93, 98
Arnold, Henry H., 67
Article 74, Army Regulations Code, 87
Atlanta Daily World, 56, 85
Aviation Squadrons (separate), 45
Axis Propaganda, 5

Babero, Bert B., 63
Bagley, Ted, 109
Baker, Newton, 10
Baldwin, Raymond, 6
Baltimore Afro-American, 101
Barnett, Claude A., 29

150   Index

Becton, J. H., 55
Benedict, Ruth, 65
Bennett, Bishop G. G., 34
Bennett, Joan, 34
Bethune, Mary McLeod, 6, 12–13, 31
Blacks, 31, 98–100
Black Americans, 1, 3, 5, 9, 15–16, 63, 108
Black Blood Donors, 75–76
Black Inductees, 6–7, 34–37
Black Leaders, 7–10, 12, 14, 69, 75, 84–85, 92, 105
Black Medical Personnel, 41–43
Black Nurses, 42–43
Black Officers, 37–41
Black Physicians and Dentists, 41–42
Black Press. See individual newspapers
Black Soldiers. See Chapter Three
Black Troops, 54, 60, 64
Black Youth, 36
Blood Plasma, 75–76
Blood Program Committee. See American Red Cross
"Blue Discharges," 71–72
Bray, Douglas, 7
Byrd, Harry F., 35

Call, The, 36
Camp Barkeley, 62
Camp Breckenridge, 58
Camp Claiborne, 67
Camp George Jordan, 64
Camp Gordon Johnston, 63
Camp Livingston, 71
Chamberlain, Edwin W., 27–28
Chicago Council of Negro Organizations, 31
Chicago Defender, 30, 101
Citizens' Nonpartisan Committee, 8
Civil Rights Movement, 108
Civilian Aides to the Secretary of War. See William H. Hastie; Truman K. Gibson, Jr.; Marcus Ray; James C. Evans
Coffin, President Henry Sloan, 34
Coiner, Richard T., 44–45
"Color Line," 64, 98

Colored Federal Employees Association, 10
Columbia University School of Medicine, 75
Commission on Civil Rights, 103
"Committee of 100," 33
Committee on Equality of Treatment and Opportunity in the Armed Services, 105
Committee on Medical Policies and Procedures of the American Red Cross, 77
Corps Area Commanders, 41
Courier's Army Bills, 3
Cramer, Myron C., 87
Crisis Magazine, 3–4
Crump, C. B., 60–61

Davis, Benjamin O., Sr., 9–10, 57, 66
Davis, John P., 31, 87
Davis, Norman H., 76
Davis-Monthan Field, 56
"Democratic rhetoric and ideology," 28
Dewey, Professor John, 34
Discrimination, 15, 64, 67–68, 73–77, 87, 98
Donor Registration Card, 77
"Double V" Campaign, 15–16, 55
Drew, Dr. Charles, 75
Du Bois, William E. B., 84–85

Early, Stephen, 8–9, 15
Edison, Charles, 33
Eisenhower Administration, 107
Ely, H. E., 2
Embree, Edwin R., 33
Esprit de Corps, 18, 54, 59, 61
Evans, James C., 47, 86, 101–02
Executive Order 8802, 33
Executive Order 9981, 105–06

Fahy, Charles, 105
First Army Headquarters, 6
Fish, Hamilton, 91–92
Ford, Sam C., 33
Forrestal, James V., 103
Fort Benning, 65

Fort Bragg, 72
Fort Clark, 66
Fort Francis E. Warren, 57
Fort Huachuca, 43, 55
Frankfurter, Felix, 11–12
Franklin, C. A., 36
"Four Freedoms," 31, 55

Gadsden Times, 34
Garvin, Roy, 35
Gerhardt, H. A., 77
Gesell, Gerhard A., 107–08
Gibson, Truman K., Jr.: Advisory Committee on Negro Troop Policy, 46, 86; black blood donors, 74–77; black fliers, 46; black medical personnel, 41–43; clash with Grant Reynolds, 104; Gillem Report, 100; recreational facilities, 59, 65; soldiers' complaints, 56
Gilbert, George R., 72
Gillem, Alvin C., Jr., 99
Gillem Report. *See* Appendix
Ginzberg, Eli, 7
Graham, President Frank P., 34
Granger, Lester, 101–02
Grube, Raymond, 40
Guenther, L. A., 65

Hampton Institute, 46–47
Harter, George J., 33
Harris, Wender H., 35
Hastie, Judge William H.: Advisory Committee on Negro Troop Policy, 47; appointment to War Department, 10–11; Army Air Corps, 43–47; black blood donors, 73–77; black combat units, 91–92; black leadership opposition, 15; black leadership support, 14; black medical personnel, 41–43; black officers, 37–41; black press opposition, 30; black press support, 29; black recruitment, 35–37; Chamberlain's reaction to Hastie Report, 28–29; General Marshall's reaction to Hastie Report, 28–29; letter from Thurgood Marshall, 11–12; military police, 67–71; New Caledonia rape case, 87–88; 1941 Report on black manpower, 25–27; power base, 13, 98; private citizen reaction to soldiers' abuse, 89–93; reaction to General Benjamin O. Davis, Sr., 57, 66–67; reaction to Stimson's appointment, 12; recreational facilities, 59–60, 65; resignation, 84–86; soldier morale, 60–66; soldiers' complaints, 56; statement to black soldiers, 14; support of black national organizations, 31–32; "The Negro Soldier," 37; troop stationing, 67–68; use of "Nigger," 56–57; white opposition, 33; white support, 33
Henderson, Algo D., 34
Hermitt, Roy, 71–72
Hersey, R. G., 57
Hershey, Lewis, B., 17
Hill, T. Arnold, 8, 12
Hillman, C. C., 76–77
Hitlerism, 16, 31
Hopkins, Harry, 10
Householder, Eugene, 29
Houston, Charles H., 2–3, 102
Howard University, 31
Hurley, Robert, 6

Illiteracy, 6–7
Institutional Racism, 31, 43, 108
Integration, 30–31, 103, 106

Jackson Air Base, 56
Japanese, 29
Jenkins, Latrophe F., 69
Jim Crow, 17, 44, 61, 101
Johnson, Campbell C., 10, 37
Johnson, F. Ernest, 34
Johnson, Jesse J., 39
Jones, Eugene K., 8

Keller, Helen, 33
Kellogg, Paul, 33
Kennedy, John F., 107
Kimble, Frederick, 86
King, Stafford, 5

Kirk, Dr. Norman, 42, 76–77
Klapper, President Paul, 34
Korean Conflict, 106

Labor and Supply Units, 1, 26, 34
La Guardia, F. H., 33
La Junta Army Field, 64
La Roe, Wilbur, 45
Lawrence, John, 106
Lee, William D., 63–64
Lewis, H. B., 34
Logan, Rayford W., 3
Louis, Joe, 62
Lovett, Robert A., 44–46
Loyal Soldier, A, 53
Lyles, Edward N., 70–71
Lynn, Winfred W., 16–17
Lythcott, Lloyd, 73

McAuliffe, Anthony C., 106
McCloy, John J., 30, 87, 99
McLean, Malcolm S., 46–47
MacLeish, Archibald, 16
McNamara, Robert S., 107
Madison Square Garden, 9
Marcantonio, Vito, 88, 103
March-On-Washington Movement, 31–32
Marshall, George, 42
Marshall, George C., 27, 56–57
Marshall, Thurgood, 4, 11–12, 37, 86, 93, 102, 108
Mason, Professor Daniel Gregory, 34
Maw, Herbert B., 33
May, Andrew J., 66
Medical Corps, 26–27, 41–43
Medical Reserve, 26–27, 41–42
Messenger, 15
Military Police, 67–69, 71
"Misfits," 102
Mitchell, Arthur W., 31
Mixed training, 7, 34, 38, 101, 106
Mixed units, 7, 34, 38, 101, 106
Morale, 61–62, 66–67
Moskowitz, Jack, 107

NAACP, 2–3, 14, 30, 36, 60–61, 86, 93, 103–04

Nash, Philleo, 104
National Association for the Advancement of Colored People. *See* NAACP
National Committee Against Jim Crow in Military Service and Training, 102–03
National Council of Negro Women, 6
National Federation for Constitutional Liberties, 42
National Negro Congress, 4, 86
National Urban League, 14, 31
Nazi philosophy, 76–77
"The Negro Soldier," 36–37
New York Age, 9, 31, 85, 101
New York Amsterdam-Star News, 29, 101
New York Daily News, 89
New York Times, 74
Nicklus, T., 68
"Nigger," 41, 56, 58, 68, 71
908th Quartermaster Company, 56
1954 Brown Decision, 108
1940 Draft Act, 3, 5, 7, 16–17, 53
1940 Presidential election, 9–10
1964 Civil Rights Act, 108
1937 mobilization plan, 2–3
99th Pursuit Squadron, 46–47
92nd Division, 104
Ninth Cavalry, 91
Norfolk Journal and Guide, 29, 35, 101

Office of War Information, 16
Officer candidate schools, 38
Olson, Culbert, 33
Osborn, General Frederick H., 36, 61–62

Pampa Army Air Field, 56
Park, Professor Marion E., 34
Parrish, Noel, 86
Patterson, Robert P., 11, 26–27, 30–32, 35–36, 41–42, 45–46, 57–58, 61, 75, 90
Paul, Willard S., 102
Pearl Harbor, 29
Personnel Division, 27, 41
Petersen, Howard C., 36, 61

Pickens, William, 15
Pittsburgh Courier, 3–5, 15, 29, 44, 84
Planning and Liaison Branch, 68
Prattis, Percival L., 5, 29, 60–61, 69
Prejudice, 5, 54, 99, 105
President's Committee on Equality of Treatment and Opportunity in the Armed Services (Fahy Committee), 105
President's Committee on Equal Opportunity in the Armed Forces (Gesell Committee), 107–08
"Project Clear," 106
Promen, Leo J., 33–34
Protests, 8, 30, 97, 102, 106
Public Relations Bureau, 34–36, 62

Quartermaster and Engineering Corps, 26

Races of Mankind, 66
Racism. *See* Discrimination; Prejudice; Segregation
Randolph, A. Philip, 8, 14, 31–33, 102–03
Rankin, John E., 34
Ransom, Samuel L., 58–59
Ray, Marcus, H., 101–02
Recruitment Formula, 35–37
Red Cross. *See* American Red Cross
Redistribution centers, 99
Reed, Thomas, Jr., 13
Reevers, Eddie W., 15
Regular Army, 25–26, 37, 39, 100
Reserve Officers, 26–27, 41–42
Resignation. *See* Hastie
Reynolds, Reverend Grant, 103–04
Richmond Times-Dispatch, 15
Ridgway, Matthew B., 106
Roosevelt, Eleanor, 6, 31–32, 55, 66, 69
Roosevelt, Franklin D., 8–10, 15, 31, 42
Royall, Kenneth, 102

Scott, Emmett J., 10
Second Cavalry Division, 89–91
Second World War, 55, 77, 99, 110

"Section VIII," 72
Segregation, 10, 27, 32, 67–68, 87
Segregationists, 35, 59
Selective Service and Training Act of 1940. *See* 1940 Draft Act
Senate Resolution 75, 32
Sengstacke, John H. H., 29–30
Shedd, William E., 41
Sheridan, Major, 58
Shock Treatment, 73
Sioux Falls, South Dakota, 58
Sissle, Noble, 62
Sloan, James, 9
Slossom, Professor Preston W., 34
Snyder, Howard MacC., 56–57
Southern politicians, 33, 34, 59
Specialist schools, 26–27, 36–38, 86
Spingarn, Arthur S., 33
Stimson, Henry L.: abusive language, 56–57; assessment of Hastie, 13, 43; black blood donors, 73–77; black leadership, 9–10; black troops in World War I, 38; Hastie's appointment letter, 12; Hastie's resignation, 84; illiteracy, 7; military police, 67–70; New Caledonia rape case, 87–88; officer candidate schools, 38; Redistribution Centers, 99; Second Cavalry Division, 89–91; stationing of black troops, 67–68; Tuskegee Air Base, 43–44
Street, St. Clair, 46
Sullivan, John L., 105
Surles, Alex P., 36
Symington, W. Stuart, 105

Talmage, Herman, 34
Tenth Cavalry, 91
Thomas, Charles M., 15
Thomas, Huntington, 11
369th Infantry, 3
333rd Fighter Squadron, 86
328th Aviation Squadron, 56
Time Magazine, 84
Truman, Harry S, 93, 99, 103–05
Tuskegee Air Base, 43–47
25th Infantry, 40
24th Infantry, 68

Ulio, James A., 75
Union of Democratic Action, 33
U.S. Air Force, 105, 109
U.S. Army, 105, 109
U.S. Congress, 108
U.S. Constitution, 54–55, 108
U.S. Marine Corps, 109
U.S. Navy, 109
U.S. Supreme Court, 17

Vann, Robert L., 3–5
Verbal abuse. *See* "Nigger"
Vietnam War, 108
Villard, Oswald Garrison, 33
Voting Rights Act of 1965, 108

Waddy, Joseph C., 102
Wagner, Walter, 34
Wailes, Sylvain, 107
Warden, John A., 57
War Department policies, 4–5; abusive language, 56–59; black blood donors, 73–77; black officers, 40; black recruitment, 34–37; Draft Boards, 6; "fair" treatment of black soldiers, 9, 38; illiterate black and white troops, 6–7; integration, 30; mixed units, 38, 101, 106; opposition to segregation and racial discrimination, 106, 108; recreational facilities, 59–60, 65; Redistribution Centers, 99; segregation, 7–8; 10 percent ratio, 26; Tuskegee Air Base, 43–47
Ware, Gilbert, 106
Washburn, Bishop Benjamin M., 34
Washington Afro-American, 84
Washington Post, 34
Washington Tribune, 15
Watson, Edwin, 4
Weaver, Robert C., 9, 108
Wesley, Charles, 31
West, Milton, 67
White civilians, 67–68
White House, 10, 103, 105
White National Organizations, 13, 98
White officers, 38–39, 44, 58–59
White press, 13, 34, 83–86
White, Walter, 3–4, 8–9, 14–15, 32, 36, 60–61
Wilkins, Roy, 3, 9, 13, 16, 31, 68, 101
Wilson, Charles, 54
Winfield, Martin, 40
Wolfe, James H., 33
Woodring, Harry H., 2–3, 5
World War I, 2–3, 5, 10
World War II, 1–2, 97, 99

Young, P. B., 29

About the Author

PHILLIP M. MCGUIRE is Associate Professor of U.S. History at the University of North Carolina at Wilmington. He is the author of *Taps for a Jim Crow Army*, and his numerous articles have appeared in such publications as the *Journal of Social and Behavioral Sciences, Military Affairs, Journal of Negro History, Phylon,* and *The Researcher.*

Recent Titles in
Contributions in Afro-American and African Studies
Series Advisers: John W. Blassingame and Henry Louis Gates, Jr.

"De Lawd": Richard B. Harrison and *The Green Pastures*
Walter C. Daniel

Health Care Issues in Black America: Policies, Problems, and Prospects
Woodrow Jones, Jr., and Mitchell F. Rice, editors

The Character of the Word: The Texts of Zora Neale Hurston
Karla F. C. Holloway

Surprizing Narrative: Olaudah Equiano and the Beginnings of Black Autobiography
Angelo Costanzo

Conscientious Sorcerers: The Black Postmodernist Fiction of Leroi Jones/Amiri Baraka, Ishmael Reed, and Samuel R. Delany
Robert Elliot Fox

Alexander Crummell: Pioneer in Nineteenth-Century Pan-African Thought
Gregory U. Rigsby

A Revolution Gone Backward: The Black Response to National Politics, 1876–1896
Bess Beatty

The Short Fiction of Rudolph Fisher
Margaret Perry, editor

Black Sailors: Afro-American Merchant Seamen and Whalemen Prior to the Civil War
Martha S. Putney

Assimilation Blues: Black Families in a White Community
Beverly Daniel Tatum

Take Five: Collected Poems
Kenneth A. McClane

Pride Against Prejudice: The Biography of Larry Doby
Joseph Thomas Moore

Sacred Symphony: The Chanted Sermon of the Black Preacher
Jon Michael Spencer